Empowering Philosophy and Science with the Art of Love

Lonergan and Deleuze in the Light of Buddhist-Christian Ethics

John Raymaker

University Press of America,® Inc.
Lanham · Boulder · New York · Toronto · Oxford

Copyright © 2006 by
University Press of America,® Inc.
4501 Forbes Boulevard
Suite 200
Lanham, Maryland 20706
UPA Acquisitions Department (301) 459-3366

PO Box 317
Oxford
OX2 9RU, UK

All rights reserved
Printed in the United States of America
British Library Cataloging in Publication Information Available

Library of Congress Control Number: 2006922196
ISBN-13: 978-0-7618-3467-0 (paperback : alk. paper)
ISBN-10: 0-7618-3467-2 (paperback : alk. paper)

∞™ The paper used in this publication meets the minimum
requirements of American National Standard for Information
Sciences—Permanence of Paper for Printed Library Materials,
ANSI Z39.48—1984

> First across the gulf we cast
> Kite-borne threads, till lines are passed,
> And habit builds the bridge at last!
>
> John Boyle O'Reilly,
> *A Builder's Lesson*

> Can a bridge be built
>   —once heartfelt spiritual threads an East-West divide
> Have spanned? In Buddhist and Christian hearts,
>   virtuous habits DO abide:
> Habits of the heart to span gaping cultural gulfs
>   —lest errant ones collide.

DEDICATION

I wish to dedicate this work to my wife Christa, and my brother Rudy (MD) and his wife Pat. This work is also dedicated to Michele Lafay (MD) for her heroic work as a medical doctor, educator and anthropologist with minority tribes in South East Asia, particularly for her 25 or more years in Mindanao, Philippines. There she has struggled in the mountains to educate the Manobo animist people.

I express particular gratitude to Joris Wiggers, MD, and Frank Braio, PhD, for their friendship and critical analyses. The shortcomings are all mine. I have plodded through uncharted fields. I hope that I have seen more than a mirage.

TABLE OF CONTENTS

Illustrations
Preface
Introduction

PART ONE
TRANS*FORM*ATIVE LOCI
POTENCY AND FORM 1

Chapter 1	An Outline for Empowering Philosophy, Artists and Science	3
Chapter 2	Trans*form*ative Potencies in our Genomes	15
Chapter 3	Trans*form*ative *Form*s in Mathematics	59

PART TWO
INTEGRATING IDEAL TRANS*FORM*ATIVE ACTIONS
IN FEEDBACK WAYS 99

Chapter 4	East-West Philosophies' Trans*form*ative Feedback, Allelic *Opera*tions	103
Chapter 5	Contextualizing and Implementing GEM Diphase Feedback's In-Betweens	111

Endnotes 151
Glossary 189
Index 191
Biography 194

ILLUSTRATIONS

Figure 1
    Trans*form*ing Deleuze and Guattari's Conceptual Triad
        with a Spiritually Open One   35

Figure 2
    Ethically and Spiritually Contextualizing Genomes
        with Meta-Substantial *Opera*tions   40

Figure 3
    Trans*form*ative Loci
        that Transcend Genetics and Conceptual Philosophies   61

Figure 4
    Objectifying Trans*form*ative Triads
        in Functional Specialties' Feedback   114

PREFACE

This book is, like my two previous books on a "spiritual genome," exploratory in nature. Circumstances such as my frequent moves between the United States of America, Japan, and Europe and my retirement from active teaching (I now live in Germany and am learning German) have made it difficult for me to consult experts in the many fields into which this book ventures.

As I indicate in the Glossary and in the text, my proposed "AIRR-4-3-5 structured spiritual genome" is this book's central claim.

AIRR is an acronym for the four imperatives, more or less consciously operative in each person: every person should be *be* A) attentive, I) intelligent, R) rational and R) responsible." These four imperatives arise on the basis of 1) experiencing, 2) asking questions so as to understand, 3) asking further questions aimed at judging what is truly so or truly worthwhile. On the basis of these three underlying operations, a person can then 4) exercise liberty in choosing. These four AIRR realities lie at the basis of Lonergan's generalized empirical method (GEM).

In an "AIRR-4-3-5 spiritual genome," "4" stands for the aforesaid AIRR *opera*tions we cannot avoid using; "3" stands for a GEM triad to be explained in the text, and "5" stands for GEM's fifth precept, *be* in love.

For Jewish rabbis, God is beyond explanation; yet, they do try to explain some of the mystical notions involving the Hebrew letters *heh* and *yod*. Rabbis touch on some traditional notions regarding these two letters that refer to God and God's creation (as implying a four-structured interpretation of time and space). They also point out that our 4-dimensional universe is to be complemented by the unknown fifth "dimension" that represents God's creating existence and sustaining act of existence. They relate our 3-dimensional space to the fourth dimension of time and the fifth dimension of spirituality.

In Kabbalah, "*ruah*" (breath, spirit, life of the soul etc.) is the uniting force between *heh* and *yod*. I was not aware of such "4-3-5 interpretations" in Judaism until I finished this book. Such venerable interpretations make me breathe a little more peacefully. The "breathing" implied in *heh* denotes God's creation; *heh-*

Preface

yod represent some of the ways we participate in that creation. Our "creative" participation involves a question-answer dialectic reminiscent of the one Bernard Lonergan has advocated throughout his writings. It also involves our ineluctable involvement in the realities of good and evil. Jewish traditional lore recalls, for me, the equally profound Hindu teachings on *Om (Aum)*.

It is in this spirit that this book approaches 4-3-5 mystical and ethical interpretations of reality in the form of interfaith, interdisciplinary and "transcultural" applications of a "4-3-5 spiritual genome" which is structured analogically to 4-3-5 physical genomes. The main difference is that physical genomes code and are often subjected to determinist interpretations. A 4-3-5 spiritual genome, on the other hand, operates or should operate in ethical ways. It frees us so that we can "breathe" creatively, that is share in God's ongoing creation through the cooperative, ethically loving ways that this book advocates.

John Raymaker,
Tallahassee, Florida
   and
Homburg (Saar), Germany
November, 2005

INTRODUCTION

This book might have been called, "Mapping a Map of Love" for it maps trans*form*ative loci influencing ethical, virtuous love. Being prone to tunnel visions, we often get so wrapped in one aspect of reality that we dismiss other aspects. Because our strengths easily "co-opt" us, pride can engender hubris. A balanced character and virtues that enable us to use our strengths so as to deal with our weaknesses are "imponderables" that can empower persons as well as philosophy and science. These are elusive notions that we can retrieve by examining how humans per*form* in various fields of activity. By studying how philosophers, mathematicians, biologists or average persons per*form* their work and respond to ethical demands, this book seeks to empower us on the model of how my *Empowering the Lonely Crowd* addressed[1] what is lacking in Riesman's *outer-directed* lonely crowd. It extends that model with an "art of love" exemplified in East-West ethics. It recovers the roots of spirituality that "civilization" tends to hide from us. Gautama and Jesus knew our weakness; they both encouraged us to follow the path of virtue. A problem is that, blinded by parochialisms, many of us are unable to transcend our own narrow self-interests.

When President Bush declared war on terrorism, some objected that you cannot declare war on a noun. A war that falls short of addressing the root causes of a problem only provokes other problems. Sadly, with such rare exceptions as Lincoln or Gandhi, politicians fail to address core[2] issues. Oblivious of ethical ideals, they ply slogans. In view of that sad reality, this book focuses on creative ethical ideals before addressing derivative constructs. It espouses a *spirit philosophy* centered on workable ideals. Recognizing that we often go awry, it delves into the mystical side and ideals that motivated the lives of such geniuses as Spinoza and Einstein, who nevertheless failed to give a satisfactory account for their belief in an immanent pantheism. It argues that the dreams of Plato and German Idealism are best rooted in the *quest* for love—loving as a *verb*, not as an "-ism noun."

We will not find the source of free action in the lofty realms of the mind or in the depths of the brain. The idealist approach of the phenomenologists is as hopeless as the positive approach of the naturalists. "To discover the sources of free action it is necessary to go outside the limits of the organism, not into the intimate sphere of the mind, but into the objective forms of social life; it is necessary to seek the source of human consciousness and freedom in the social history of humanity. To find the soul it is necessary to lose it."[3] I argue that a paradoxical loss of self is often necessary—as taught by Buddha and Jesus[4] and lived out by such great leaders as Lincoln or John F. Kennedy.

The human mind is "portable"; it engenders trans*form*ative and viable ideals. If alleles (allelo*morph*s) are any of a group of possible mutational *forms* of a gene, I study groups of philosophical concepts' possible mutations so as to find hope for our sometimes chaotic lives. In previous books, I sought to reconcile East-West thought by linking the trans*form*ative loci" of genetics and of mathematical thought. This book probes such loci anew with a view to bridging religious-secularist divides exacerbated by postmodernism. For cognitive linguists, our conceptual schemas arise from embodied experience; they fail to identify cognition's deeper "verb structures."

Rather than directly empowering disciplines, *Empowering Philosophy and Science* seeks to empower the *practitioners* of these disciplines by having them pay heed to the art of an ethical virtue enjoined in the two great biblical commandments and in Buddhism. It explores insights into our physical genome and mathematics that I "translate" into an empowering ethics, that is, into the "trans*form*ative allelic loci" of a social ethics. I argue that an empowering ethical love is an "art *form*" and that a Buddhist-Christian ethics helps us "spiritualize" secularist insights. Noting that bees outstrip us in zeal, that worms are as agile as we, Schiller rhapsodizes that only art distinguishes humans. I write of ethical artists who practice love even in the face of deception. Such artists may lack politicians' clout or legendary heroes' fame, but their heart is in the right place. By living out their ideals in the face of evils, they build empowering bridges rooted in the deeper psyche. Some disdain ideals because they are aware of only one side of a gulf to be bridged. The heart can reach out across the divide to link up with other hearts—but only if we first balance the trans*form*ative and *invariant* aspects of our cognition and of our feelings. In genetics and mathematics, loci are functional in nature, but the loci of cognition and spirituality are *foundational*; functional and foundational loci differ radically; they do share analogical properties.

As in my previous books, I seek to enlarge Bernard Lonergan's method with a bridge to East-West ways of thinking—a foundational bridge latent within us, waiting to be discovered so that we may "tick." A bridge built on "trans*form*ative ideal loci" locates thought's foundations in our cognitive *opera*tions. It links past traditions to future needs. Conflicting theories and beliefs stem from the insights that begot them. Insights allow us to inquire into theories while serving as trans*form*ative loci for new insights. This book's Chapter 1 suggests that science, philosophy and art can be enriched by "allelic loci" (potentially) at work in human persons. Chapters 2 and 3 explore notions of allelic loci in genetics and of loci in mathematics, both of which imply trans*form*ations. Chapters 4 and 5

Introduction

seek to integrate philosophy and science with daily life by spelling out an ethical notion of what "makes us tick." Self-transcendence implies being open to a Higher Power's subtle trans*form*ations. On second thought, before starting to speak about ideals that can make us "tick," it may help to let *naive* realists have their say. Non-critical "realists" may argue that I assume too many optimal conditions. Accordingly, I shall append to each chapter some conversational notes, where a "realist can have it out" with me (John) in testing trans*form*ative ideals. I use "get real" dialectics to "shock" one into appropriating one's own transcultural bridge and the full panoply of one's emotions. I argue that no one can explore anything, "tick" nor trans*form* self or one's life without implicitly using the trans*form*ative ability that in*form*s their knowing-doing oper*a*tions.

*A "Let's Get Real" Objection to a Trans*formative *Dialectic*

A Realist's view: "John, what are you saying—this talk about 'ticking' and a bridge? Get real, will you. What does "integrating the full panoply of our emotions" mean? Dang it, John, you know most of us have to struggle all our lives. It hardly ever goes the way one wants. Of course, it is *nice* to be blessed with parents and friends able and willing to pull one through. But still, John, get real, won't you? Many people just survive; they can't achieve much. What about them?

John: Diplomats focus on what can "work" in a troubled world. In family life or in peace-building we must go beyond what "works" and address such intangibles as character, a balanced perspective and the virtues. Such often-neglected intangibles are indispensable to ironing out everyday life's give and take. By addressing personal shortcomings, they can help achieve "breakthroughs" in human relations.

Part One

TRANS*FORM*ATIVE LOCI

CHAPTER 1

AN OUTLINE FOR EMPOWERING PHILOSOPHY AND SCIENCE WITH LOVE

This chapter outlines my project which depends on fathoming the depth of our knowing-doing *opera*tions' allelic loci, what I call our "spiritual genome" that makes us "tick." I remember going to a party one evening with a beautiful woman who drank and talked endlessly. After the party, as I drove her home, in the wee-hours of the morning, the besotted gal began to insist that I let her take the wheel. Knowing that I was the designated driver, I had kept sober. As we drove along, the more I refused to let her drive, the more she began to browbeat me. Fortunately, I managed not to give in. Many a time, I have wondered what had "gotten into" her. By recalling the drunken woman's basic goodness, I dealt with her dark side. What leads people to become self-destructive? Do we have enough dedicated groups such as the Red Cross and Alcoholic Anonymous—or persons able to address problems caused by such "imponderables" as a lack of character? Biographers often dwell on how character influences their subject's lifework. Einstein was a "sharp-tongued cynic at times, a self-centered man who could serve humanity" well but not those close to him.[1] How do we get to the essence of character? How do we deal with our flaws? What makes us "tick"? How assess the philosophical, scientific and religious insights that can empower us humans in the spiritual and political areas of our lives?

To answer such questions, we would do well to consider the ways of scientific procedures and the insights of philosophers and religious thinkers. Humans are complicated beings, subject to contradictions as expressed in many of the sutras or in the works of Poe, Kafka, and Beckett. Our race has taken over the reins of the planet, but it often seems too drunk to drive. As a result, we face possible disaster in the social and environmental facets of our lives. We let short-term profits beguile us into ignoring long-term consequences. The rain forests in Brazil are burned or felled and not restored. Such are a few of the imponderables facing humans as decision makers. We cannot but benefit from understanding a method that integrates today's revolutionary changes within a framework of invariant givens in our nature. To find solutions to our social and environmental problems, we first have to go back to the "basics." Lonergan's *Insight* and its generalized empirical method (GEM) helps us do this.

An "In-between Allelic Loci Shorthand" Mediating between Philosophy and Science

I often find myself talking about Lonergan's "GEM" with my friends and acquaintances. On one such occasion, when asked by my physician what GEM is all about, I answered that it goes into the data of sense and into how we understand these data, judge and act on the data. He answered "That sounds like what I do everyday." He had grasped that GEM deals with what makes us "tick" and that these four levels *opera*ting on data are a simple, yet profound key to explain everyday experience. GEM is a transcendental method based on the cognitional makeup of a normal person born and raised in any land or culture: it is a set of trans*form*ative *opera*tions[2] in*form*ing four transcendental "AIRR" ideal imperatives that urge each person to "*be* A) attentive, I) intelligent, R) rational and R) responsible." AIRR means *living* our four *opera*tions in *ideal* ways but this depends, I argue, upon GEM's fifth imperative, "be loving," which is a key to a viable ethics.

Joris Wiggers, a young psychiatrist friend of mine, helped me reconsider the brain-mind problem when he critiqued my *Buddhist-Christian Logic of the Heart*'s notion that all humans are endowed with an inbuilt, spiritually genomic bridge based on our common AIRR *opera*tions. The bridge is possible, I explained, since all A) humans *attend* to data of sense and of consciousness and I) *intelligently form*ulate concepts; they R) *rationally* judge about the validity of concepts or derived systems before R) *responsibly* acting upon their experienced, understood and reflected upon data. In answer, Wiggers wrote: "Why should the cell and its machinery offer such a nicely fitting analogy for spirituality? Is it a coincidence or a clever application of one set of data to another? A use of one complex system to give meaning to another system, whereby apples and oranges still remain different and unrelated?" Is there an underlying principle binding the two seemingly unrelated spheres of cellular mechanics/molecular biology and the psyche-spirit? Is it similar to the brain-mind problem (the inexplicable correspondence of mind and brain [ineffable qualia vs. quantifiable matter])? Some argue for an emergent mind, (the brain creating emergent mind as greater than its parts). Rejecting a causal path from physical to psychical, others suggest an acausal, circular correspondence. In either case, he writes, "this line of thinking approximates the idea of an inbuilt bridge in a way that suggests more than a facile application of one narrative onto another. If we push to the limits of credibility and hold that all reality" is subjectively idealist, the duality angle allows for a "bridge" that quells his original skepticism that DNA and spirit must not be compared. Many people are, at first, skeptical of an inbuilt spiritual genome (which I take to be more than a mere metaphor). To these, I reply that God, the Master Builder, may have used analogous designs to activate our biological and spiritual genomes. GEM transposes *empiricism*: our AIRR *opera*tions are and have in-between (= bridging) feedback abilities. Still, one may ask how can an AIRR ideal feedback be reconciled with the claims of science? I argue that just as most living beings' physical genome is constituted of genes and cells, so our spiritually genomic actions play a role analogous to cells. In cells, alleles are one of the possible mutational states of a gene. Genes are functional units with fixed allelic *loci* on chromosomes. If a locus is the site or place on a chromosome where a particular gene is located, or if the complex nature of cells' DNA-RNA has a self-directed causality, our "AIRR allelic loci" are a spiritually genomic power "AIRR-located" in our experiencing-understanding-judging-deciding-based *opera*tions but in need of an ideal of love. The three cognitional *opera*tions of experiencing, understanding and reflecting and the fourth *opera*tion of deciding are the basic, reduplicative elements of intentional consciousness that GEM thematizes and which give rise to the AIRR imperatives that I treat as "AIRR verbs" in this book.

Great is our ignorance on many subjects. The world needs police, arms and fences to keep peace. In academia, fields of study overlap; academics are given to ever more arcane types of specialization. The hundreds of languages people speak, the issues of poverty and taxation cause further problems. While the capital sins tempt us all, virtue helps us convert and transmute such a powerful emotion as anger into a force for "AIRR allelic wisdom."[3] Transcendental GEM, based on our pattern of recurrent and related AIRR *opera*tions, is a normative method that yields cumulative and progressive results. Its AIRR levels of conscious intentionality work analogously to the adenine, thymine, guanine and cytosine (ATGC) nucleotide bases that trans*form* genomes.[4]

I use a shorthand abbreviation to refer to how our AIRR *opera*tions deal with the data of sense and consciousness and with the ideals implied in these *opera*tions. One applies in feedback ways one's *opera*tions as intentional to the *opera*tions as conscious as follows: one A) is *attentive* to one's experiencing, understanding, judging and deciding; I) *intelligently* understands the unity and relations of one's experienced experiencing, understanding, judging, deciding; R) *rationally* affirms the reality of one's experienced and understood experiencing, understanding, judging, deciding; R) *responsibly* decides to *opera*te in accord with the norms immanent in the spontaneous relatedness of one's experienced, understood, affirmed experiencing, understanding, judging and deciding.[5] Most of us want to be attentive, intelligent, rational, responsible, but often *fail* to live up to AIRR ideals. Lonergan's *Method in Theology* develops eight functional specialties that enable specialists of all fields to co*opera*te in a feedback deployment of this single AIRR method. One may claim that I "mix" apples (AIRR ideals) with oranges (coded ATGC nucleotides). What I seek to do is to develop an analogy between our physical and spiritual genomes that compares the misuses of our AIRR *opera*tions with how cancer is induced by malfunctions in ATGC bases. As an analogy should show that analogous properties are relevant and differences, irrelevant, I seek to show that AIRR spiritually allelic processes leading to good or evil are subject to culturo-ethical influences and to irrational factors not unlike how ATGC mutation in genes can cause cancer. I root an ethic relevant for today in the religio-philosophical insights of Pythagoras Socrates, Buddha and Jesus.

AIRR imperatives can guide us in daily life or when engaging in interdisciplinary studies. While Milesian philosophers viewed nature as transcendent, Parmenides and Zeno of Elea, sought transcendence within our own depths. GEM does this, too, by thematizing *insight into insight*. By having correct insights, we practice GEM. To explain what insights are, however, is an uneasy path. The path has to address such problematics as the influence of Pythagoras[6] on Plato's treatment of ideal *form*s and our own ability to practice loving ideals. My doctor was correct in saying that he practices AIRR in his daily work; but one must add that we can flounder in that task. To address such issues, I develop a category of AIRR "*allelic in-betweens*" that *oscillate* between life's ideals and its evils, between the concrete and the abstract, between our conscious or unconscious memories, between the generations or the sexes, between nationalism and hopes for a just world, between the handicapped and the elite. Addressing in-between life settings of texts (*Sitz im Leben*), I apply them to our own lives to help us reflect on ethics. Allelic AIRR in-betweens *concretely* mediate both the personal and social levels of human interactions. They refer to gray areas of life and to *ideally* feasible solutions. More profoundly, they reflect Plato's notion of an "in-between metaxy" of love that Eric Voegelin reinstated into political science so as to mediate between the *apeiron* (depths) and the heights of the Beyond. In the *Symposium* (202d-203), Eros is defined as a great *daimon* mediating between God and mortals. Such a metaxy is a symbol that mysteriously mediates ideals and acquires love's ontological rank. Consciousness is a luminous metaxic reality occurring within a more comprehensive reality reducible to neither intentionality's subject nor its object pole. For Voegelin, the *Timaeus*' demiurge better mediates nature and ultimate reality to us[7] than does Hegel's reason. If the reasons of our hearts better address our contradictions than does a "detached" reason (Pascal), this book's AIRR spiritual genome analogy empowers the heart; its AIRR ideals use "in-between categories" to mediate our personal and societal complexities. If geneticists study mutational analysis of RNA, I study society and culture across the globe to claim not a self-directed causality but love's in-between ethical ideals.

Robert Magliola suggests a deconstructionist Buddhist logic focusing on the metaxic in-betweens of Nagarjuna's "void."[8] I defer further treatment of this void to Part Two; at this stage, I simply note that, as humor capitalizes on the absurd "in-betweens" of situations, so GEM explores consciousness' luminosity. It asks about being inasmuch as it is open to the in-betweens of being and of a trans*form*ing "*void*." Being realizes itself when inquiry leads to discovery. I seek to link the implausible ideals of two metaxies, those of Greco-Christian insights into love and of Buddhist insights into a void *interrelating* persons and things. Deconstructionists study tensions between memory, fidelity to tradition and the heterogeneity of the new. GEM maps in-betweens of data and of trans*form*ative ideals. By our scientific standards, the *Timaeus'* account of biology is badly flawed; but it does close with an inspiring paean on the Beyond. I explore modern genetics, but I cannot outdo Plato, Pascal or the Buddhists in their inspiring accounts of the Ultimate. Some question the notion of an ideal. If for Heidegger, everything toward which we comport ourselves is being, this book's Part One explains the rationale for an AIRR shorthand that sublates[9] some of his insights into such comportment.[10] Part Two uses GEM's trans*form*ative feedback ability to mediate our ambiguities with the ideals of metaxic love. We are "AIRR reasonable" when we correctly understand, judge and act upon the data we experience. Yet, "imponderables" stalk us at every turn. Like those undone by alcohol, we, too, experience the conflicting demands of feelings and reason, strength and weakness. We sway between reasonable love and deep-seated fears. AIRR ideals *can* guide us through our crises—*if* we grasp and implement our common AIRR bridge. If concepts overlap in their meaning, our AIRR *opera*tions permit us to act in ethical ways; these *opera*tions must be understood in AIRR verb instantiations rather than as nouns or concepts.

Dobzhansky and Mayr revolutionized genetics by showing that variations can occur in a genome over the span of a single generation. GEM revolutionizes philosophy by AIRR-integrating the metaxic aspects of a relational, loving ethics. To grasp this notion, let us recall the alcoholic woman and my doctor's reactions upon hearing of "AIRR." Alcoholics Anonymous (AA) tells us that even when at the end of one's rope, God speaks to us. But this involves certain conditions such as following all its twelve Steps; the first step is admitting that one has a problem. Grasping that our postmodern world has a problem due to false theories of knowledge is our first AIRR step.

Physical and Spiritual Alleles and Deleuze and Guattari's Postmodernist Philosophy

We humans reasonably interact by using our AIRR *opera*tions' feedback ability. In cases of a single person or of many interacting persons, our experiencing-understanding-judging-acting ideal *opera*tions (when used in ethical feedback fashion) can resolve the tensions between feeling-reason, wisdom-folly alleles. This book explores basic conditions of spiritual healing in the light of a Buddhist-Christian ethics; it alludes to influential thinkers who, in attempts to resolve our tensions, invoke Spinoza but overlook the contradictions between his sublime teaching on feelings and his *axioms* on a monist substance. Spinoza's pantheist *Ethics* puts the cart before the horse[11] by effectively abrogating freedom. Trans*form*ative AIRR *opera*tions empower us inasmuch as we can confront the group interests and political coercions militating against the common good. To address our contradictions, I generalize GEM's insights into science, religion, philosophy and the arts by interpreting it as a "spiritual genome" whose "alleles" (congruent with how we arrive at knowledge) can help us responsibly address reality. GEM helps us by having appropriate our inbuilt set of AIRR *opera*tions and pursue trans*form*ative, interdisciplinary feedback. Scientists can now make synthetic nucleotides, manipulate natural nucleotides, or even alter our physical genomes. But are we too drunk to drive? Do our egoisms not turn us upon ourselves? We can only tick if we understand the basics of human knowing and respect ideals. Buddha and Jesus both enjoined a world community ethic whose allelic virtues I invoke in spite of postmodernist thought.

In *What is Philosophy*? Deleuze and Guattari argue that philosophy often fails to reach its intended wisdom; as remedy, they propose a triad: 1) plane of immanence 2) philosophy as the art of *form*ing, inventing and fabricating concepts and 3) conceptual personae. For them, concepts cannot be reduced to an object of science nor to the functions of scientific propositions. Concepts' *becoming* involves relations with other concepts on the same plane. Concepts support one another and belong to the same philosophy despite their different contours; related to other concepts, their partially overlapping threshold of indiscernibility makes their components inseparable. Scientific notions, however, are not defined by philosophical concepts but by functions or propositions that enable the sciences to communicate. Because objects such as geometrical spaces are scientifically constructed by functions, their philosophical concept, which is by no means given in a function, must be discovered. Conceptual personae are the subjects of a philosophy, on a par with the philosopher whose destiny is to become his conceptual personae or something other than what he is historically or mythologically. They "have a hazy" (61) existence halfway between concept and preconceptual plane. Passing from one to the other, they create concepts by interfacing with the plane of immanence. Deleuze and Guattari laud "idiots" who think for themselves. The old "idiot" (Descartes) wanted truth; "new idiots" like Kierkegaard and Nietzsche do not need the indubitable truths of mathematics. They want to turn "the absurd into the highest power of thought—in other words to create" (62). If Nietzsche signed himself "the Antichrist," "Dionysus crucified," Cusa and Descartes should have signed themselves "the Idiot.'" The new idiot is more like Job than Socrates. I sublate Deleuze and Guattari's triad and their reliance on Spinoza's pantheism and Nietzsche's atheism with GEM's triadic potency-*form*-act conjugate structure. Their view of "concept" includes what GEM studies as *form*ulations of insights. Unlike a Nietzschean *axi*ology (study of values) that prioritizes art but attacks the ascetic ideal, I defend ascetics. Potencies-*forms*-acts are "*metaphysical elements*" (a triadic unity in a *known*) equivalent to the experiencing-understanding-judging triad (a unity in *knowing*: *Insight*, 431). I interpret AIRR ideals as including metaxic in-betweens with which GEM's immanent cognitional structure addresses human events. Immanence, for GEM, is not restricted to "private" thinking as in Plato's Socrates or Descartes' "idiot"; it encompasses the self-transcendent AIRR ideals grounding social ethics or the sciences.

GEM refutes Hume by showing that the things skeptics doubt are, in fact, preconditions for skepticism to make sense. It challenges Kant's autonomous ideal which also led to skepticism (as in H. Kleist) and his moral *axio*ms that influenced *axio*logy's problematic foundations. For Kant, "transcendental" means the prior thought *forms*, the innate principles that give the mind its ability to *for*mulate perceptions and make experience intelligible. GEM's "*axio*logy" reintegrates our AIRR feelings-reason alleles that Descartes separated and Spinoza sought to reintegrate. It helps us settle our conflicts and to evaluate ongoing revolutions in any field of activity. Seeking congruences between philosophy, science and religion, I study how people per*form* in such fields. Arguing that a spiritual genome is analogous to our physical genome, I compare the way ideals link us to God with how ATGC nucleotide bases work in DNA. Unlike Kant, GEM "AIRR-links" percepts with values. It remains "ambivalent" about both by retaining their trans*form*ative power. If we are daily faced with patterns of evil that philosophers cannot explain away,[12] we must advert to the ways we exploit nature if and when ideals are left unintegrated. I use "AIRR in-betweens" to "sublate" ethical ambiguities in positive ways so that *axio*logies and the oppressive measures of totalitarian regimes recover their AIRR ideals—lost in Kantian *axio*ms and in ensuing *axio*logies.

Unlike coded nucleotides, AIRR loci lead to self-transcending, ethical actions and enable us to evaluate such actions. GEM "locates" immanence in our ideal AIRR *opera*tions that pivot on our direct, inverse and reflective insights. This is a fine but important point. Socrates attributed his genius (*daimon*) to an inner voice that issued prohibitory messages. To him, being wise meant knowing he was unwise. GEM adds that living out a self-transcending ethics is a way of wisdom. Voegelin focuses on Plato's ideal of love (a luminous, spiritual metaxic event occurring within a more comprehensive reality never reducible to intentionality's subject or object poles). I develop a Socratic midwife method that may guide us into the depths of a spiritual art of ethical love so as to help us recover Socrates' view that philosophy is about virtue. I also evaluate and complement Deleuze and Guattari's restrictive immanentism with an AIRR immanence open to the numinous.

Socrates sought to educate by birthing a spiritual fire in our souls. GEM does not estrange AIRR practical from pure reason. It helps us birth *within us* a transcultural method able to remedy Deleuze and Guattari's failure to give us and adequate criteria for judging. They do not explain how they can reconcile their acceptance of Spinoza's immanentism and Kant's transcendentalism. They laud Kant's *Critique of Judgment* (one of his last works in which the mind overcomes the limits that Kant had so carefully laid down in his earlier works), but fail to see that a Spinozist monism contradicts Kant's pluralist views. Kant ignores Spinoza's deductivist order of ideas as the order of things. Lonergan addresses Spinoza and Kant's failures to develop adequate theories of being. Kant does not explain how we generate categories, how series of judgments constitute a fact, arrive at objectivity and lay a verification plane a critical philosophy calls for (*Insight*, 339).

In his Foreword to Deleuze and Guattari's *A Thousand Plateaus*, Brian Massumi touches on the authors' nomadic thought that replaces the closed equation of representation. For them, it is not the points but the *ponts* (bridges) that count. I argue that GEM's AIRR *pont*-bridge is able to order the nomadic chaos of Deleuze and Guattari's immanence-concept-conceptual personae triad *and* to map the undefined points that mathematics organizes into loci (systems). A rhizome is an expanding root system with a vast network of shoots difficult to uproot. Deleuze and Guattari's notion of rhizome is not a tracing mechanism, but a *map* with multiple entry points for dislodging preconceived ideas. It is a multiplicity without any unity that could fix a subject or object. For them, psychoanalysis represents the subconscious existing prior to any tracing. Tracing does not create anything new. Mapping[13] constructs the unconscious; it orients us toward an experimental contact with the real. GEM maps East and West's multiple entry points into psyche and mind. In GEM, images are presentations or heuristic symbols in which insights grasp what is real; they are a source of unity in the subject. So as not to limit mapping to tracing functions, I focus on how East-West thinkers have objectified experience. GEM's "meta-nomadic" AIRR horizon maps how mathematicians think, how they can be open to the transcendent. For example, Fourier's work in thermodynamics (series representing functions in practical ways subject only to very general conditions) reinforced his view that God is immanent to a creation he transcends. For Deleuze and Guattari, their rhizome can dislodge preconceived ideas; yet, their fluid notion of conceptual personae cannot ground East or West spiritualities. This book inquires into how GEM maps images and the representations of sense in ways that parallel, but sublate how Kant uses symbolic representation to link unconditional categorical imperatives with finitude. It remaps Deleuze and Guattari's thought-as-rhizome from a moving point of view that integrates Western personalism with Eastern cosmic views. Chapter 2 grounds my analogy between our physical and spiritual genomes. Chapter 3 studies mathematical loci so as to fashion a spiritual topology. Part Two argues that approaches to loci in biochemistry, mathematics, Nishida and GEM reinforce one another and thus can be related in AIRR feedback ways. It integrates a Buddhist, impersonal field of immanence through an ethically based ongoing feedback whose objectivity lies in nomadic subjects' AIRR loci.

AIRR point-loci sets have subsets *open* in their intersecting sets of *operations*; such allelic loci function through a potency-*form*-act *triad* emergent in our minds. While ATGC nucleotides *code* our genome (using sets of correspondences between DNA nucleotide pair triplets and amino acids in proteins) AIRR ideals permit us to be creatively *free*. By ethically empowering others, we spiritually become "greater" than the parts that constitute our bodies or minds. GEM can dialogue with postmodern views for it exposes secularists' hidden presuppositions. Deleuze and Guattari ably relate philosophy to art's intricate percepts: art "*thinks*" with its percepts and affects, just as much as philosophy does with its concepts; but they fail to explain how their use of Nietzsche's esthetic model justifies their philosophy of immanence. Nietzsche and Foucault's view the actual differently. For Nietzsche, we use an intuition specific to concepts: a field, a plane or ground that must not be confused with them but that shelters their seeds and the personae who cultivate them. "For Foucault, what matters is the difference between the present"[14] and what we become. GEM judges concepts; it integrates chaos and percepts within a plane of immanent self-transcendence.

Deleuze and Guattari see philosophers as "plunging into chaos" so as to extract the determinations with which to produce the diagrammatic features of a plane of immanence. For them, every *form* taking shape within chaos vanishes with "infinite speed." Chaos is not disorder, nor a nothingness but a *virtual*, containing all possible particles and drawing out all possible forms without reference or consistency. Science, on the other hand, relinquishes thought's infinite speed so as to arrive at reference, that is, a relationship between a variable's values. By setting a limit to chaos, the sciences can *form* a variable determined as abscissa while the limit *form*s a universal constant that cannot be gone beyond. The first functives of science are therefore the limit and the variable; "reference is a relationship between values of the variable" (118). By going beyond this notion of reference, philosophy's plane of immanence retains infinite possibilities; its concepts give consistency to the virtual. If *form*s can lead to changes *open* to infinity, and if Cezanne found mystic meanings hidden in the "chaos" he painted, I seek to ground chaotic immanence with self-transcendent AIRR meaning. For GEM, in judgment, one arrives at a virtually unconditioned that I relate to Deleuze and Guattari's notion of a *virtual open* to the infinite. Complex judgments grasp evidence as sufficient for the virtually unconditioned of other prospective judgments. Affirming a known involves three elements: a conditioned, a *link* between the conditioned and its conditions and the fulfillment of the conditions. Merely asking questions for reflection involves a conditioned. Prospective judgments become virtually unconditioned if the conditions are fulfilled. Conditions are known when one grasps the link between a conditioned and its conditions.[15]

Like GEM, Deleuze and Guattari argue that we master human rationality's diversity by constantly reappropriating one's subjectivity; unlike GEM, they rely on a (Kantian) notion that intellect intuits essences. As postmodernists, they question the subject's ability to be independent either of the body's "deceptions" or of the tyranny imposed by historico-cultural conditions. At best, one attains a relational I-unity in a visual field's subjective sensation. Relying on Spinoza and Fichte's attempts to arrive "at mental objects determinable as real beings" (207), they combine concepts (as mathematicians combine sets of objects into subsets without regard to order); they explore how art, philosophy and science interface by analyzing the problems of interference (215) among the plane of immanence of philosophy, the plane of composition of art and the plane of reference of science. They conclude that many of these interferences are extrinsic and "cannot be localized." In contrast, I argue that our *opera*tional AIRR loci help us localize planes' interferences and their interconnections.

Besides enabling us to actually carry on co*opera*tive ventures in all facets of life, our AIRR feedback *opera*tions underlie and mediate conceptual triads. Potency, in GEM, denotes what is *to be known* in fully explanatory knowledge. It corresponds to Deleuze and Guattari's plane of immanence in that it applies to all possible knowledge within their plane. *Form* denotes what is to be known by understanding things fully in *relation* to *one another*; it corresponds to their notion of concept. Act (what is to be known in a fully validated act of judgment) incorporates but expands on their "conceptual personae."[16] In everyday life, we apprehend reality in 3-dimensional terms; but in fact, this is subject to a feedback intellectual-spiritual framework (Part Two). GEM's feedback framework can effect an ethical, mutually beneficial encounter between East-West philosophies in ways that Deleuze and Guattari fail to do. *Yana* can mean a noun (as in *Mahayana* "greater" vehicle) or a verb ("going, moving"). In both Hinduism and Buddhism, *yana* and *marga* express the metaphor of spiritual practice as a path or journey—not unlike that of a Chinese *Tao*.

Deleuze and Guattari lay an important basis for East-West discussions by arguing that the void is *not* nothingness. For them, Sartre's presupposition of an impersonal transcendental field restored the rights of immanence. Yet, for two millennia, Taoists and Buddhists have enunciated analogical views of immanence. One way to lay out a transcendental field that restores the rights of immanence (in a Buddhist, meta-Sartrean way) is to compare East-West artistic perspectives. Artists embody humanity's desire to invent and perfect.[17] This desire bore fruit, in the West, in a painting's vanishing point (one or more imaginary points toward which our eyes are invited), and in China, in a way of painting that combines parallel perspective with a viewpoint from above. We artists (in the broad sense) should integrate our lives along the lines of a *loving harmony*. Just as East-West artists use different *forms* to achieve perspective in ways that graphically depict three-dimensional relationships on a two-dimensional plane, so East and West's complementary views of being and *nothingness*, can serve as intellectual *forms* for integrating their ethical and mystical perspectives in trans-*form*ative ways. As crossfertilization succeeds by uniting gametes, so I seek to crossfertilize the AIRR foundational perspectives of Buddhist-Christian thought. Buddhist "nothingness" is not mere nihility; it is a relational allelic template virtually interrelating all beings. Chinese have associated it with "non-self, non-action" relating us to deeper realities. I refer to it in this text as "void" (emptiness = *sunya(ta)*), close to a mystical Taoist Way.

For Deleuze and Guattari, the universals of contemplation, reflection and communication explored in the three eras of the Eidetic, Critical, and Phenomenological are inseparable from the long history of the "illusion" of transcendence. Kierkegaard leaps outside the plane of immanence. What is restored to him in this suspension is "existence on the plane of immanence." For when we "encounter the transcendent within immanence, all we do is recharge the plane of immanence with immanence itself." What constantly reaffirms sciences' opposition to religion,[18] "and at the same time, happily makes the unification of science impossible is the substitution of reference for all transcendence" (*Philosophy*, 125). What brings the two together is that functives are not concepts but figures defined by a spiritual tension rather than by a spatial intuition. Husserl set the tone for modern philosophy by conceiving immanence "as that of the flux lived by subjectivity" (47) wherein the transcendent is to be found within immanence itself—a theme GEM also pursues—in open ways. GEM, like Brentano and Husserl, studies our minds' intentional acts rather than their contents; scientific method supplies philosophy "with instances of the heuristic structures which a metaphysics integrates into a single view of the concrete universe."[19] Science seeks to universalize a single law, a single force. As an intellectualist (*non*-conceptualist) method, GEM overcomes oppositions between science and religion; it locates intelligibility in the AIRR set of basic terms and relations *opera*ting in scientists and in religious thinkers. Making possible the specialized acts of understanding, in which particular types of *form*s are grasped in their actual intelligibility, is a person's more general set of AIRR ideals. Lonergan's *Insight* pivots on this set whose undefined terms and relations dynamically "bind cognitional operations together."[20] Because it is *undefined*, our AIRR set of ideals enables philosophers, artists and scientists to co*opera*te if and when they "appropriate" their own set. By appropriating one's AIRR ideals, one knows in ways iso*morph*ic with what is known. Knowing is a related set of acts; the known is the related set of contents of these acts. The pattern of the relations between AIRR acts is similar in *form* to the pattern of the relations between the contents of the acts due to an *isomorphism* between our AIRR structure of knowing and structures of the known. *Preconceptual* insights grasp in images intelligible possibilities that may be relevant to an understanding of data. This permits a transition from latent to explicit metaphysics realized in a *series* of affirmations of concrete and recurring structures in self-affirming subjects (*Insight*, 399).

GEM helps us "AIRR appropriate" what is *not* confined to the visual field or an I-unity. As with Freud, it sees human thought and speech as not *merely* rational but as also governed by our psyche moved by our feelings' inherent contradictions. Mere logical negation does not convey anything 'real.' Logic need not touch the concrete being of a table or a desk; the psyche wants a real situation that it can embrace in all its glaring contradictions. Naive realists cannot remain "naive" if they acknowledge the psychological facts. "For them knowing is a matter of taking a good look; objectivity is a matter of seeing just what is there to be seen. For them my account of human understanding would appear to present intelligence as subjective,"[21] empiricist or idealist. GEM does not leap into transcendence; it focuses on correct insights. It stresses that our intellects do *not* intuit essences. Modern art seeks to evoke the abyss of being in lines, colors and plastic *form*s; the sciences approximate an ideal of complete explanation. GEM links philosophical and artistic *form*s with the AIRR criteria of scientific and hermeneutic methods.

A First "Let's Get Real" Concurrent Dialectic

"Realist": John, you start off talking about a tipsy woman. You ask about what makes one tick. But then look at all the stuff you throw in there. John are you for real? You don't know what "ticking" *means*! I just want to have my fun and be left alone after a hard day's work, you know?

John (sticking to his ideals): I grant you that self-transcendence (trans*form*ative AIRR loci) involves abstraction. Because of this, I use a spiritual genome analogy to recast the brain-mind "problem" in terms of our organic, intellectual *and spiritual* development. Trans*form*ative love is possible inasmuch as we appropriate ethical (religious) ideals in GEM's heuristic way. As those in power influence the political process in subtle (unfair?) ways, so we need to identify why a genius like Gauss or philosophers of science have insisted on the twin aspects of the inductive-deductive method. This book seeks to empower us by mapping our AIRR *opera*tions' trans*form*ative abilities.

CHAPTER 2

TRANSF*ORM*ATIVE POTENCIES IN OUR GENOMES

*The Case for an Analogy
between Physical and Spiritual Genomes*

Pursuing the goals of my *Empowering the Lonely Crowd*, this book explores allelic *loci* in biology, in mathematics and in Nishida's thought. This chapter seeks to establish an analogy between how the adenine, thymine, guanine and cytosine (ATGC) bases code a physical genome, on one hand, and how our AIRR *opera*tions trans*form*atively course between the alleles of faith and reason (enabling our self-centered natures to act in benevolent ways) on the other. It develops my ATGC-AIRR analogy by arguing that while there are genetic instructions in the cell nucleus that control proteins' makeup, GEM "locates" our spiritual alleles in our AIRR ideals and in a generalized, *intellectualist* potency-*form*-act triad that effectively sublates Deleuze and Guattari's *conceptualist* triad. By clarifying brain-mind problems, GEM grounds a self-transcendent ethics and spirituality.

Does conscious experience arise in a brain or does a brain "arise" in conscious experience? Like Husserl, GEM opts for the latter. While psychophysics and neuroscience seek to empirically demonstrate the unity of mind and body by relating increases in bodily energy to corresponding increases in mental activity, I seek to establish a case for an analogy between our physical genome and a trans*form*ative, spiritual one that, arising in conscious experience and *opera*ting through our "AIRR allelic in-betweens," helps us interrelate our various sciences with ethics and daily life. If lasers use the basic principle that atoms and molecules can be excited to higher energy levels, a spiritual genome raises us to higher *forms* of allelic reason-faith consciousness and of spirituality. If in electronics, a feedback circuit determines the frequency of wave oscillations, my analogies compare cycles such as those of cells or waves so as to "AIRR-feedback guide" our mind-spirits; if in a helium-neon laser, helium catalyzes an energy input to the neon, GEM "meta-catalyzes" us.

What is the underlying principle binding the seemingly unrelated spheres of cellular processes and the psyche? Empiricists, uninterested in *spirit*, fail to reconcile the mind's ineffable qualia with the quantifiable matter of the brain. GEM's potency-*form*-act conjugate triad allows for the traditional body-mind spirituality "*triad*." These triads can guide us through the shoals of privatizing egoisms that exploit legal loopholes. Rather than explaining a causal path from the physical to the psychical, a trans*form*ative ethics argues that there is more than a circular, acausal correspondence between body, psyche and spirit. Our bodies need enzymes (proteins that enable chemical reactions involved in living organisms' metabolism by acting as biological catalysts); our mind-spirits need AIRR ideals—rooted in, but not reducible to molecular processes.

Our complementary AIRR *opera*tions guide our spirits. Yet, we know that there is a gap between our AIRR ideal *opera*tions and how we act; fallible, we often fail to live up to these ideals. Do the gaps existing between our actual functioning and AIRR ideals allow any solution? I suggest that trans*form*ative AIRR loci are part of an answer to confronting evil. Such allelic in-between loci go beyond empiricism; they o*pera*te on the cognitive data and actions of persons' own AIRR *opera*tional loci as functionally "integrative pivots" inviting conversion and ethical coo*pera*tion. AIRR mental acts are very complex. Relying on Lonergan's explanation of these acts, I develop them as allelic loci that can be and are sublated in spirituality, as e. g. summarized by Nishida and his Kyoto School disciple, Nishitani. In these two men's' philosophies, "locus" is a way to virtually draw out all possible *forms* that build society and to ground or transcend mere "subjects." Figures 1 to 4 illustrate my strategy of relating our AIRR mental loci to those of biology, mathematics or ethics.

Knowledge is a self-corrective process anchored in the virtually unconditioned, but it is reinforced with a virtue ethics that promotes the greater good. The theological virtues of faith, hope and love (reason's alleles) have a crucial role in inspiring us to commit ourselves to such a greater good. If ideological biases co-opt youths' development, GEM allelic loci of love can free youths. Let me unpack the above assertions by relating the structural and trans*form*ational elements of physical and spiritual genomes' unique feedback abilities by way of three interludes. A first interlude links discoveries in genetics and physics with creative insights and with virtue. The second interlude on Wilfred Bion's grid categorizes all events in human interactions with vertical-horizontal axes—a procedure analogous to a Cartesian mapping of analytic geometry. The third interlude touches on Pythagorean notions underlying numbers. The three interludes seek to help us locate or map the AIRR loci that can integrate" our outside with our inside by duly recognizing the non-reducible domain of religion problematized by Kant's immanental *axio*ms on "reality."

First Interlude:
4-3-5 Feedback Structures and Transformative Loci's Mediations

Scientists ask heuristic questions, per*form* experiments, confirm or reject hypotheses; they reach knowing by classifying data by sensible similarity, correlating data and verifying systems of correlations. Correlating acts and contents of knowing involves 3 possibilities: 1) one correlates contents to one another, which yields *pure* (explanatory) conjugates—terms defined implicitly by empirically established[1] laws; 2) one prescinds from contents and correlates *acts* of knowing so as to obtain *special pure* conjugates—an original GEM insight; 3) one correlates acts and contents that yield *experiential* conjugates or correlatives whose meaning appeals to the data of our senses and to the content of our experience (as verified by scientists or in common experience). In the third case, one is working toward either a scientific goal or GEM's overall goal of appropriating one's AIRR ideals so as to orderly deal with recurrent chaos. To explain all data one moves *from* experiential *to* explanatory conjugates. By relating AIRR *opera*tions as they *opera*te through conjugate triadic structures (analogously to how amino acid triplets affect DNA's nucleotides), GEM can trans*form* any discipline *if* its practitioners appropriate their *opera*tions' feedback ability; they can do so by reaching out through spiritual conjugates guided by a socioethical map of love.

Reductionists use theory to reduce our AIRR loci feedback ability to brain-mind structures, an extreme *form* of which occurs in behaviorists' stimulus-response views based on balancing pleasure and pain (on our minds' "inputs and outputs"). They take for granted the working of their own AIRR *opera*tions in futile attempts to reduce the *opera*tions to brain-mind so as to eliminate the reality of spirit. They overlook life's ambiguous realities as well as our spirits' deeper spiritual trans*form*ations. I shall briefly explain the set of our 4-3-5 ethically trans*form*ative loci *opera*ting in our spiritual genome and contrast this ethical set with reductionist or analytical too limiting "quantifying" mental sets.

1. ATGC bases code our physical genome as mediated by molecular chains of proteins built from 20 different types of amino acid triplets. ATGC bases need these triplets' mediation to code a genome in what I call a 4-3-5 feedback structure. In a physical genome, "4-3-5 structure" refers to DNA's 4 ATGC bases (4), to series of mediating amino acid triads (3) and to the RNA template for protein synthesis when uracil (U) substitutes for thymine (5). In a spiritual genome, "4" stands for the AIRR *opera*tions we cannot avoid using; "3", for the GEM potency-*form*-act triad conjugates, "5" for GEM's fifth precept, be in love. If ATGC-U is a code directing physical life,[2] AIRR loci "lead to" a 4-3-5 foundational ideal of love enabling us to live ethical lives. "AIRR-love" and "4-3-5 GEM" are equivalent expressions for mapping a GEM map of love. ATGC-U's GC bases have a GEM "analogue" in sensory-theoretical knowledge (statistical-classical

methods); AT-U bases are "analogous" to judging-acting-loving. If ATGC bases are complemented by uracil (in RNA), our AIRR opera*t*ions are complemented by a 4-3-5 ethical metaxy that, I argue, Taoists, Pythagoreans and Buddhists located in a cosmic mysticism, and that GEM locates in the AIRR-love actions any person per*form*s. As RNA is a 4-3-5 template, so love is a template activated by the trans*form*ative 4-3-5 ideals of Buddhist-Christian ethical precepts.[3] I develop a "4-3-5-enabled" transcultural ethics, that, with Aristotle, seeks to avoid infinite regress.[4] Such an ethics focuses on ideal AIRR loci that help us choose the good and reject evil within one's horizon as enriched by 4-3-5 ethico-religious convictions. Since human activity is challenged by a higher good, I transpose Plato's metaxic *daimon* (partially based on the gods' whims) to our own AIRR (4-3-5) actions.

Virtues trans*form* our lives by enabling us to find a middle ground that ethically mediates between extremes. In a physical genome, the locus of a gene on its chromosome can mean the gene itself. In a spiritual genome, the analogues of genes are ideal AIRR opera*t*ional feedback loci affected by good-evil, interiority-exteriority or reason-faith allelic loci. Such feedback loci can be linked through some of the "in-between" triadic functions as proposed in GEM, in various philosophers' triads and in mathematics. If ATGC-U bases trans*form* us physically, AIRR-love opera*t*ions are in-between ideal loci that transcend DNA-RNA structures as they 4-3-5 mediate between a Buddhist "*void*"[5] and a Christian art of love with AIRR ideals that seek to re-empower our distorted ideals. An *ideal* functioning of AIRR opera*t*ions is rare; virtues and ethics are necessary to restore ideals.

2. 4-3-4 models, impervious to 4-3-5 trans*form*ative ways of opposing evil, are restricted to the AIRR feedback which humans cannot avoid using; yet, unless AIRR opera*t*ions opera*t*e with a love-interrelatedness metaxy ideal, they can be co-opted. In *Insight*, Lonergan focused on his triads; in *Method*, he broadened that focus by studying self-transcendent love's role in a foundational 4-3-5 feedback method. A 4-3-5 shorthand helps me relate GEM's AIRR levels *and* their in-betweens to concrete situations, to reductionist claims and to 4-3-4 analyses. The latter two's pertinent trans*form*ative loci lack 4-3-5 feedback (a grounded method mediating between our AIRR ideals and a 4-3-5 reason-faith allelic stance subtended by love and hope); theirs are would-be solutions. GEM 4-3-5 plunges into chaos so as to retrieve ordered AIRR-4-3-5 feedback possibilities with virtue's ideals using the virtually unconditioned of judgment. Nietzsche, in "*Genealogy of Morals*" (second essay) takes on an almost prayerful tone as he pleads for an Antichrist's "sublime wickedness" and the "nausea" of nihilism. I view his "prayerful" plea as a 4-3-4, quasi-4-3-5 ideal quest. Nietzscheans and atheists misunderstand prayer, but it is implicit in their thinking. It is not inherent in the data of sense, but may well influence how researchers conduct their investigations. GEM's 4-3-5 feedback structure differs from ATGC-U's 4-3-5 structure for, unlike the latter, it is not coded. If physical alleles guide bodily development, AIRR opera*t*ions need love's allelic ability to bridge atheist gaps by evaluating

the past in the light of the future. Such an evaluation requires untold trillions of cooperative decisions. I argue that "4-3-5 faith-hope-love" are part of persons' antecedent willingness to transcend self, a view that justifies a notion of spiritual transformative allelic loci. I study the ideals and mental acuity of geniuses and of ordinary folk so as to link their AIRR-love loci. All humans rely on the empirical data of sense and of consciousness. GEM extends AIRR data to include those of 4-3-5 consciousness. Glenn Gould reinvigorated music with the computer; John Cage helped us hear music anew. GEM helps us hear atheist *axio*logies anew as a pining for 4-3-5 ideals. A 4-3-5 *axio*logy addresses the drawbacks of Spinozan monism and of Hegelian immanence as "quasi-4-3-5 stances" that nurture our present chaotic conditions in that they reduce 4-3-5 values to claims of "4-3-4 self-sufficiency" (as do Nietzsche and Deleuze). In *Die Geburt der Tragödie aus dem Geist der Musik*, Nietzsche set up a model that led to his genealogy (*Entstehung, Herkunft, Abkunft*) of a courageous becoming. An ideals-based map of love (4-3-5 *axio*logy of "becoming") also fosters courage; it rejects neither self-transcendence nor teleology even as it accepts Goethe or Bateson's *Gestalt morph*ologies of 4-3-4 cultural patterns.

3. 4-2 reductionists overlook the set of our 4-3-5 trans*form*ative loci and reduce our AIRR-love abilities to body-mind automatisms—a theoretical position that covertly turns our ineffable 4-3-5 qualia into "4-2 quanta" in failed attempts to do away with spirituality. Neither of our 4-3-5 structured physical or spiritual genomes can be reduced to analytico-synthetic structures. Kant's disputed synthetic a priori[6] set the stage for these 4-2 quantified logics that deal with spatial arrangements by isolating AIRR-4-3-5 ideals. A Nietzschean set of partially trans*form*ative 4-3-4 loci invites a chaos that leads to totalitarianisms. Nietzsche, a non-mathematician, was unfamiliar with modern chaos theory's *axio*m of "No Ultimate Truth." His *axio*logy does open up a 4-2 chaotic *aporia* from which we must be saved. GEM's poly*morph*ism of human consciousness, "the one and only key" to philosophy,"[7] saves us from such *aporia* by investigating the roots of science and mathematics. Trans*form*atively sublating 4-2 reductionism and other "isms" is a GEM forte. If numbers can be reduced to sets (and number theory to set theory) and if chemical properties like valence can be reduced to properties of molecules and atoms, GEM corrects 4-2 reductionisms that reduce the special sciences to a theorized "unity of science" with AIRR science-faith feedback.

Alleles are one of the different *form*s of a gene or DNA sequence that can exist at a single locus (some of which are *not* expressed in a heterozygote). GEM orders our AIRR *opera*tions on the model of how mathematicians handle the loci of points' infinite possibilities. A locus is any system of points, lines or curves that satisfy one or more conditions. If a set of points consists of only those points whose coordinates satisfy an equation, then that set is the locus of the equation, the equation being that of the locus. AIRR loci are sublatable alleles (not reducible to systems). Lacking a foundational 4-3-5 metaxy to convert or trans*form* AIRR loci and to deploy reason-faith alleles, 4-3-4 modes cannot refute 4-2 reductionisms. They are like cells that, bereft of necessary trans*form*ing properties, fail as cells. Against those who reduce us to cellular functions (supposing that matter can create thought or intent), cognitive and AI (artificial intelligence) theorists argue that a model of consciousness must first solve the problem of where it fits in the brain and what functions it per*form*s before devising any model.[8] GEM's functional specialties critically appraise self-transcending actions so as to avoid 4-2 cultural relativism. While the latter lack insights into "relational feedback," a 4-3-5 GEM ethics finds solutions to life's stresses: AIRR cognitional levels are mediated by a body-mind spirituality. Probing molecular mechanisms to effect physical healing is one thing; ethics and spiritual healing are another. If a genome is the complete DNA content of an organism and if it is restricted to codes, a spiritual genome "AIRR-enables" us to achieve mutual transself quests by taming unruly ego's and reconciling selves by way of free 4-3-5 spiritualities—as is here "feedback illustrated":

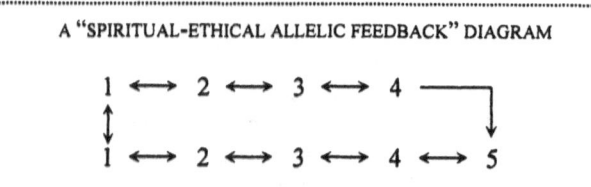

A "SPIRITUAL-ETHICAL ALLELIC FEEDBACK" DIAGRAM

This spiritual-ethical allelic feedback is to be applied in fig. 1-4 to illustrate what I mean in the entire text by 4-3-5 allelic loci that, through their feedback potential (rooted in GEM conversions), may help tame unruly ego's.

Second Interlude:
Bion's Categorizations of Human Interactions

Bion explored the psyche's deep and *form*less infinite with his notions of trans*form*ations in "O" (Ultimate Truth, Absolute Reality). His subjective science is an objective and numinous psychoanalytic theory that parallels my efforts to relate East-West 4-3-5 notions of the absolute.

Bion eschews words that may lock the reader into preconceived ideas. Instead, he "mathematically expresses" his deeply held psychogenetic-spiritual notions. The vertical axis of his grid is his "genetic axis" categorizing (A-H) levels of complexity from A) Kantian noumena (beta elements) to thoughts (alpha elements) to dreams to preconceptions (collection of thoughts) to abstract concepts on to H) algebraic calculus. The horizontal axis involves a random selection of possible uses (1-6 . . . n) of his vertical scheme, which includes hypothesizing, false *form*ulations, notation, attention, inquiry and action, . . . n. This axis has n number of possible columns. Bion encourages us to try to apply his vertical axis to all sorts of mental experience, n . . .; his vertical axis is that of genetic "mentation". It includes protomental, unconscious processes such as dreams (that do affect what the mind does). During a psychoanalytic session, each event might be found on a ground and designated by letter and number. So Beta-element Action (A-6) describes unconscious activity without reflection or thought automatism. B6 describes conscious action with awareness. B2 thoughts would tend toward a false hypothesis. While G1 would be an entire abstract hypothetical system of scientific thoughts (excluding calculus and algebra) and be valid, G2 thoughts are false.[9]

Bion's general approach is consistent with GEM. I interpret both as spiritually genomic structural-trans*form*ative efforts. Bion's vertical axis is "equivalent" to GEM's 4-3-5 trans*form*ative, "genetic" aspect. His horizontal axis and his caesura of birth and postnatal development parallel some of the GEM insights I include in allegedly "irrelevant," in-between and mystic metaxies of a Buddhist-Christian ethic. A 4-3-5 *form*ula is not a spiritual genie out of a 4-2 bottle; rather, it translates body-mind reductionisms into a body-mind-spirit triad compatible with higher virtues. The cardinal virtues are pivots on the natural plane, but there emerges the need for the higher plane of faith, hope and love. This book pivots on the empowering, trans*form*ative loci of a faith-hope-love triad, a triad that Bion's categorization of human interactions bolsters with a grid that mediates a caesura. If "caesura" usually refers to a pause or break in music or poetry, for Bion, it refers to the *break* in one's being caused by the act of birth and by our initiation into numinous trans*form*ations. Faith is a leaven that influences society. Bion's grid reconciles present realities with a wisdom mediated by the 4 cardinal virtues or by Buddhism's three refuges (the Buddha, the *dharma*, and the *sangha* community). Too often, some writers seem compelled to claim a quasi-omniscience in discoursing about a given subject. They must appear godlike in that they cannot make or admit a mistake lest they be pilloried. A GEM metaxy makes room for the right ways of thinking and acting advocated by both Aristotle and Buddhism. It assumes that we are fallible and that we need one another in innumerable ways to survive. GEM complements the ways Bion interrelates his caesura-grids' knowledge interactions. If a psychotherapist's role is helping a patient, GEM's role is helping us co*operate* in virtuous ways. Whether it be a Zen that helps people act decisively, activists who promote equal justice for all, or Levinas-Derrida based efforts to locate the basis of ethics from a phenomenological or a deconstructionist standpoint, many seek ethical ideals. If Bion's grid evaluates our knowing's trans*form*ational and structural loci, GEM grounds his grid.

Given life's rational and irrational in-betweens, chapter 3's spiritual topology links psyche and spirit through our spiritual AIRR ideals in ways analogical to Bion's grid. Our AIRR acts are involved even in our patterns of sleep or meditation which are part of a continuum of sensibility open to ideals. Dreams of the night and heuristic "dreams" of the day are integral to working out AIRR ideals.[10] If poststructralists seek alternative texts in any discourse, GEM and Bion's grid help us see multifarious sides of a text or a person's intention. Our task is to contextualize in-between allelic loci in reality and in thought. As geneticists map genes or mathematicians map functions, I map allelic AIRR loci. If a function maps a number in one set to another number in another set, I map AIRR alleles *opera*tive in all our knowing-doing into "loving sets" that allow us to ethically 4-3-5 reorient our lives. This involves con-textualizing transcultural AIRR alleles and remapping them in feedback ways: AIRR ideals *opera*te as in-between loci in search of a loving, foundational 4-3-5 ethics. GEM distinguishes between classical culture as single universal norm and culture as it is empirically studied (summarized in Geertz's phrase "local culture"). It goes beyond classical culture to address transculturally (allelically relate) real situations in local cultures or in religion.[11] The first two interludes on 4-3-5 foundations and Bion's grids lead to notions of AIRR harmony.

Third Interlude:
4-3-5 Pythagorean-AIRR Notions of Harmony in Numbers

Just as ATGC-uracil codes by way of proteins built from amino acid triplets, so "AIRR+love" mediates meanings. GEM studies how a faith-hope-love triad helps us interrelate our lives with God and others. Reducing free will or consciousness to a strictly causal approach overlooks the subjective nature of mind and its need of virtue. A 4-3-5 GEM "bridges" nature's irrational and rational sides. Like many other problems, that of irrational numbers was introduced by the Greeks who had long adhered to the rational number line model of continuity. Consider a 4-3-5 right angle, with sides 4 and 3 whose hypotenuse is the *rational* number 5. Rational numbers were the basis of the Pythagoreans' finely tuned view of the universe as one physically and metaphysically describable by whole numbers. They relied on their theorem that says that the length of any third side of a square-cornered triangle can be calculated if one knows the lengths of the other two sides. One day, some Pythagoreans were asked to solve an overtly simple problem: how long would a fence be that cuts a measured square plot of land diagonally into two triangles? They were unable to measure the fence in ways that would yield the precise numerical ratio in question. It would be almost, but not exactly 3/2 the expected length. Having the *irrational* square root of 2 (1.4142), its hypotenuse was "irrational" in two ways: 1) it was not a ratio of whole numbers; 2) it failed to fit within their conceptual realm. Pythagoreans' belief that "all things are numbers"[12] influenced many philosophers (up to Spinoza and Leibniz) to unduly blend religion and reasoning.

GEM does not do so; rather, it focuses on the trans*form*ative loci of our AIRR *opera*tions. Both our physical and spiritual genomes have analogical 4-3-5 trans*form*ative, "disruptive," yet structured patterns that function in unique ways. Feynman's *QED* (quantum electrodynamics) uses the Pythagorean theorem to locate points in three-dimensional space by combining amplitude arrows to explain photons and electrons in one dimensional space; he calls it "an absurd" process. I map AIRR alleles mediating Feynman's "absurd"[13] approximations and the modest genius' play on words. A scalar field assigns a single number (scalar) to every point in space (n-dimensional space with a real or complex number attached to each point in the space). Scalar fields indicate, for instance, a temperature distribution throughout space or the air pressure. I use 4-3-5 loci to remap neuroscience's complexification of our physico-psychic reality. The in-betweens of real (rational and complex) numbers, of Feynman diagrams or of 4-3-5 loci are relevant issues. GEM's ethical 4-3-5 in-betweens mediate between the transcendent and the physical. I locate trans*form*ative in-betweens that enable us to deal with our irrationalities. Pythagorean triples are integers a, b, c (e. g. 4-3-5) satisfying a + b = c. There are infinitely many such triples which we can generate. I focus on the 4-3-5 nuanced loci that imply the in-betweens of the symmetry and asymmetry, the rationality and irrationality of the human mind and its relation to material bodies and spiritual possibilities; an AIRR spirit philosophy seeks to link the in-betweens of 4-3-4 models and 4-3-5 genomes. As the Greek crisis of irrationals led to a focus from numbers to geometry, so today we "algebraize" geometry. If irrational numbers have approximate roots, I seek to "approximate" 4-3-5 foundations. In projective geometry, right angles and circles lose their Euclidean properties; this allows for a more efficient trans*form*ation of coordinates that focuses on projective features left invariant. An orthogonal matrix (a real matrix that is equal to the inverse of its transpose) leaves the quadratic *form* invariant. Approximations are a fact of life in physics which recognizes that orthogonality in a linear set may not mean the same as perpendicularity. Milo Wolff's spherical standing waves (with presence everywhere in space) are also approximations. 4-3-5 foundations must also "approximate," that is, one must transpose the analogue of a real matrix to a GEM AIRR-4-3-5 feedback matrix where "absurdity" and an uncertainty principle are recognized as facts of life.

These three interludes illustrate my strategy for a GEM mediation of what is in-between 1) our individual lives, each caught up in one's relative milieu, 2) mirror reflections or mental images that are quite different from that of the objects they reflect and 3) mathematicians' 4-3-4 invariant correlations. I seek to ground a 4-3-5 analogy in our two genomes' particularities (chapter 2). A 4-3-5 spiritual topology (chapter 3) presupposes that abstract laws do not depend on such particularities. A 4-3-5 spirit philosophy studies how GEM faces such issues as each person's individuality (the general, invariant AIRR mental acts of all observers) and the nature of theorizing. Moving beyond the algorithms of repetitive processes, chapter 4 uses mutually reinforcing loci in Buddhism and GEM to explore "grounds" for a trans*form*ative feedback built on the in-between variations within AIRR invariance allowing us to address human policies in ethical ways. Chapter 5 then explores a spirituality that *transposes* our intellectual (mathematical) patterns of experience in 4-3-5 feedback ways.

Anticipating how we Locate
4-3-5 Spiritual Allelic Loci's Immaterial Aspects

For Platonists, the soul or *psyche* was the locus of thought and emotion.

Hume's "bundle theory of mind" denied the Cartesian view that experiences belong to an immaterial soul. I locate mind-*psyche* in our "4-3-5 spirit" (including our will, soul, emotions, feelings) as linked to one's body within spacetime. Spirit trans*form*atively integrates body-mind interactions, as suggested in St. Teresa of Avila's stress on our need of a *spirit* of "interior recollection"[14] that helps one meet life's demands. A 4-3-5 spirit, as in*form*ed by mind (soul) and body, helps one coordinate various external input with the subjective reality of one's inner world. Going beyond body-mind dualisms, unable to integrate our in-between immaterial loci, a 4-3-5 spirituality can help us relate sleep and meditation as these are affected by alpha-theta brainwaves. In prayer, whether directed to inward or outward reality, 4-3-5 spiritually allelic loci are a guiding influence. If "we live in a world of forms, not the Platonic forms or ideas, but solid forms"[15] of palpable space, AIRR-4-3-5 spiritual in-betweens are solid trans*form*ative "*forms*" that mediate the ideals of Buddhist-Christian virtues. Such ideals are best integrated within feedback patterns of 4-3-5 trans*form*ations (Part Two). I turn to explore issues that affect locating our allelic AIRR-4-3-5 loci's trans*forma*tive, ethical abilities.

John Eccles anchored his concept of self to brain *opera*tions, namely the microphysiology of synapses. He endorsed Popper's philosophic, non-scientific aspects of dualist interactionism that postulates the three world of physical states (World 1), of consciousness states (World 2) and of objective knowledge (World 3). "Each of these three worlds requires the *opera*tional existence of the other. Popperian dualist interactionism prevented Eccles from developing a theory of non-material systems"[16] *opera*tionally independent of material systems. Without this, there can be no scientific theory of the survival of the self after the body's death—which Eccles upheld. Can research on brainwaves help us clarify a body-mind-spirit triad? Our brain is an electrochemical organ with very low frequency rhythmic wave fluctuations[17] of electric potential between parts of the brain; it requires rest and restoration. Active cells build up chemical deposits. Sleep removes waste products from the nervous system such as the build-up of neurotransmitters and hormones between cells.

Using computers to study brainwaves and on the basis of electro-encephalograms (EEG's), researchers identify four stages in sleep. Underlying the jagged, irregular pattern of brainwaves' desynchronized marks is a base rhythm called beta waves which are from 15 to 38 cycles per second (cps). Beta waves occur in alert stages; delta waves, in deep sleep; alpha waves, in relaxed meditation; theta waves, in light sleep or creative insights. When one begins to relax and empties one's mind, one generates alpha waves (8 to 14 cps)—in a pattern of smooth, regular electrical oscillations. This is the pleasant stage of "alpha rhythm,"[18] one akin to what occurs in meditation. During sleep, neurons lose their normal waking patterns. "Some are going slow, some faster; and there is some chaos taking over, with firing in bursts. Sleep doesn't mean cessation of activity but it is something much more like disordered activity."[19] When alert, "yet momentarily not thinking about anything in particular, beta waves become synchronized, and you can see the beta wave pattern on the EEG."[20] The brain's electrons are energy quanta located in the space around an atomic nucleus (a "probability cloud"). Brains exhibit chaotic behavior (determined but not random). Even if we knew all of a brain's determining factors, we could not predict its course because different causes interact unpredictably. Quantum physicists posit an energy foundation for all material reality.

4-3-5 GEM explains how our cognition depends on objects of perception but needs a foundation that links yet distinguishes physical and spiritual energies. In response to the language games that box in 4-2 analysts, I argue that the quantum dynamic processes of photons underlying our four types of brainwaves manifested in thought, dreams or meditation are aspects of our spiritually genomic structure that is perfected in the freedom of our will—"irrelevant" in-between aspects illustrated in Feynman's "absurd" photon arrows. His arrows suggest to me that there is an ideal aspect to reality which science can only partially bridge. The success of films such as *Star Wars* or *Lord of the Rings* suggest that moderns believe in a universal energy of life charging the body for a variety of mental and spiritual tasks. Hindus call it *prana*, the Chinese and Japanese, *chi*, *ki*, Hebrews, *ruach*, the Greeks, *pneuma*. I interpret such "energy" with an underlying conversion *form*ula. If brainwaves are energy packets or quanta, they are only a substrate for deeper reason-faith allelic action. Just a relaxed state helps us synchronize our waking consciousness enabling us to be more attuned to the rhythms of life, so dreams help us trans*form* our lives. Dreams occur after stage four of sleep during *stage one emergent* or rapid eye movement (REM). I suggest that alpha and theta waves may be a sign of the as-yet-little-understood aspects of a 4-3-5 spirituality that motivates some to great love.

*Opera*ting on one's *own* experienced-and-properly-understood-evaluated-and-acted-upon data enables a person to live ethically. Our AIRR acts can transpose the universality of ethics since these acts are the subject pole of our inbuilt bridge that objectifies intersubjectivity on the object pole. The poles work in an upper-lower-blade scissors fashion; the lower blade rises from data through measurements and curve-fitting to *form*ulae. The upper blade moves downward "from differential and operator equations and from postulates of invariance and equivalence."[21] Those able to access their feelings through dreams or friendship may be predisposed to meditate in ways that generate ethical ideals in valid 4-3-5 poly*morph*ic ways. In terms of Bion's grid, this poly*morph*ism indicates the vertical, genetic axis (how the mind generates any mentation). The vertical axis is in constant interplay with Bion's structural, horizontal axis that corresponds to GEM's iso*morph*ism between knowing and known. GEM provides foundations for Bion's grid by identifying a feedback that can reasonably ground both personal and social interchanges as well as Eccles' spirituality.

For Eccles, mental events and outer and inner sensory experiences are a composite with different levels of intensity, reciprocally linked, in some unitary manner, to a bundle of dendrites by way of unit "psychons." Since Eccles had no scientific theory of spirit to guide him, Donald Watson proposes a Theory of En*form*ed Systems (TES), not induced from introspection or observation, but focusing on the self, not on mind. In empirically testable TES, a self per*form*s all the *opera*tions attributed to mind. Using Eccles' hypothetico-deductive method, TES posits a basic capacity to organize, denoted by the term en*form*y. Opposing the disorganizing operations "implied by the second law of thermodynamics, enformy organizes" and sustains 4-dimensional fields of non-random domains of influence named SELFs (Singular, Enformed Living Fields) to indicate they are sustained by en*form*y and able to reproduce and evolve. SELFs explain the continuity of mental experiences by bridging unconscious gaps. Eccles' notion of psychons is consistent with one of SELFs' behaviors under TES, namely "cohering in spacetime."[22] Psychons are not *perceptual* paths to experiences but are experiential *opera*tions linked to the spiritual.

Such a holistic view revises Descartes' *Cogito* which did not locate thinking[23] in its proper origin of a conscious context. Psychons are consistent with the fundamental behaviors of SELFs except that SELFs are not contents but containers. TES helps us "locate" a 4-3-5 metaxy of love in the immaterial aspects of our spiritual allelic loci. Like TES, GEM has an en*form*y, a basic AIRR trans*for*mative capacity to organize that this book stresses by italicizing *form*, *morph* and the "*opera*" of *opera*tion. SELF bridges unconscious gaps by explaining the continuity of mental experiences. Bion uses a grid to mediate the break in one's being caused by the act of birth with the reality of numinous trans*form*ations. I study how our AIRR *opera*tions move from data to a universal ethics. GEM, TES and Bion help remedy Eccles' inability to develop a spirituality *opera*tionally independent of material systems. Mathematicians use simple equations that produce complex chaotic input; they reach for an infinity they cannot attain. Cusa focused on mathematics' inadequacies (e. g. inscribing a polygon within a circle). I argue that our minds' seeming chaos (as reflected in sleep or brainwaves) is a portal to God's mystery of love. I develop a spiritual *docta ignorantia* to trans*form*atively integrate East-West ways of thinking. Agnostics belittle self-giving love but can appreciate the soothing effects of music on our brain.[24] Binaural beats in the brain resonate with different frequencies. Brain-mind interaction remains mysterious, but research on sleep and meditation do not contradict "a *chaotically* freeing" 4-3-5 body-mind spirituality. Dreams and insights are examples of an in-between creativity, a bridge between the material and spiritual. Direct, reflexive, ethical and spiritual insights, as well as dreams, are "matrices" that can help us overcome egotist delusions. Rather than study physiology, I seek a spiritual matrix to interrelate AIRR acts with love ideals—one that, by becoming "greater" than its parts, helps us integrate the allelic in-betweens of being-relatedness and reason-faith. If RNA mediates[25] between proteins and DNA, allelic AIRR-love (in*form*ed by relevant dream and ethical patterns) mediates between reason and faith.

While some speak of the "illusion" of transcendence or of experience itself, I appeal to the insights of such artists as Goya, Blake or Ensor who explored their private, "illusory" dreams. The impressionists studied sensible impressions that classical norms had long stifled. In projecting their introjected experience, Cezanne and Van Gogh "imagined themselves as *being* the landscapes"[26] they painted. Our youths, exposed to materialist 4-2 programming, are spiritually handicapped. In the light of this, I pursue a 4-3-5 task of clarifying how physical and spiritual allelic loci work in feedback ways. If we can appropriate our metaxic, trans*form*ative 4-3-5 loci, we shall realize that they *form* a unity of identity (classical anticipations) and non-identity (randomness) that occurs in all of our human knowing. Sublating phenomenological interpretations, GEM establishes this unity by moving from conscious interiority back to common sense and theory. Trans*form*ing Cartesian method without identifying the natural sciences with technical interests, it reconstructs underlying experiences of our history and leads to new stages of human self-reflection.[27] While Dilthey clarified how the human and physical sciences differ in their approaches, GEM confronts issues dividing scholars and scientists by developing criteria and norms that show how these approaches differ, yet complement one another. Our dreams projected in art offer a link beyond what some see as the illusion of transcendence; transcendence is not illusion but a source of art and ethics. If John Cage hears music anew by *questioning sounds*, I probe reason-faith's 4-3-5 (ethical) in-betweens.

*For*mation of RNA secondary structures is an example of the sequence-structure problem. If some phase problems of self-attracting RNA remain problematical, GEM is a diphase[28] heuristic structure that postulates an iso*morph*ism between our AIRR *knowing* structure and our *knowns*—a structure in part due to our poly*morph*ic consciousness. We iso*morph*ically 4-3-4 know spacetime through our poly*morph*ic AIRR structure. GEM has us ask ever more questions until we reach answers in a diphase feedback process. It helps us apply general AIRR structural *form*s within 4-3-5 ethical communities. Its trans*form*ative ability applies to both practical life and to philosophical or scientific domains. It helps families, groups or nation-states foster a world ethics. Analogously to ATGC-U trans*form*ative loci, GEM helps us be ethical in that our poly*morph*ic consciousness can use processes of adaptation to attain and successively trans*form* our iso*morph*ic knowing-knowns.

Processes of adaptation, whether in married couples, in associated groups or in biological *morph*osis, involve trans*form*ations. *Morph*ology, the study of word *form*ation should be studied in contexts of AIRR trans*form*ative loci—*not* vice versa. Our poly*morph*ic consciousness is the *key* to philosophy, a key that GEM uses to iso*morph*ically link linguistic *morph*ologies. It links them first through its triadic conjugate structure, then by relating the triad to its AIRR base which it then trans*form*s into a 4-3-5 immanent metaxy that faces chaos. This conjugate structure replaces notions of "substance"[29] with a central potency, central *form* and central act triad that works analogously to how RNA's uracil trans*form*atively substitutes DNA's thymine base by way of auxiliary amino acid triplets. GEM's precept, "be in love," is an analogue of RNA's uracil base.

In occurrence, acting lovingly is rarer than uracil; it is an ideal! When it occurs, it puts everything on a basis of conversion (appropriating one's AIRR feedback *opera*tions). Just as uracil and being in love are the trans*form*ative agents within physical and spiritual genomes, so per*form*ative self-transcendence (as having a "real" influence on the psychosocial processes of human life) suggests that one can plausibly postulate allelic analogues in our physical and spiritual genomes that *can in*f*orm* both our bodily needs and our self-transcendent acts. Such "in*form*ing" involves dynamic trans*form*ational elements that I seek to link and map by way of a compact, de-complexifying 4-3-5 conjugate *form*ula applicable to and interrelating each of our two genomes.[30]

*Damasio's Emotions-Feelings-Brain Triad and GEM's Trans*form*ative Spirituality*[31]

To empower science, artists and philosophy, we must cross disputed territory such as what links faith, emotions and reason. Probing into body-mind relations, Antonio Damasio deftly links emotions, feelings and reason, on one hand, and body, brain and mind, on the other. "All living organisms from the humble amoeba to the human are born with devices designed to solve *automatically*, no proper reasoning required, the basic problems of life." Emotions that play out in the theater of the body can be made visible with scientific probes. Feelings remain hidden in the theater of our minds but they reflect emotions which are "automata" built from simple reactions promoting an organism's survival. For GEM, emotion-feeling alleles can foster a spiritually-based coop*era*tion; its potency-*form*-act and body-mind-spirit triads can mediate Damasio's emotions-feelings-brain and body-brain-mind triads. Damasio offers a setting for such mediation: "Because the mind arises in a brain that is integral to the organism, the mind is part of that well-woven apparatus. Body, brain and mind are manifestations of a single organism. We dissect them under the microscope, but they are inseparable under normal operating circumstances. Our affects are not to be taken for granted nor are they Cartesian automata. The presence in the brain of dynamic neural patterns related to an object or event is "a necessary but not sufficient basis to explain the mental images of the said object or event."[32] Consciousness studies focus on the issue of getting from described neural patterns to introspective images; yet, no one has clinically shown how this happens. GEM has not shown this either, but it sets up parameters by investigating insights into imaginal phantasms that serve as heuristic symbols in neurologically mapping understood images. Insights map imaginative representations. Series of insights lead to ever larger maps (viewpoints) that I seek to link in a 4-3-5 East-West ethics that does not confuse science and symbols with myth. A map of love 4-3-5 converts more than meets the eye.

Damasio perceptively links our emotion-feeling-reason triad, but misdiagnoses the impact of Proposition 18, Part IV of Spinoza's *Ethics* that says that the very foundation of happiness and virtue lie in the endeavor (*conatus*) to preserve one's self. *Conatus* is the aggregate of dispositions "laid down in brain circuitry" (36). Damasio notes that the *Ethics* may sound like a prescription for today's selfish culture but he argues that it "is a cornerstone for a generous ethical system ... an affirmation that at the base of whatever rules of behavior we may ask humanity to follow, there is something inalienable."[33] I argue that our AIRR ideals correct a *conatus* that lets the self bathe in the ether of the One Substance. GEM enables us to meet the unrelenting demands of the concrete by having us live out AIRR ideals so as to trans*form* our degenerate habits or irrational emotions.

Damasio's "nesting principle" analyzes our seemingly unified affects and our underlying emotions; feelings support homeostatic regulation by incorporating in their "machinery" lesser drives and motivations such as those revolving around metabolic processes. We might expect that philosophers would help non-experts fathom Spinoza's presuppositions, but Deleuze fails in this task. If Damasio and Deleuze accept a Spinozist immanentism that would reduce the transcendent to what is immanent, I argue that GEM's trans*form*ative ethic deepens feelings-virtues alleles by rooting them in our immanent AIRR structure—not in an immanentist pantheism. AIRR *opera*tions are an underlying nesting, trans*form*ative principle. Damasio ends his *Spinoza* by arguing that Spinoza prefigured many of neurobiology's findings, but that one needs a more flexible spirituality than one finds in Spinoza. A 4-3-5 trans*form*ative GEM is such a spirituality. Our sense of wonder, our dreams and hopes mediate between our immanent desires and AIRR ideals; they allow persons to transcend themselves in feedback ways that dialectically avoid neuroscientific 4-2 dualisms such as physicalism, epiphenomenalism, genetic reductionism or biological determinism.

The trans*form*ative allelic *loci* of East-West thought, exemplified in GEM, can reconcile reason-faith alleles and move us beyond Spinoza's ethics. GEM's potency-*form*-act triad is "4-3-5 activated" in the various conversions that trans*form* a nomadic humanism intent on self. It has an ethical potential for achieving the higher reality of a 4-3-5 spirit-filled realm. It can help us *tick* for it roots us in a body-mind-spirit triad that affects and is affected by the trans*form*ative *opera*tional triad of reason-feeling-faith. Such GEM triads can help us explain the in-betweens of emotions, feelings and reason. In GEM, feelings involve intentional responses that are distinct from such non-intentional states as fatigue, irritability or anxiety. While states simply have causes, feelings involve goals and such "ontic" values as persons or qualitative values "as beauty . . . truth, virtuous acts and noble deeds."[34] GEM AIRR nests Damasio's reason-feeling-emotion triad and applies the *nested triads* to the lives of normal human beings by way of "4-3-5 in-between" ethical virtues.

For Deleuze and Guattari, we reach the ideal, implied in the virtual, through concepts; but their triad begs the question on how our AIRR *opera*tions *opera*te. For them, philosophers plunge into chaos[35] by way of concepts, but science remains on the plane of reference. Their notion of plunging, restricted to the plane of immanence, partly relies on G. G. Granger's view of the virtual as a knowledge of the lived inasmuch as it constitutes a "virtual totality"[36] in the transition from scientific to philosophic knowledge. I argue that this notion of the virtual has aspects in common with GEM. In *Insight*, Lonergan explains how we arrive at knowledge through the virtually unconditioned. Unlike Kant, who incompletely rejects naive views on objectivity and fails to find the virtually unconditioned as constitutive of judgment, GEM lets sensitive consciousness[37] integrate otherwise coincidental neural manifolds. Its judgments include *opera*tional distinctions that are *prior* to theory—a fact that enables it to sublate metaphysics and objectify faith realities. As complex as life processes are, our mental and spiritual functions are not to be 4-2 reduced to such processes. Rather, just as DNA synthesis is able to proofread and repair errant encoding processes,[38] so, humans can ethically and spiritually trans*form* society. With Deleuze and Guattari, I "plunge into chaos" so as to extract a way of reaching a virtual that trans*form*s all *form*s. Many nations are plunged into chaos. The Palestinians, faced with calculated land grabs, still retain hope. Willing to admit partial defeat for the sake of their children, they address chaos constructively—a less than ideal, but realist willingness to implement the structure of their AIRR-4-3-5 *opera*tions so as to confront an unforgiving world order. Many persons, too, are mired in chaos— victims of circumstances or of their own failings. How then can we implement the real structure of our AIRR-love *opera*tions, when love lags and confusion and/or chaos seem to reign?

Genetics and an Analogical 4-3-5 Transformative Spirituality

Rather than studying DNA-RNA, I map our minds and hearts' heuristics. In the face of many uncertainties, humans can adapt or freeze; adapting to intersubjectivity's realities is one facet of the allelic and flexible schemes of recurrence that GEM recognizes as opening us to the spiritual. GEM helps us reach out across the divides so as to "4-3-5 link up" with other hearts.

In *DNA*, James Watson recounts that his interest in DNA began when he read the physicist Schrödinger's suggestion, in *What is Life*, that genetics is probably guided by a code-script. The solution to that code, however, was long stymied. Biologists long believed that proteins, rather than nucleic acids, would eventually be identified as the primary bearers of genetic instructions. Proteins are molecular chains built from the 20 different building blocks of amino acid triplets. Because permutations in the order of amino acids along the chain are virtually infinite, it seemed plausible that proteins could encode the in*form*ation underpinning life's extraordinary diversity. It remained unclear just how the ATGC deoxynucleotide bases of the DNA molecule were linked chemically. For decades after DNA's discovery, chemists were unable to analyze DNA molecules' immense size and complexity. If DNA were indeed Schrödinger's script, a DNA molecule would have to be capable of existing "in an immense number of different *form*s. But back then it was still considered a possibility that one simple sequence like ATGC might be repeated over and over along the entire length of DNA chains."[39]

Finally, in 1944, Oswald Avery's group discovered that the composition of the surface coats of pneumonia bacteria could be changed through the agency of DNA—thus proving that DNA is the trans*form*ing principle. Watson and Crick discovered the roles of ATGC nucleotides and of the double helix in such a trans-*form*ation. Analogously, GEM's study of the basic AIRR *opera*tional structure of our minds directs us in living out the 4-3-5 ethical trans*form*ative actions demanded in our world society. ATGC bases *code* biological processes, but our ideal AIRR *opera*tional structure *frees* us to engage in needed co*opera*tive ethical actions.[40]

After DNA's discovery, RNA's role in life was still unclear. It was thought that RNA was involved in protein synthesis, since cells that made lots of proteins were always RNA-rich. The physicist Gamow suggested in a letter to Watson and Crick that all organisms used a simple code of four that was determined by the order of recurring triplet nucleotides, the basic components of DNA. Gamow had become interested in DNA even before the link between DNA and the amino acid sequence of proteins had been proved. Transposing his insights into the universe's makeup to the new field of DNA biochemistry, he suggested to Watson and Crick that amino acids use RNA molecules as templates during protein synthesis, but his letter was "odd," for he was an inveterate joker. This caused Watson and Crick to be at first dubious, but the other side of his personality soon won them over. Gamow was the first to theorize about a *form*al scheme of overlapping triads of DNA bases that served to specify certain amino acids. His notion of a 4-3-5 "genetic code" anticipated the central dogma of molecular genetics: "DNA makes RNA, which makes proteins." DNA's genetic in*form*ation is used to make RNA chains of complementary sequences which serve to 4-3-5 specify the order of amino acids in their respective proteins. This view won the day after the 1959 discovery of the enzyme RNA polymerase which catalyzes the production of single-stranded 4-3-5 RNA chains from double-stranded DNA templates. RNA's central role in producing proteins raised another long-unanswered question as to *why* the in*form*ation in DNA must go through a 4-3-5 RNA intermediate before being translated into a polypeptide sequence.[41] If, in polymerase chain reactions, sequential steps activate defined DNA regions, GEM focuses on our free *opera*tions; it links knowable *forms*, related to being, to mystic "*form*less *form*alyzables."

Since the genetic code has no internal punctuation, Crick argued that there must be an *adaptor* RNA molecule covalently binding to an amino acid, yet capable of hydrogen bonding to a nucleotide sequence. To transcribe DNA, 3 types of RNA are synthesized, converting chemical in*form*ation to the amino acids to produce proteins. DNA is transcribed in the cell's nucleus into messenger RNA (mRNA) which is then exported to the cytoplasm for translation into protein. By proving that this occurs in ribosomes (rRNA), Harry Noller solved the riddle of which came first proteins or DNA. An RNA matrix helps create life when peptide bonds are catalyzed; transfer RNA (tRNA complementary to mRNA's triple-base codon sequences) delivers amino acids which are bonded together in a protein chain. Before Noller's proof, molecular biology had been stuck in a chicken-and-egg problem of the origin of life—nonplused by a general assumption that a DNA molecule gave rise to life; this had posed a contradiction since DNA cannot assemble itself: DNA cannot exist without proteins, but proteins depend on DNA. Since 4-3-5 RNA is the equivalent of DNA (it can store and replicate genetic in*form*ation) and the equivalent of protein (it catalyzes chemical reactions), it is both the chicken and the egg.[42] I argue that, just as mRNA synthesizes proteins in ribosomes' molecular factories, so a GEM metaxy helps us understand how our genetic and spiritual 4-3-5 structures "trans*form*" us. RNA templates *form* amino acid triads, but insights, virtues and AIRR-love ideals act as trans*form*ative 4-3-5 templates in our spiritual lives. As the solution to the genetic code was long stymied by a focus on proteins rather than on nucleic acids, so many persons' search for truth is too focused on linguistic "per*form*ance." I use insights into DNA-RNA to "provoke interest" in our own trans*form*ative AIRR loci. In this context, Deleuze and Guattari's notion of a *virtual* that contains all possible elements and draws out all possible *forms* is helpful. It can help contextualize GEM's virtually unconditioned with the example of how Crick and Gamow made correct judgments in resolving DNA-RNA problems; it suggests how virtuous persons overcome ambiguities in reaching out for self-transcendent ideals. If Gamow transposed his insights from physics to genetics, I transpose insights into mathematical loci and ATGC loci into mediating AIRR loci analogously to how homozygous-heterozygous alleles work. Analogous to ATGC-U bases, AIRR trans*form*ative ideals transpose brain-mind reductionisms. "4-3-5 GEM transpositions" extend the allelic principle to *remapping* the range and domain of AIRR ethical loci.

In Watson's *DNA*, a chapter "Playing God" compares recombinant's DNA's ability to cut, paste and copy DNA to a word processor's analogous ability. GEM goes beyond such an ability. It does not play God; it submits to divine love. Ironically, while genetics has alerted us to the 4-3-5 nature of our physical genome, many lose sight of their 4-3-5 spiritual genome. Victims to a Tower of Babel hubris, they let theories make them forget their own heart's 4-3-5 ideals.

While it had occurred to Watson (prior to the proof) that it was likely that the genetic information in chromosomal DNA was used to make RNA chains of complementary sequences, he could not reach a virtually unconditioned judgment on his hunch. GEM links the process of how we reach a virtually unconditioned in all aspects of life. Just as there is a trans*form*ative interaction between DNA and RNA whereby RNA chains serve as templates specifying amino acids, and just as scientists use the iso*morph*ism between our AIRR *knowing* structure and *knowns*, so there are trans*form*ative interactions among persons wrestling with the in-betweens of vice and virtue; a trans*form*ative AIRR-loci matrix links our in-between ability to respect virtuous proprieties in life.

GEM mediates the body-mind problem with trans*form*ative ideals. Our AIRR loci (a set of basic terms and relations) are analogous to the ATGC nucleotide bases that trans*form* genomes. Lonergan's *Method in Theology* clarified how

AIRR loci work in four trans*form*ative feedback levels arranged in "functional specialties." *Ceteris paribus*, a functional specialties' AIRR trans*form*ative feedback approach can be used in all disciplines—as I shall try to show in Part Two. A focus on the in-betweens of GEM's insights allows us to interrelate our bodily and spiritual needs by mediating opposed theories or ideologies with a trans*form*atively poly*morph*ic-iso*morph*ic AIRR feedback.

Allelic in-betweens 4-3-5 Sublate
Fichte, Hegel or Peirce's Revisions of Kant

We are spirits, caught in the in-betweens of our bodily needs and of transcendence. GEM reconciles experience and theory. Our AIRR trans*form*ative feedback structure lets us, in principle, understand, reach for or even attain self-transcendent love. What is the role of a 4-3-5 love metaxy? It may seem that GEM's focus on retrieving intelligibility[43] borders on obscure corrections of scholastic issues. But if politicians fail to address core issues in their use of slogans, GEM challenges us with ideals that do address what plagues our world. It replaces Aristotelian, Lockean and Spinozan notions of substance with *conjugates* in which one grasps a concrete and intelligible unity, identity whole.[44] Such conjugates are the essential features of intelligibility. I seek to retrieve what is "in between" immanence and transcendence, namely the AIRR ideals and ethical *verbs* (virtues) that can guide us. Virtuous ideals are located in an immanent 4-3-5 metaxy of ethical love not cut off from transcendence. If in sleep, neurons lose their normal waking patterns in that some go slower, some faster (yielding temporary chaos) I seek patterns that can help us cope with chaotic pluralism. Consider modern art. Impressionists had abandoned Rafael and Da Vinci's scientific perspective only to have Cezanne and Gauguin reject the Impressionists' view of nature as a naturalism that would dominate human sensibility. If Cezanne combined the principles of air-based light with a more structured style that paved the way for Cubism, and if Cubists depicted fragmented objects with their several sides seen simultaneously, GEM helps us grasp love's complexities. As Cezanne discovered new harmonies in the iridescent chaos he painted, so I seek a Buddhist-Christian ethics whose in-between 4-3-5 love metaxy can help us integrate our pluralist world without excluding transcendence. By exploring how analogically structured 4-3-5 triads affect ATGC bases and AIRR ideals, I seek to transcend the bounds within which Deleuze and Guattari restrict themselves. The two men cannot access 4-3-5 virtues that address virtual chaos with self-transcendence.

GEM moves beyond Hegel and Peirce's triads.[45] Hegel's triadic process challenged Fichte who sought to reconstruct Kantian thought with his obscure "fact-act" (*Tathandlung*) or "science of science." He later sought to underpin reason with faith. Hegel forged dialectical oppositions based on contradictions within the conceptual field. His successive conceptual triads and relations of opposition and sublation between concepts are claimed to be "necessary."

GEM's higher viewpoints transpose Hegel's *an sich, fur sich* and *an und fur sich* triads with a movement from the objects of mathematical, scientific and common-sense understanding, through the acts of understanding (*Insight*, 374). GEM differs from Hegel's closed, immanental dialectic that deals with conceptual, determinate contents. It addresses, not such contents, but heuristically defined anticipations. Its *intellectualist* potency-*form*-act triads are open, factual and normative. Its "dialectical opposition is the conflict between the pure desire to know and other desires" (421); so far from fixing the concepts that will meet the anticipations, it awaits from nature and from history a succession of tentative solutions viewed as products of a cumulative succession of insights—such as 4-3-5 trans*form*ations, etc. Peirce's triad (Firstness, Secondness, Thirdness or Quality, Relation, Representation) rethinks Kant's categories; it refers to the relationship of a self, a thing, a word: a self names an object, using symbols to stand for or represent things in one's world. GEM triads lead to a dialectic, allelic ability to relate linked but opposed principles. Like Kandinsky, GEM disengages nature's potentialities; it, too, knows that "civilization" can destroy our awareness of an all-pervading spiritual force. Like Boulez' music, it seeks to integrate cultural *form*s so that we may 4-3-5 reach realities that transcend half-truthful popularizations. It trans*form*s artists of love through a 4-3-5 metaxy not dominated by nature. If "civilized" societies use the force of law, law itself must uncover the true good in opposing evil.

Touching on the question of boundaries, Peirce asks what demarcates a black spot from its white background (1893: 98). If topologically, a black spot owns its boundary,[46] GEM shows us how to own our own limitations. Mathematics is restricted by logic and an incompleteness theorem (Gödel), but neither our psyche nor ethics is subject to system. A 4-3-5 spirit philosophy lifts the virtually unconditioned of virtue toward an ethical consciousness of world solidarity. It transcends the opposition between the individual and society by showing how individuals can transcend reductionisms by being judiciously open. It confirms the virtues practiced by GEM artists in their spiritual, poetic dreams of building an East-West ethics. GEM artists respect faith-reason alleles; their art of love foregoes dubious goals for the greater good of viable ideals; 4-3-5 ideals help resolve systemic limitations as they move us beyond a pragmatic logic. Part Two will show how feeling, decision and the functional specialties play pivotal roles in grounding a 4-3-5 metaxic feedback way to ethically redress human chaos. By going beyond the problems of self-reference and second-order variables, GEM uses the laws of probability to address and ground science's inductive forte; its qualitative predicates trans*form* logic's mere 4-3-4 quantitative ones.

Derrida subscribes to Peirce's notion that one sign is explicated by another, which in turn demands a third or endless allelic play of *differance*. While physical genomes are coded by allelic variations, AIRR alleles "*differantiate*" disciplines' methods in ways that transcend postmodernist claims. 4-3-5 *differance* differs from Nietzchean-Deleuzean-Derridean 4-3-4 *differance*s in its radical openness to faith. One cannot negate the allelic *differances* of grammar and semantics, but our structured AIRR acts are an invariant grid that ethically links humans. If ATGC bases need RNA's uracil and amino acids' triadic codes to function, AIRR alleles rely on a potency-*form*-act triad's feedback. If Cezanne and Gauguin's art studies nature so as to inspire viewers, a GEM metaxy 4-3-5 trans*forms* us with love. Let us clarify how such a metaxy based on an analogical genetic and spiritual process *morph*s our set of basic AIRR terms and relations into an ethical role. I map a map love that first locates AIRR loci, then identifies their 4-3-5 *differantial* ethical abilities.

A Deterritorializing 4-3-4 Geophilosophy or an Ethical 4-3-5 Spirit Philosophy?

For Deleuze and Guattari, the world of the lived is like the earth; philosophical concepts need a 4-3-4 geophilosophy that territorializes and deterritoriali-

---

Fig. 1. 4-3-5 TRANSFORMING DELEUZE AND GUATTARI'S CONCEPTUAL TRIAD WITH A SPIRITUALLY OPEN ONE

Deleuze and Guattari triad	GEM's quasi-infinite Modal AIRR operators	Concretizing AIRR operations' Quasi-infinite "Facial" 4-3-5 Plasticity ★47a
Plane of immanence 4-3-4 concepts	Quasi-infinite plasticity Images-percepts-forms	Potency-finality-experiential conjugates Insights-formulations-systematizations
Conceptual personae	Ethics empowering persons	Transformatively foundational act-loci

GEM's transformative AIR-loci work as spiritual-ethical 4-3-5 alleles in the feedback pattern (as illustrated pg. 20). This feedback pattern is a first step in mapping the in-between alleles of (violent) reality and of thinking with transformative 4-3-5 loci. Such loci do not rule out (as does 4-2 science) our data of consciousness; they leave one open to the quasi-infinite loving plasticity of conversion.

---

zes—notions that they derive from animals' habit of *form*ing territories. They project a territorializing habit into the hominid "who from its act of birth deterritorializes its front paw...and reterritorializes it on branches and tools."[47] GEM relocates all concepts in our creative insights' AIRR process—rather than in Deleuze and Guattari's interpretation of that process. Not only creative geniuses, but even ordinary beings are endowed with a potency-*form*-act triad that each person is invited to understand. Animals *form* territories; humans consciously or implicitly *form* various potency-*form*-act triads. Our higher *opera*tional AIRR levels sublate and surpass lower levels: one's experience is put on a *new* basis that preserves and empowers what is sublated and carries lower levels forward to fuller realizations in ongoing feedback ways.

GEM probes the trans*form*ative realities in*form*ing progress and decline. My analogy between trans*form*ations in ATGC-U bases and AIRR-love *opera*tions depends on 4-3-5 processes. Figure 1 is the first of 4 diagrams illustrating our AIRR quasi-infinite feedback ability to relate spirit to the world of matter. It is based on a GEM iso*morph*ism between our knowing structure and knowns which can lead to ethical modes of feedback co*opera*tion. For Levinas, ethics addresses one's way of talking about the encounter between the self and the other; it calls into question one's own spontaneity due to the presence of the Other. With Plato and Descartes, he argues that an encounter with infinity trumps any primacy of the self/same over the other. Deleuze and Guattari's approach to spirit and matter overlooks a notion of the primacy of ethics over ontology held by Levinas and GEM; it needs trans*form*ative ideals' AIRR feedback. This book builds analogies between physical and spiritual process, only to distinguish the two. While many fail to associate spirituality with ethics, GEM does so. In a diagram (page 20) I suggested how GEM feedback applies to the foundational ethical element stressed by Levinas. The "5" in that diagram is the key trans*form*ative pivot permitting me to compare physical and spiritual genomes. As an *opera*tor indicates *opera*tions to be per*form*ed,[48] so figure 1 pivots on Levinas' "facial encounter." To speak of one's encounter with infinity, Levinas analyzes the encounter of the self with the "*face*" of the Other. Like ethics, face is, for Levinas, a technical term; it is the "way the other presents himself, exceeding the idea of the other in me."[49] Infinity exceeds the *idea* of infinity. The series of 1-2-3, 1-2-3-4 or 1-2-3-4-5 feedback *opera*tions in figures 1-4 are "series" comprising a quasi-infinite numbers of *opera*tors that are to be spiritually *and* ethically grounded (as in Levinas). Levinas' facial encounter addresses the problem of totality, the primordial manifestation of violence manifested in the "*il y a*" (what *is* before there are separate existents—beyond a "being-in-the-world"). "Contrary to Hegel's account of the evolution of the absolute, the "*il y a*" remains present in the absence of things as a field of forces, an ontological 'black hole,' the sheer fact of being when there is nothing at all. Yet, *before* there is alterity and negation, the *il y a* is seething with the promise of violence "as signified in apocalyptic literature."[50]

Seeking to "tame" violent reality with invariant AIRR *opera*tors mediating between endless variations, figure 1 trans*form*s Deleuze and Guattari's hazy conceptual personae with a 3-4-5 ability, that is with GEM's quasi-infinite *opera*tors that mediate between the polarities inbuilt in our plane of immanence. *Opera*tor indicates an *opera*tion to be per*form*ed—a Newtonian notion in analytical dynamics that opened a new path to the idea that *form*s and *opera*tors are ordered sets that we can express through *opera*tions. GEM adapts Newton's notion; potency-*form*-act triads and AIRR ideals are dynamic *opera*tional sets that continually map but sublate changing cultural contexts. Figures 1-4 map such changes with the contextual alleles of reality and thought in ways that preserve, extend and apply foundational AIRR loci to new contexts; they locate our AIRR ideals' ability to trans*form*atively mediate our contradictory 4-2 in-betweens. I use a notion of "4-3-5 *differance*" *opera*tive in GEM's quasi-infinite *opera*tors, namely the in-between immanent-transcendent ethical virtues that trans*form* us. GEM radicalizes the fourth level of intentionality, freeing it for a 4-3-5 ethics. It lets one *opera*te on one's AIRR *opera*tional loci so as to co-*opera*te with others. Figure 2 will transpose GEM and Deleuze and Guattari's triads by using an analogy between our physical and spiritual genomes. Figures 3-4 will, in turn, transpose figures 1-2 with a spirit philosophy that compares and relates Buddhist and Christian ethics. In figures 1-4, arrows indicate a dispositional feedback between AIRR *opera*tions and the 4-3-5 functional specialties. GEM's criteria of knowledge (objectivity, truth, reality and value) are immanent in AIRR loci that *opera*te through the *opera*tors that ask questions, but they preserve our foundational ability to be open to the infinite.

Bion writes of a restless patient in psychoanalysis who had a dream which is in fact a sensuous experience. "The patient then has to find a dream which is more in conformity with what he thinks is expected of him by the analyst. He will often betray the fact that it is not an ordinary dream by the absence of free associations."[51] Unlike Lacan, Bion does not read into dreams a notion of an irretrievable unconscious.[52] GEM empathizes with dreamers as it draws out the dynamic aspects of *opera*tional sets.

I pursue this GEM forte through my analogy between our physical and spiritual genomes. If 20 amino acid triplets serve as bases for DNA-RNA trans*forma*tions, our images-percepts-*forms* triad trans*forms* us through dreams and/or a 4-3-5 ethics. Our minds are not *merely* rational; influenced by dreams, they should be ethically political. If we compare the political orientations of Deleuze and Derrida, the latter's appeal to a pure *form* of existing concepts (absolute hospitality and pure forgiveness)[53] parallels Deleuze and Guattari's distinction between relative and absolute "deterritorialization." Rather than stressing *form*s of the concept as the condition of the possibility of change, *GEM*, a per*form*atively trans*form*ative *method*, focuses on how insights help *form*/ trans*form* concepts; it explains how our AIRR *opera*tions *opera*te in *generalized* ways as we "dream" political dreams. For GEM, the empirical methods are "in search of the intelligibility and order that, when combined with the empirical residue in the data of their several domains, will provide a complete and definitive explanation of those data."[54] This includes the data of science or of our everyday lives. GEM's intellectualist account of our trans*form*ative AIRR feedback ability invigorates conceptualist *forms* by enabling us to trans*form* Aristotelian or other conceptualist *forms*. Along with relocating the creative process in AIRR *opera*tional ideals, this book seeks to vivify

Deleuze and Guattari's anemic geophilosophy with a 4-3-5 spirit philosophy (figure 1) that integrates feelings with allelic reason without falling into Spinozan deductivism or Kantian-Hegelian idealisms.[55] As the ancient painting technique of gouache produces an opaque rather than a transparent effect or as Gounod combined melodious inventiveness and *naiveté* in style to produce the "pure" drama of *Faust*, so GEM in-betweens use the dramatic opaqueness of our lives to respond to God's love. To address the face of violence, GEM and Levinas go beyond the German idealist tradition (from Kant to Husserl) which takes intelligibility as the end-point of the acts of consciousness that correlate the data of things with one another. GEM and Levinas do not reduce the alterity of the other, but respects it.

An analogy brings out similarities and differences between one or more entities. Our 4-3-5 physical and spiritual genomes are alike in that trans*form*ative allelic loci are at work in the domain of genetics and in our spirits. But while physical genomes are coded scripts, a spiritual genome focuses on the allelic loci of reason and faith, emotions and judgments, being and "nothingness." Psychically, scientifically and spiritually, humans effect psychosomatic and other changes in physical allelic loci. Triadic amino acids "co*opera*te" within physical genomes; helping persons *appropriate* their own AIRR *opera*tional loci can foster co*opera*tion in many fields of human endeavor in 4-3-5 feedback fashion. This is one of GEM's great merits. Or again, just as proteins are the business end of cellular process, and genes are the source of cell in*form*ation, so a spiritual genome analogy is a lovingly ethical way to AIRR-4-3-5 integrate interdisciplinary studies.

Similarities within "Differences"
in a 4-3-5 Transformative Genomic Analogy

One of Mendel's laws states that a pair of alleles (or homologous chromosomes) separate during meiosis (gamete *form*ation) and admit of no in-betweens. Recent genetics has gone beyond Mendel by its discovery of multiple alleles. GEM's 4-3-5 trans*form*ative spiritual structure is not limited by a determinist genetics. It detects the allelic in-betweens needed to address the complex issues and dilemmas we meet in life and in academia.

Just as nature religions learned to negotiate the in-between thresholds of the seasons or as *Feng-shui* appreciates nature's harmonies,[56] so I argue that spirituality "harmonizes" body and mind. For GEM, in any plant, animal or person there is to be affirmed an individual existing unity which it "4-3-5 integrates" through its complex notion of conjugate and central triads. GEM's study of biological purposiveness, genetic method and the processes of development takes us beyond genetics. "Just as the conjugate form, mass, was reached by Newton, inasmuch as he reduced Kepler's planetary scheme of recurrence to his abstract laws of motion and gravitation, so also the conjugate forms of the organism, the psyche, and intelligence are to be discovered by proceeding from the schemes of organic, psychic, and intellectual recurrence to the underlying correlations."[57] The correlations enable one to work out, map various schemes of recurrence that include both the *fixed*, rigid periodicity of the planetary system, as well as the *flexible* circle of ranges of schemes that characterize the psychic acts of perception, conation and intellectual acts. Psychic acts (which account for the higher integrations) open the way for a non-reductionist 4-3-5 structured ethical and spiritual account of body-mind interactions.

While 4-2 reductionists allow for no spiritual in-betweens that can guide our minds and in*form* our bodies, GEM's allelic in-betweens address the thresholds between good and evil. By so doing, one can negotiate the misunderstandings arising from cultural differences, age, class disparities or social standing through a spiritual give-and-take which transcends mind and body. Spirituality is itself a 4-3-5 allelic in-between that taps the deeper resources of the human spirit—resources that the banality of mass culture often leaves dormant or represses. In response to our crises, GEM can galvanize Buddhist-Christian wisdom as a moral dynamism of the human spirit.

A "4-3-5 Spiritual Spindle" Strategy that Contextualizes an East-West Ethics

A cell cycle progresses from a period of chromosomal DNA replication to the segregation of chromosomes into two nuclei. In mitosis, cell division produces two identical daughter cells without changing a cell's 46-chromosome ploidy; daughter cells, derived from the original one, retain one part of each chromosome. In meiosis, two separate haploid gametes (building on genetic alleles) are produced, and a cell's ploidy is changed. In both processes, cells assemble a *thread*-like spindle[58] made up of microtubules around *loci* called centromeres; genes interface on the spindle from prophase to telophase. Chromosomes attach to the spindle and are pulled to the spindle's poles. A physical genome depends on chromosomes' spindles. I map an analogy between how our physical and spiritual genomes function. Figure 2 illustrates or "maps" the analogy between the functions which include the roles of amino acid triads in molecules and of potency-*form*-act interrelatedness triads and patterns of experience in GEM. Scientists pursue knowledge; common sense develops by changing the subjective term in the object-to-subject relations that it knows.

Our stream of consciousness occurs in a temporal succession of different contents; it requires striving and effort. A notion of biological, esthetic, intellectual and dramatic patterns of experience helps us organize various elements in our experience, unifying them into dynamic manifolds. A pattern of experience is the *form*ulation of an insight which "arises from sensitive or imaginative presentations."[59] The relevant presentations are the various elements in the experience organized by a pattern. Patterns help us contextualize issues by differentiating between scientific and common-sense accumulations of insights.

In GEM, such an accumulation of insights is as crucial as the spindle is in the cell cycle. The cell cycle depends" on codon triplets as it progresses from chromosomal DNA replication involving a segregation into two nuclei. Whereas philosophy often ignores the source of self-transcending love, a 4-3-5 spindle notion relies on allelic, ethical ideals to build an analogy between cell cycles and a self-transcending feedback. In a spiritual genome, conversions are a "spindle" for locating a metaxy of love whose healing ability links one's inside and outside

---

Fig. 2 ETHICALLY AND SPIRITUALLY CONTEXTUALIZING GENOMES
WITH META-SUBSTANTIAL 4-3-5 OPERATIONS

BIOCHEMICAL PROCESSES		GEM ALLELIC, TRANSFORMATIVE AIRR-LOCI PROCESSES
Cells, whose level-5 uracil informs all life processes, have some "freedom": spindle action and various phases	R LEVEL	effective freedom of 4-3-4 act-actions as underpinned by a fifth ideal of metaxic love: a "diphase 4-3-5 spiritual spindle" interrelates thinkers' phases
Chromosomes-spindle and DNA-RNA transformations mediated by ATGC-U bases	R LEVEL	transformative, creative insights and an AIRR cooperative (possibly graced) "feedback spindle" that ethically "differantiates" judgments of value
Genes and their allelic loci Proteins-enzymes and Amino acid triads in molecules	I LEVEL	operations' AIRR allelic loci formed within patterns of experience consonant with potency-form-act interrelatedness triads
Atoms and subatomic particles such as leptons, quarks, mesons as potentially understood	A LEVEL	sensations, presentations, images and representations

GEM's allelic, transformative air-loci (illustrated pg. 20) are one way to map, transpose feedback contextual alleles of reality and thought by comparing-contrasting genetic-spiritual transformative 4-3-5 operations. GEM allows for a 4-3-5 transcendence "ploidy" that transforms 4-3-4 immanental concepts as well as 4-3-5 DNA-RNA. ∗57a

---

with those of others in creative ways—as Lonergan suggests.[60] A spiritual writer has said that God has sent us the flax, we must make the spindle. Figure 1 depicted the triadic process moving from potency-finality through *forms* and acts. If geneticists use linkage analysis to locate genes, figure 2 maps AIRR-4-3-5 loci on a spiritual spindle based on analogical ATGC-U alleles. It outlines ethically ideal, 4-3-5 trans*form*ations involving feedback between patterns of experience; it allows one's spiritual pattern to interface with differently expressed patterns. Insights into a co*opera*tive ethics find a parallel in the role of a chromosome's spindle on which genes interface. If the biological *opera*tor is a higher system on the move, the ground of the flexible circle of schemes of recurrence for organic functioning, a 4-3-5 spiritual spindle ethically trans*form*s us. If viruses highjack cells, GEM confronts evil by 4-3-5 mapping an ethics that promotes solidarity.

Many genetic processes such as inversions on chromosomes or transcription (transfer of genetic in*form*ation from DNA by a synthesis of an RNA molecule copied from a DNA template) are involved in transmitting life. As DNA-RNA templates are mutually trans*form*ative, so are AIRR ideals and 4-3-5 love. Chapter 4's feedback matrix highlights such trans*form*ations which figure 2 specifies in terms of an ATGC-AIRR loci analogy so as to help us compare constructive changes effected by 4-3-5 love with the DNA-RNA processes within our cells. Genetics and spiritual life are both subject to constraints. Psychic 4-2 adaptative mechanisms influence our allelic AIRR *opera*tions as we adapt to or change the environment. As there are physical mutations and a regulation through negative controls whereby a group of genes is expressed together as a unit, so humans use group regulations that often favor the privileged. In the light of genetic, psychic and political constraints and in the interest of a just peace, I explore how our AIRR-love *opera*tions can help us resist evils.

In analogy to the coded synapse-*locus* fusion of chromosomes in meiosis, figures 1-4 map an AIRR feedback spindle that integrates Deleuze and Guat-tari's conceptual triad with GEM's more basic potency-*form*-act triad. This basic concrete triad (and AIRR *opera*tions) yield 4-3-5 spiritual conjugates that transpose postmodernist views into ones that can guide the future by putting picturesque realities in their place. In mitosis, daughter cells retain ploidy while haploid, allelic gametes change it. GEM allows for a 4-3-4-immanence-4-3-5 transcendence "ploidy-analogue."[61] In cell cycles, an interphase occurs between the two gaps as DNA replicates; meiotic-mitotic phases allow haploid gametes to *form* a diploid zygote. Unlike viral trans*form*ative loci, AIRR trans*form*ative loci yield a diphase feedback allowing for ethical co*opera*tion. Analogous to how ATGC is coded by way of RNA-uracil templates, a 4-3-5 map of love staves off biased, egotist mutagens; its allelic, transcendental dynamic co*opera*tive action sublates 4-3-4 immanentisms.

Figure 1 sought to trans*form* Deleuze and Guattari's conceptual triad with a spiritually open potency-*form*-act triad. Figure 2, suggests how one can ethically-spiritually contextualize our two genomes. It is to be read from the bottom up so as to understand how, in both our genomes, the simpler affects the more complex. It compares DNA-RNA and a 4-3-5 ethics' complementarities. DNA translates in*form*ation. A physical genome's trans*form*ative loci are its ATGC-U bases that allow chromosomes to interface on a spindle. These bases work through such *opera*tional amino acid triplets as asparagine (AAC or AAU) or cysteine (UGC or UGU)—genetic codings triads that, I argue, have GEM allelic counterparts manifested in our dreams or reflected in the potencies of our brains' wave patterns whose *form*s we actualize. Chromosomes break apart and re-*form* as they produce sperm and egg cells—they recombine in different combinations. Figure 2's allusion to meiotic-mitotic spindles highlights the transsexual 4-3-5 metaxic in-betweens of an ethical love that transposes trans*form*ative AIRR loci into 4-3-5 processes. Socrates, Jesus, Lincoln, Gandhi, Martin Luther King and Rabin died for their "unusual" ethical views. Buddha and Mandela were not slain, but they have shown us a way. Figure 2's AI-levels in*form* the ways we spin 4-3-5 threads on a spiritual spindle—involving the spiritual, metaxic in-betweens of Buddha's enlightenment, Socrates' *daimon*, Jesus' beatitudes, Martin Luther King's dream or Rabin's courage; such in-betweens include developmental phases that are to be related on a 4-3-5 feedback spindle (Chapter 5). The phases implement a spindle analogy between cellular and AIRR processes as a way to bridge the irrational and rational sides of our nature. Spindles are agents or a medium for effecting trans*form*ative changes in our two genomes.

As quarks, genomes and thinkers have phases, so diphase GEM bridges physico-spiritual phases. Its 4-3-5 spiritual spindle goes beyond meiotic-mitotic phases; it helps us ethically trans*form* self. The *Phaedrus* recounts that Socrates saw himself as a seer who faults writing for replacing living memory with a mnemonic device —a theme revived by Derrida. 4-3-5 GEM is aware of what is in-between living memory and our discourses about it. It locates the *differance* in our spiritual genome, a *differance* that I *"differantiate"* or transpose into an interdisciplinary, interfaith higher key. A fifth ideal metaxic eye of enlightened love is an in-between key or "tool" that mediates *differances*.[62]

Figure 2's spindle analogy is a key to this book's strategy that is based on 4-3-5 similarities within difference between our genetic and spiritual genomes' trans*form*ative abilities. A physical genome is a given; figure 2 suggests that a 4-3-5 genomic metaxy is an analogy that holds even if one goes into such cellular processes as the cell cycle's diploid-haploid numbers or cytoplasmic fibrils (spindle fibers *form*ed during cell division and involved in the separation of chromatids at anaphase and their movement toward opposite poles in the cell). Biochemists know much about proteins but little about a spiritual genome; to understand how proteins' DNA and other biological molecules "catch rides" on the various transportation systems inside cells, they study quantum dots made up of tiny specs such as silicon. GEM AIRR feedback involves "transportation systems" whereby our minds and 4-3-5 spirits "give rides" to insights and ideals. DNA-RNA trans*form*ations depend on mitotic-meiotic phases involving ATGC-U. While cells have some "freedom," persons are ideally free; they are not pulled to a spindle, but retain an AIRR-*loci* ploidy open to God's grace. A GEM feedback matrix allows us to integrate the complementary aspects of a Buddhist-Christian ethics. If Nietzsche and postmodernists have set us on a cynical course oblivious of ideals, GEM recovers the insights and ideals of Buddhist-Christian traditions so as to bridge their ethical views.

Human concern is a privileged instance of a developing universe. While 4-2 reductionists tend to *eliminate* the 4-3-5 structural basis of mind and brain rooted in spirit in favor of a strictly causal brain-mind dualism, GEM stresses mind's subjective nature and our dependence on ethics, and society. It studies classical and statistical intelligibilities that inquire into what functions; it probes into genetic and dialectical intelligibilities that study what develops over time. In genetic intelligibility, one uses models of stars, plants, human intelligence, morality, etc to study the developmental phases they undergo. Direct and inverse insights help us study two basic kinds of development. Inverse insights grasp that there is no single driving factor that keeps a development moving. Like direct insights, an inverse insight presupposes a positive content had in the data of sense or of consciousness, but it is a negative moment in abstraction: one grasps that "the point is that there is no point, that the solution is to deny a solution, ... that the rationality of the real admits of distinctions and qualifications."[63]

Lacking direct intelligible content, an inverse insight grasps only that the intelligibly anticipated in the inquiry is not to be found. But it exploits this negative aspect. Prescinding from particulars, it focuses only on relations of things to one another. I use our 4-3-5 in-betweens (that differentiate between mind and spirituality in ordering AIRR ideals) to derive the judgments that interrelated persons can and should make to arrive at trans*form*ative modes of human behavior. GEM artists use their AIRR *opera*tions to 4-3-5 trans*form* what needs to be trans*form*ed and to preserve what needs preserving. Just as DNA and RNA use a spindle to bring about trans*form*ations in our physical genomes, so we freely use an allelic reason-faith spindle to order our AIRR-love ideals in judging about the necessity of 4-3-5 ethical co*opera*tion.

It is noteworthy that it was not biochemists but rather a physicist, Francis Crick, and a biologist, James Watson, who first identified DNA's double helix. Other physicists such as Teller, Schrödinger, Gamow, and Feynman played key roles in inspiring biochemists' views of the physical genome. Perhaps it is because physicists are trained to study elementary particles' most general functions that their insights are so fruitful. If Watson appreciated Feynman's "creative imagination,"[64] I seek to relate how GEM's creative ideals can 4-3-5 guide our minds and spirits through trans*form*ative insights. Insights help discipline our imaginations' musings and permit us to partially attain certain self-transcending goals (or allelic in-betweens). GEM trains us in AIRR ideals' general aspects. Let us consider five aspects that apply to but *differantiate* ATGC-uracil and AIRR-love's 4-3-5 structures inasmuch as both involve analogous, creative trans*form*ations.

A first differentiating aspect of an ATGC-AIRR analogy stems from the fact that DNA's ATGC nucleotides need RNA's uracil (U) for DNA to per*form* its trans*form*ative task. I use the example of how DNA's thymine, T, is replaced with RNA's U as an analogy to explain how in an AIRR *opera*tional structure, concepts must go undergo the probative trans*form*ation of being verified in judgments. This verification process occurs through AIRR reflection as (often) aided through the further trans*form*ative ability of "allelic grace." If 4-3-5 RNA trans*form*s DNA, GEM explains how persons open to faith and reason are trans*form*ed through psychic, intellectual, moral and religious conversions. Unlike our coded DNA-RNA molecular bases, our conscious levels of intentionality *can* freely combine the alleles of personal faith with Western philosophies of being and with Eastern philosophies such as those of Buddhism or Taoism. Because GEM's notions of being or of metaphysics are *grounded* in self-affirmation, it avoids Derridean criticism. It can be related to the Buddhist "void" (or emptiness = *sunya(ta)*) or to a mystical Taoist Way in which the mind reaches the *void* of "pure consciousness" when emptied of all particular objects. The conceivable is relative. The absolute *inconceivable* truth is *sunya(ta)* as mystical "void." In tearing away illusory false "truths," we discover a Buddhist abyss as standpoint of enlightenment. One achieves *sunya* enlightenment by becoming detached from all clinging—freed from multiples.

A second differentiating aspect of an ATGC-AIRR analogy contrasts a genome's haploid sets of chromosomes (male-female alleles) with our allelic AIRR *opera*tions' trans*form*ative ability as worked out in GEM's functional specialties (chapter 5). By appropriating our AIRR *opera*tional levels, one realizes that a loving ethics can help cross-fertilize East-West ways of doing or praying. This helps us build a 4-3-5 "world bridge" based on the knowing and *opera*tions of all women and men willing to co*opera*te. GEM empowers us by seamlessly rooting one's outer self *in* one's own *inner self*. Its two-phase 4-3-5 feedback ability is analogous to DNA-RNA's two sets of ATGC-U nucleotides. GEM sublates Kantian reflection by having us objectify our own 4-3-5 interiority and by AIRR-linking us with the greater world. We reassess our goals as we interact with others in self-transcendent ways. We live out an integral body-mind spirituality by meeting our needs and those of others through ethico-spiritual discernment carried through East-West AIRR feedback.

A third differentiating aspect of an ATGC-AIRR analogy regards freedom. Some argue that cells are "free"[65] in transmitting life. I argue that cells' "freedom" can only be analogical to the freedom we humans enjoy in principle. Genetic processes are characterized by the interaction of homologous or non-homologous chromosomes in accordance with the loci of given alleles. If cell cycles control physical genomes, conversion-based actions imply an ethics; confronting evil, GEM links *related*-yet-otherwise-*unrelatable* realities with the "allelic phase boundaries" between *uncoded* thinking and *codes*. While two genomic haploid sets of chromosomes combine to *form* a diploid germ cell, GEM disciplines ego's. It links *uncoded* process by grounding our praxis, not in our chromosomes, but in ethical persons who understand, judge, interact and struggle for a just world. DNA nucleotides and their double helix encode by way of phases in which codons leave room for non-coding introns within genes. Figures 2-4 compare that encoding process with GEM by objectifying the trans*form*ative spindle actions in our two genomes; this enables us to compare the cell as a unit of biological process with our daily (ethical) AIRR trans*form*ative actions. While biofascists would reduce us to cells, a GEM spindle spiritually/ ethically frees us with 4-3-5 ideals.

A fourth aspect touches on the *morph*ic, insidious ways of abusing power. Democracy has incorporated a fragile system of checks and balances between the legislative, executive and judicial branches of government. In the name of "freedom", opponents of gun control defeat measures that would rein in street violence. In Russia, Putin uses his executive power to undercut other branches of government. If powerful elites ignore the in-betweens of checks and balances in governing, GEM touches on the genetic aspects of alienation in Hegel, Kierkegaard, Freud or Sartre[66] based on both the continuities and discontinuities of our physical and spiritual genomes. AIRR-4-3-5 trans*form*ations do not neglect ethics in legislative, executive and judicial processes that must consider the variables of human nature and of spirituality in making and executing laws.

A fifth aspect compares intangible aspects embodied in some of recent Nobel prize laureates. The 2003 Prize for Medicine went to men who studied how cells are efficient "suicide machines," *programmed* to die. As snakes shed their skin, so cell suicide is necessary to life; it keeps the body in cellular balance, shapes developing tissues and organs and refines the central nervous system by letting living cells absorb a dead cell's parts. The 2004 Prize for Chemistry went to ubiquitin's discoverers; cells are equipped with ubiquitin, a protein of just 76 amino acids that function as a "kiss of death" destroying unneeded proteins. This protein-destroying process plays important roles in cell division, in the cell cycle and in protecting us against certain cancers. The 2003 Prize for Literature was awarded to John Coetzee for exposing the hidden violence in human situations. Artists and moralists explore our hearts' intangible "in-between" wisdom or blindspots. We often overlook these intangibles. An ATGC-AIRR analogy calls attention to spindle actions in both our genomes' trans*form*ative processes.[67] It aligns the physical and ethical aspects of our lives, so as to interrelate them with some of the major insights I use in this book (such as Bion's grid and Gauss' insistence on the twin aspects of inductive-deductive methods). These five aspects of ATGC-AIRR analogical 4-3-5 structures help ex-plain how our AIRR allelic loci (common to all persons) *can* lead to a co*opera*tive interaction—but only if we responsibly live out the ideals implied in AIRR ope*ra*tions.[68] I use a GEM 4-3-5 feedback spindle analogy that comple-ments our coded, "programmed" cells. Part One has been outlining trans*form*ative grids, spindles and matrices that illustrate aspects of such feedback (GEM's first phase). Part Two converts such grids, spindles and matrices with GEM's second phase feedback ability that 4-3-5 ethically trans*form*s a genetic analogy. How do our 4-3-5 structured AIRR *opera*-tions(analogous to ATGC-U process) enable GEM to trans*form* empiricism and to empower us with 4-3-5 intangibles hidden in our hearts? How do our common AIRR *opera*tions go a step beyond postmodernists in rescuing objectivity?

"Objectivity" in Deleuze and Guattari and in GEM's Reflective Method

Deleuze and Guattari seek to go beyond subject-object poles with a concept-immanence-conceptual personae triad that "belongs" to a subject, but *not* to a set; they seek to reterritorialize immanence. Like them, I seek to discover at the "heart of the immanence of the lived" a subject's "acts of transcendence as capable of constituting new functions of variables" or conceptual references (*Philosophy*, 142) so that the subject be transcendental rather than solipsist or empirical. Part One is preparing the ground to show how GEM reterritorializes geophilosophy by locating conceptual triads in our AIRR ability to act in self-transcending ways. There is a precarious balance between scientifico-logical concepts and phenomenological-philosophical concepts. For Deleuze and Guattari, logical and scientific concepts allow for philosophical functions in a third autonomous zone facilitated by fuzzy logic which provides a relevant framework for dealing with vague imprecision. Most sets of real objects do not readily fall into the logical universe of what belongs or does not belong to a given set. In reality, the transition from membership in a set of objects to non-membership is gradual: a 70-year old man can be said to be 70% old and 30% young. Fuzzy logic treats truth-values as fuzzy sets where rules of inference are approximations. In our everyday lives we rely on allelic AIRR in-betweens that fuzzily evaluate persons or vexing circumstances. GEM's potency-*form*-act and body-mind-spirit triads locate human creativity within a cognition that leads to higher (non-fuzzy) viewpoints through successive levels of higher systematizations. Successive, distinct autonomous sciences are related as higher view-points that emerge through insights that arise according to the *opera*tions of former rules expressed in other, emerging rules. Grasping the lack of intelligibility in a situation, inverse insights complement the emergence of higher viewpoints within an emerging context. In *Insight*, Lonergan had shown that objective process does not use a blueprint but is "the cumulation of a conditioned series of things and schemes of recurrence in accord with successive schedules of probabilities."[69] Such process is open, fluid, in tension; it achieves a higher reality. For GEM, higher viewpoints are springboards to order lower-level aggregates of acts/events/things; it integrates these through further in-sights that illuminate higher *forms*. In *Method in Theology*, Lonergan outlines GEM's co*opera*tive potential for achieving the higher reality of a 4-3-5 spirit-filled realm. A notion of spiritual alleles considers how feelings and emotions can affect a "geophilosophical immanence." Conceptual personae can be energized with GEM's AIRR-4-3-5 trans*form*ative feedback that deepens one's loving awareness of self and others. GEM enables caring persons to avoid Spinozist depersonalization or Nietzschean atheism. Rather than purging philosophy of its openness to God, GEM triads reinstate the "purged" openness with personalist categories[70] able to dialogue with the insights of 4-3-5 philosophies.

Secularists deny sin or mystical experience's "in-betweens" that GEM locates in our hearts. GEM "feedback moves" beyond a solipsist subject by inscribing the in-between of immanence and transcendence in human subjectivity itself without "projecting" the latter into the former. The novels of Francois Mauriac, Graham Greene and Endo Shusaku hint at our "allelic, spiritual in-betweens." These writers were all sensitive to how God works even in the tangle of deceitful evil that often besieges the human heart in its struggles against sin or evil. GEM is a 4-3-5 body-mind spirituality that mediates subjectivity and objectivity in artistic, ethical and philosophical ways. It maps, locates this spirituality in the immanent creativity of persons who manage to mediate and trans*form* life's "4-3-5 intangibles"[71] in objective self-transcendent ways.

GEM explains how we arrive at objectivity or determine contingent beings or events. Just as "knowing" means both experiential knowing and a verified knowing, so *object* may refer either to an unmediated knowing of the data of sense or of consciousness, or to a world mediated by meaning. Our questions immediately relate us to objects; our AIRR *opera*tions relate us to objects as mediated by our answers. Answers refer to objects only *by way of* a subject's questions and his/her immediate data of sense and of consciousness. The allelic "in-betweens" of mathematical continuities reside in real, rational or irrational numbers—as mediated by one's AIRR *opera*tions that seek and discover ever new continuities without exhausting their source. Anchored in one's intentional heuristic structure, one seeks after verifiable theories; we mediate subjectivity and objectivity in artistic, philosophical and ethical ways. One reaches objectivity in two ways. In the world of immediacy, one reaches objectivity by being a normally functioning animal; in the world mediated by meaning we rely on objectivity's three experiential, normative and absolute components. Experiential objectivity is constituted by the givenness of the data of sense and consciousness; this level deals with the *givenness* of reality. Normative objectivity is constituted by the exigences of our intelligence and the reasonableness of its insights. Absolute objectivity is a combination of experiential and normative objectivity.[72] We "AIRR avoid" 4-2 reductionisms, since objects we intend in our questions are then understood, affirmed, decided and acted upon. We do more than "AIRR avoid." G*E*M is a precious gem that, by definition, is *open* to the *empirical*; it enables us to reach feedback-processed 4-3-5 foundations. Accommodating the transcendent and religious facets of our lives, it empowers philosophy and science by helping us advert to our trans*form*ative allelic AIRR ethical ideals. Stemming from the exigencies of our 4-3-5 *opera*tional modes of knowing, these ideals blend the allelic facets of faith and reason.

GEM agrees with Deleuze and Guattari that the philosophical concept must not be confused with the merely lived, for the "lived" only furnishes variables, whereas concepts must still define true functions. With them, it does not let science arrogate the concept to itself, but adds that we cannot let philosophy arrogate the plane of immanence to itself either. For Deleuze and Guattari, this plane is not "a *method*." For GEM, however, the plane of immanence is cut off from neither transcendence nor method. As a general empirical *method* of self-transcendent immanence, GE*M* can guide us in our lives. It can also help methodologists 4-3-5 trans*form* empiricism by linking it with transcendence in AIRR allelic ways.

For Deleuze and Guattari, every great philosopher has laid out a new way of explaining what it means to think; yet, GEM insists that each such great thinker has had to resort to the same set of four AIRR *opera*tions at work in ordinary human beings. Strangely, Deleuze and Guattari's conceptual personae are impersonal. I seek to "4-3-5 personalize" their depersonalized persons with GEM's empowering, character-building method. GEM is not concerned with the content of thought so much as with the method of securing foundations for types of thoughts. It studies our patterns of experience, our insights into the data of sense and of consciousness, correct judgments and other criteria—all of which are necessary, if one is to arrive at a notion of authentic interiority. For GEM, what characterizes the great thinker is using AIRR opera*t*ions in a new, original way. Is philosophy only a friend, as Deleuze and Guattari argue, or can we empower it in ways that do not suffocate transcendence a la Spinoza or Nietzsche? What is wanted is not a foundation suffocating on concepts, but one that lets one breathe by giving full scope to reflective judgments.

GEM's focus on the patterns of experience has us consciously experience how we come to know and act in trans*form*ative AIRR feedback ways. We understand by reflecting on the data we experience. Through correct judgments, we then take proper action, both in our own personal lives, and in interfaith, transcultural or interdisciplinary contexts. I now offer five examples of locating AIRR trans*form*ative reflectivity within a 4-3-5 GEM feedback (Part Two).

The first example has to do with number theory and integers. Mathematicians of the early nineteenth century still regarded complex numbers with suspicion. In 1831, Gauss showed that complex numbers with the square root of -1 (*i*) can be regarded as ordered pairs of real numbers for which opera*t*ions of addition and multiplication are defined in terms of the pair's component parts. *Form*ulating the theory of congruences, he arrived at the absolute value (modulus) of a complex number. Adopting Plato's cave metaphor, he "understood his complex numbers to be shadows reflecting a complex of physical actions (action acting on action). This complex action reflected a power greater"[73] than the triply extended action characterizing a manifold's visible space. In giving the first known proof of the fundamental theorem of algebra by substituting a complex number, a + b*i*, for the unknown of the equation, Gauss separated the real and imaginary parts of the result. He showed that the two resulting functions of a and b are zero for some pairs of values of a and b. His implicit use of the notion of the reflexivity of numbers (x = x, for all x) and his use of the principle of squaring (quadrature) demonstrated that the meaning of the square root of 1 lies not in the visible domain of squares but in the cognitive realm. In effect, he realized that the Pythagorean theorem is derived from Euclidean geometry but that physical space is not always Euclidean. Today, the Pythagorean theorem is generalized in many mathematical areas such as the cosine law. While linear trans*form*ations in one dimension involve an arbitrary nonzero constant, GEM considers mathematics' limit points in carrying out rules of procedures.

If the Pythagoreans discovered the reality of irrational numbers, or if doctors and engineers use contact topologies, a spiritual topology suggests that AIRR ideals can effectively "4-3-5 transcend" the ordered sets of 4-3-4 *form*s and op*er*ators. By introducing ideal numbers (a subgroup of a ring) into mathematics, Kummer extended the fundamental theorem of arithmetic to complex number fields. His generalizations of complex numbers depend on the basis Galois gave for the imaginary roots of an irreducible congruence. If ideal numbers guide the arithmetic of algebraic numbers, 4-3-5 ideals help us live ethically.[74] The life of Evariste Galois, group theory's founder, illustrates human glory and frailty. Killed at the age of 20 in a frivolous duel, on the night before his death, he jotted down his insights into group theory—groups of auto*morph*isms that adjoin the roots of equations. Mathematics focuses on the general, the complete, the ideal; it is not concerned with the existent as such. GEM goes beyond mathematics' serially analytic principles and its range of possible systems that scientists may reflectively verify (*Insight*, 314). It focuses on the real world 4-3-4 analyzed in mathematics. I locate our AIRR ope*ra*tions and their underlying potency-*form*-act conjugates to include our in-between allelic abilities that reflect on, link our lives' 4-3-5 phases.

A second example of locating trans*form*ative reflectivity occurs in works by Fichte, Jean Nabert and Nishida. Nabert used Fichtean reflexivity in critiquing the limits of reason to arrive at the category of absolute evil. In one of his transitional phases, Nishida used Fichtean reflexivity before devising his mature philosophy of the locus (based on a trans*form*ative adaptation of Plato's cave metaphor). GEM grounds reflexivity in ways parallel to Nabert's use of a criteriology of the divine, and to Nishida's use of "nothingness" to ground moral or religious conscience. I map a map love that invites persons to live the virtues and to learn past traditions' wisdom. Appropriating traditions is complex. Nishida and Heidegger were both ambivalent in how they appropriated their traditions in the light of reigning Fascist ideologies. GEM trans*form*s Fichte's absolute ego by keeping us humble in how we appropriate our own ego in the face of violence. Like Kant and Fichte, GEM grounds autonomy and objectivity in valid AIRR judgments; it also speaks of the trans*form*ation of consciousness as being aware of one's innermost nature. I seek the in-between AIRR loci allowing such trans*form*ation to occur within 4-3-5 ethical-spiritual contexts.

A third example of locating GEM 4-3-5 reflectivity is to ascertain how our consciousness "localizes" dreams. W. Pauli and C. G. Jung exchanged letters concerning possible causal relations between one's dreams and the outer occurences that dreams sometimes anticipate or reflect. If, for example, upon dreaming of a fox or when recalling such a dream, a fox appears in one's vicinity, the fox and its symbols are not to be linked causally but are to be located in what Jung and Pauli called a "unified psychophysical reality" or the principle of synchronicity that can transcend matter-psyche splits. It involves a trans*form*ation of consciousness or of the God image. Jung called it the trans*form*ation of the Self or a potential world of causeless new creations; this potential world may incarnate into the concrete, such as when the fox appears, enabling[75] the dreamer upon explanation, to realize that he/she can recover a lost insight. If neuroscientists seek to localize the trans*form*ative loci of consciousness in our brains, with Jung and Pauli, a 4-3-5 metaxy reappropriates extra-causal life events so as to convert an acquisitive society too focused on material gains. In his efforts to find an alternative to Descartes and Leibniz's a "universal language," Swedenborg's "correspondence" theory localized mental processes; he anticipated Freud by interpreting his own dreams.[76] I interpret dreams as trans*form*ative loci mediated by an AIRR language or by the tentative ideals that motivated such men as Swedenborg, Freud, Jung, Pauli and H. Hesse. Analysis led Hesse to search for an in-between awareness beyond givens. Our two genomes use the analogical in-betweens of such awareness or of uracil to trans*form* us. Some speculate that, in addition to chromosomes' DNA strands, there are virtual strands that need to be activated into our 3-dimensional physical framework—as influenced by emotions or feelings. As we saw, Bion's grid categorizes all events in human interactions. Can such "events' brain-waves" be interpreted with Feynman diagrams since they involve electrons?

Brainwaves are energy packets; yet, they are subject to spiritual influences—a view that influenced Jung's break with Freud, in 1912, in favor of a "psychic energy" not reducible to sexual energy. While the early Freud saw dreams as a "system-topography"; his later *topiques* led him to phylogenetic-childhood views on dreams and to call id, ego and superego as "precipitates"[77] of primaeval, antiquated religious experiences. Preserving a notion of spirituality within psychic energy, Jung knew that uncontrolled psychic energy could lead to psychosis. For Jung, the "Self" appears in dreams or other *form*s of expression and embraces what the ego cannot; this Self is not a transcendent entity, but remains on the intra-psychic level. There is no way to get at the thing in itself extra-psychically. Like Jung, GEM revises Freud's enlightenment model that denies the origins of its own categories. Turning Freud's ego *topiques* into *non-determinist* potentialities, it recognizes dreams as trans*form*ative. As opposed to Jung, for both Levinas and GEM, God *is*. God is not confined within the intra-psychic. One "discovers" God by living out the immanent source of transcendence (the pure desire to know) or by discovering a love without restriction. Allowing for the subjectivity of dreams, a 4-3-5 bridge "trans*form*s" our physical realities. It helps us locate an in-between foundational space for spiritual-ethical trans*form*ations. Just as one's dreams reflect and influence one's behavior, so M. L. King's dream helped trans*form* a whole generation. King's Gandhian politics helped reshape the politics of his country.

A fourth example regards Husserl-GEM analogies. Western philosophy can be outlined as moves from Plato's world of Ideas to Aristotle's substance, to Kant's turn to the subject, to the German Idealists and, finally, to today's "end of philosophy."[78] GEM initiates us into a metaphysics, that, mediating an allelic "being-void manifold," integrates East-West philosophies allowing them to incorporate reason-faith imperatives in trans*form*ative ways. Like Kant and Schopenhauer, it begins with the notion that all that we know are objects in relation to a subject. If Kant cuts us off from "noumena," and if Schopenhauer postulates an arbitrary will (*Wille*) and idea (*Vorstellung*), GEM grounds AIRR ideals—not unlike Eastern approaches that we shall study in Part Two.

Hoping to overcome Descartes' idealism that claimed that we could doubt the existence of matter and Berkeley's dogmatic (quasi-solipsist) idealism that denied the existence of matter, Kant tried to show how concepts are related to lived experience through a priori propositions and judgments (as functions of a whole of possible experience). Basing himself on pure intuitions of space and time, he strove to validate the contents of our knowledge. Subsuming judgment under rules that do not clearly distinguish AIRR *opera*tions, understanding is, for him, the faculty of rules that passes "judgment upon the nature of things." Like Plato, he wants to bring ideas to bear upon our practical freedom as rooted in reason, but he transcendentally stymies our thinking. For him, the transcendental ego constructs knowledge from sense impressions and from the universal concepts that it imposes upon these impressions. His transcendental idealism sees ideas as raw matter of knowledge due to realities existing independently of human minds; such ideas only give us access to things as phenomena. "Things-in-themselves" remain forever unknowable to us.[79]

A hundred years after Kant, Husserl sought to solve philosophy's crises by contrasting its critical attitude with the positivist, naive attitude of natural science. To show that meaning is not arbitrary, he develops a transcendental epoche (reduction) to allow theoretical reason to put one's practical concerns in "brackets." In Greek philosophy, epoche had meant suspending judgment; but he raises epoche to the level of a technique more fundamental than that of abstraction. By practicing a sort of Cartesian methodic doubt in regard to common-sense beliefs, his epoche highlights consciousness. He focuses on it as intentional in approaching the thorny subject of "objectivity" (*Logical Investigations*,1900-01). In *Ideen, I*, (1913) he seeks to refute those who read into his use of the term "object" implications that every thought turns into a thing. His *Crisis of Philosophy* reexamines philosophy's claim to be a rigorous science so as to make possible an ethical life regulated by rational norms.

Complaining that *Investigations* had been misunderstood as advocating a Platonic realism, Husserl uses a transcendental phenomenology to analyze meaning and to clarify subject-objects relationships with an appeal to an intuition of a *necessary essence*. He examines the ways in which various modes of establishing unity in our consciousness can be correlated. These modes include the factual unity of things and states of affairs, the eidetic unity of essences and the living unity of consciousness that flow in one's stream of experiences.[80] His notions of "being in the world" and ideality express acts of self-transcendent thought. In his "immanent perceptivo-affective fusional sets," he thought he had discovered the triple root of acts of transcendence (thought) through which the subject constitutes first of all a sensory world filled with objects, "then an intersubjective world occupied by the other, and finally a common ideal world ... occupied by scientific, mathematical, and logical formations."[81] Yet, what seemed to be a strong point—clarifying the meaning of objectivity—proved to be a major weakness. It was unclear whether his epoche allowed "meaning" to be anything other than what an interpreter might choose it to mean. Husserl's neglect of history only reinforced that weakness. Hegel and Husserl's phenomenologies both seek to synthesize the subject and object. GEM revises their projects by clarifying how a subject reflectively *posits* synthetic judgments. Like Husserl, Lonergan set out to save philosophy from a naturalist psychologism and from positivism that reduces method to the sciences. Both rethink Kant's transcendental ego. For Kant, the transcendental ego is necessary to unify one's empirical self-consciousness. It synthesizes sensations according to the categories of the understanding but nothing can be known of this ego because it is a *condition*, not an object, of knowledge. GEM revises this view by reconnecting pure and practical reason with one's feelings. If positivism's attack on metaphysics had questioned any kind of continuity or structure, GEM restores both by locating the sources of objectivity in a structured AIRR (ethical) methodology.

While Husserl refuses to let God into philosophy, a reading of St. Augustine might have taught him that the world, as I know it, may be created by God independently of my knowing it; "it is not a world for me until I know it, and it is only in constituting it that I know it."[82] Husserl's transcendental ego is pure consciousness, for which everything that exists *is an object*; the ego is the ground for the constitution of all meaning. Any conclusion in any field, such as the meaning of force or acceleration in physics, the notion of right and obligations in law or the execution of an artistic work, depends on one's judgment.[83] Yet, GEM is close to Eastern philosophies, in not excluding religion when analyzing consciousness; its judgments are open to mystic insights that lead to self-transcendence. Since the world, as I know it, is created by God, independently of my knowing it, and since it takes my use of a complex structure of embodied intentionality that responds to God's love for me to constitute that world, GEM serves as an in-between metaxy in search of relational[84] love. In constituting cultural objects, our judgments help us encounter the totally Other.

GEM saves us from mere 4-2 techniques and from Husserlian intuition by having us *affirm* our actions as our own. The world, as I know it, is not a world for me until I know it by "constituting" it. Knowledge is discursive, not intuitive; the intelligible is what we expect to grasp, when we ask how new things emerge out of the old. Emergence is the process in which "otherwise coincidental manifolds of lower conjugate acts invite the higher integration effected by higher conjugate *forms*.[85] Aggregates of acts of knowing are taken up into successively higher *forms* of syntheses. Within this perspective, potency-*form*-act triads take on a special meaning. Potency encompasses all the possibilities latent in given realities that are or can become intelligible elements within higher systems' potencies. If Husserl was concerned that his *Investigations* had been misunderstood as advocating a Platonic realism for which he substituted an eidetic unity of essences (ideality of self-transcendent thought), GEM deepens the eidetic function with 4-3-5 ideals. It does so through trans*form*ative conjugates that AIRR-transpose Spinozan substantialism.

A fifth example of GEM reflectivity occurs in how it explains virtues' 4-3-5 trans*form*ative mediation of tunnel visions. Spinoza restricts free will; virtue means "intellectually" loving a God deduced as infinite substance.

GEM's develops ethics within an explanatory context of the good. Goodness in the universe emerges from potencies. Human concern, mystic insights and morality are all privileged instances within a universe *in process* that GEM calls *finality*—a notion as broad as being that refers to the incomplete aspect of all things-in-potency moving toward being or to reality as an upwardly directed dynamism. Such a dynamic finality implies an AIRR iso*morph*ism between the mind and proportionate being. If Bion's vertical axis is equivalent to GEM's genetic aspect and his horizontal axis represents GEM's structural foundation, I seek to outline ways to distinguish, yet interweave a spirit philosophy that can differentiate GEM's trans*form*ative and structural aspects. Unlike Spinozan pantheism, such a philosophy is abductively foundational. It provisionally adopts hypotheses and perseveres until reaching a foundation. The universe is not at rest but *in process*. Present reality and knowing are only *moments* in the trans*form*ative *process* that emerges in the field of proportionate being within creative relational process. GEM identifies a potential good with a potential intelligibility that can become an actual good. Its generalized emergent probability (the immanent intelligible order of the universe and the ground for its unity) supplies the initial coincidental manifolds of events in which higher conjugates emerge. GEM's conditioned series of things and schemes of recurrence in developing organisms help us explain how perceptual beings successfully develop or function in emerging environments. The intelligible orders that our AIRR *opera*tions achieve are realizations of prehuman intelligible orders within the universal order of generalized emergent probability. If mRNA-tRNA abet DNA trans*form*ations (by way of allelic loci), I locate GEM's intelligible orders in the trans*form*ative AIRR allelic *loci* of East-West thought. Trans*form*ative loci, inherent in all researchers, reflect the AIRR iso*morph*ism between our minds and the reality we discover; we use such loci to reconcile the concrete "things" of daily life with a pluralist realism. As empowering, trans*form*ative loci, they illustrate how GEM per*form*ance AIRR-trans*forms* linguistic per*form*atives and accounts for personal and group action.

Rethinking Galileo and
4-2 and 4-3-4 Formulations

Despite their genius, Galileo and Descartes gave rise to untenable 4-2 views; this has led Snow to speak of our "two cultures."[86] While Galileo held that there is extension and duration if there is matter and motion whether or not any animals with their sensitive experiences exist, GEM holds parallel distinctions between how we or other animals experience extension or duration and how scientists 4-2 *form*ulate their notions of color, sounds or electric phenomena. GEM verifies the contents of our everyday experience (red as seen, extension as touched); it correlates such experienced contents with the potential correlatives established by science. Both our everyday experience of things and science' *for*-

*mu*lations of timespace include experiential and explanatory conjugates; experiential conjugates' meaning appeals to the content of our experience; explanatory conjugates are terms defined implicitly by empirically established laws. Explanation of all data consists in moving *from* experiential *to* explanatory conjugates. Insofar as experiential and pure conjugates *are* verified, *both* types, as *given* in our data of consciousness, can be reasonably AIRR affirmed. By rejecting the Aristotelian method of inquiring about the *nature* of an object and by specifying correlations, Galileo initiated modern science; but by rejecting the relations of things to our senses in explaining the relations of things to one another, he 4-2 *reduced* merely "apparent" secondary qualities to their "real and objective" source in primary qualities For GEM, truth is to be reached not merely in contents of our 4-2 experience, nor in their potential correlatives, but in *combinations* of such contents and correlatives. Verified correlations are those terms we can *implicitly define* and correlate; they do *not* involve more than such implicitly defined terms as related, for what is verified accurately are not particular propositions but the *abstract proposition* on which ranges of particular propositions[87] converge. The 4-3-4 spacetime of relativity stands to the extensions and durations of experience in the same relations as wave lengths of light "stand to experiences of color, as longitudinal waves in air stand to experience of sound, as the type of energy defined by the first law of thermodynamics stands to experiences of heat."[88]

Conjugate *form*s (terms implicitly defined by empirically verified and explanatory relations) are one with *potency*, the component of proportionate being that seeks to know in intellectually patterned experiences of the empirical residue; such *form*s are also one with our knowing acts. Potency is known by experience; it merely presents what *form* will define and what judgment will affirm to be in act. From this potency-*form*-act triad, GEM "AIRR-moves" on to a fourth level of intentional consciousness as modulated by a 4-3-5 ethical doing whose feedback spindle I am investigating.

Descartes' mind-matter split reflects Galileo's inversion of the roles of primary AIRR structures and secondary linguistic ones. Static ideas came to replace the dynamic nature of our intellects. In fact, scientists do use secondary qua-lities as they verify the correlations of things to one another. GEM reverses the inversion with AIRR primary structures that respect and integrate primary and secondary qualities; it verifies terms and correlations in conjugate *form*s. One's verified *inner* data respect reality. By rescuing *all* secondary qualities, GEM sublates "value-free" approaches that shortcircuit AIRR *primary* structures' s secondary qualities. It integrates our experience with God and neighbor by linking faith to explanatory conjugates. Unlike Galileo and Locke, it *return*s to objects of sensation, to our minds' *opera*tions. It leaves out neither our data of consciousness nor the secondary qualities of things as *related to us*. Its return to things as related to us "re-stitches" the gaps introduced by Galileo and preserves notions of unity by linking concepts and individual data. Analogously to nucleoproteins (conjugated proteins linking DNA and 4-3-5 RNA), GEM relines persons on the basis of allelic conjugates that initiate us into ethics.

The heart has reasons reason cannot understand (Pascal). Terrorists reach for perceived immediate advantages, but a 4-3-5 spiritual genome advocates the ideals of Buddha and of Jesus; it seeks 4-3-5 spiritual liberation. It reaches for infinity by implementing the in-between alleles of reason and faith, good and bad feelings and many other allelic loci open to trans*form*ative meaning and values in the interest of all. "In the interest of *all*" is an ideal norm by which lesser interests are to be adjudicated. As uracil *forms* A-U base pairs to trans*form* DNA, so AIRR acts trans*form* dated extra-scientific philosophical views such as those of Galileo and Descartes in rebuilding society.

The fact that insights are both intellectual and reflective suggests their crucial roles in trans*form*ing meaning. If RNA has a catalytic role of mediating between DNA and proteins,[89] so insights have a "supra-catalytic" role. They mediate between evil and 4-3-5 good trans*form*ative processes within and among humans. Meaning is constitutive; it mediates the mediator to him/herself giving rise to a nuanced feedback meaning. Time is not just a measurable quantity; it involves the "now" in the flow of our conscious-intentional acts that historians can investigate.[90]

Some question whether our analytical-theoretic frameworks actually represent an identity with observational constructs. To unmask 4-2 reductionisms, GEM probes how our first three cognitional levels use data of sense and consciousness to attain certitude. It asks and answers 3 basic questions: 1) "what am I doing when I seek to know?" (cognitional theory); 2) "why is that doing that knowing?" (epistemology); 3) "what do I know when I do it?" (metaphysics). Being is all that is known and remains to be known. Our poly*morph*ic AIRR consciousness knows knowns iso*morph*ically. Events complement conjugates; such a complementarily (that of metaphysical equivalence)[91] involves a *rule of concreteness* allowing us to use general concepts to refer to *concrete* potency-*form*-act conjugates. These three conjugates lead to knowledge, but point to in-between known unknowns to be known heuristically through our invariant *op-erat*ions. Some reduce GEM's metaphysical equivalence and GEM itself to a natural theology. I go beyond 4-3-4 spacetime views to include a fifth metaxic ideal of ethical love. We progress from a cognitional theory to a metaphysics by way of epistemology. GEM's metaphysical equivalence allows one to establish an analogy between genetic and 4-3-5 spiritual processes with conjugates that bypass "substance." GEM conjugates (AIRR-4-3-5 acts) yield a "chicken and egg" knowledge: their AIRR feedback ability trans*form*s meaning; it grounds 4-3-5 ethical spiritualities as loci of conversion.

Deleuze and Guattari would have us be nomads. Does that mean giving up the familiar comfort of known terrain so as to be absorbed in Spinoza's substance or in Nietzschean will? Are we to order our artistic-scientific symbols in Nietzsche's Dionysian terms for lack of spiritual convictions? Or can we muster courage to nurture the planet for future generations and to rethink Nietzsche's 4-3-4 critical "higher morality"? GEM conversion can help us act authentically within circles of friends open to the good. Its potency-*form*-act triad complements Deleuze and Guattari's would-be 4-3-4 self-sufficient, immanent triad so that our AIRR ideals of being attentive, intelligent, rational and responsible can lead us to a more humble attitude converting us to mystery, to acknowledging that no matter how much we know, or "control" nature, we are dependent creatures, yet able to co*opera*te so as move beyond tunnel visions.

Some genetic mutations in the base sequence of DNA molecules are heritable and stable, but oncogenic mutations (mutagens) alter a cell's genetic constitution and cause cancer. Likewise, sinful, evil "mutagens" wreak havoc. Not being coded, AIRR *loci* are more prone to evil mutagens than are ATGC; but since they *are free*, they allow us to empower one another *or* to distort AIRR for malign uses. In the face of scientifico-philosophical dogmas that would 4-2 *shortcircuit* the full 4-3-5 dynamism of our basic knowing-doing AIRR *opera*tions, I study how GEM reverses such dogmas. As enzymes direct and catalyze a host of biochemical reactions within genes' DNA, so GEM trans*form*s us.[92] Enzymes greatly hasten body processes. GEM helps us duly reflect so as to achieve *slow* trans*form*ations—as occurred in the past and still occurs. Art, literature, ethics or religion *can* promote self-transcendent 4-3-5 virtuous authenticity in persons, young and old; as "trans*form*ative matrices" in*form*ing our struggles against biased evils, they can help us fashion more comprehensive "4-3-5 in-between ideals" to bridge East-West ethics. If nature uses 4-3-5 RNA to trans*form*atively propagate life, authentic persons, in touch with their inner life, are the ethical artists humanity needs to motivate others.

As RNA molecules are a template that amino acids use for protein synthesis, and as DNA needs to go through an RNA intermediate before it can be translated into a polypeptide sequence, so we can learn to integrate our inner and outer life on the model of East-West mystics. Built atop our DNA-RNA genome, our spiritual AIRR alleles are a source empowerment. In our psychological development we first become aware of what is outside of us before discovering one's inner self. This tends to lead an inside-outside dualism. It is perhaps such a dualism that Buddhists, Spinoza, Deleuze and Guattari have sought to overcome by appeals to an immanentism. GEM has the often-overlooked ability to reintegrate us mystically and *ethically* by helping us appropriate *our own* inbuilt 4-3-5 bridge. Feedback AIRR *opera*tions in intending subjects are immanent "*opera*tors" guiding us to the transcendent. They can integrate the world. AIRR *ideal* imperatives imply love—inasmuch as we act on them. It is because such imperatives are attainable ideals that they serve as East-West metaxic foundations that promote us all by furthering (world) ethical co*opera*tion.

While mRNA produces polypeptide chains by synthesizing nucleotides' ATGC "words" (phosphate esters of nucleosides that contain nitrogen) into nucleic acid "sentences," AIRR *loci* use psychogenetic-spiritual processes to trans*form* egoists through 4-3-5 conversions.[93] Viruses and postmodernism both *lack life*—unless respectively guided by cellular or trans*form*ative processes. A virus hijacks host cells. GEM's ideal diphase feedback moves us beyond diploid cells (in which we are rooted) toward godly action. Just as invaded host cells fight back, so AIRR ideals "4-3-5 repel" evils' virulent infectiousness. Our spiritual genome's AIRR *opera*tions are "pivotal alleles" that work in self-transcending feedback to promote a dynamic, conscious development in persons. As cells' surface proteins are involved in the acceptance or rejection of tissue and organ grafts, so our 4-3-5 authentic *or* inauthentic actions make the difference in striving for a just peace based on justice.[94] Our AIRR imperatives are loci that pursue or reject ideals: they are located in a spiritual 4-3-5 genome's allelic loci on the analogy of how ATGC-U nucleotides genetically trans*form* us. They promote us from being subjects as objects, to being self-transcendent "subjects as subjects."

A Second "Let's Get Real" Concurrent Dialectic

"Realist": Oh, I see! We are rooted in a biology different from what's going on in our heads. What about mathematicians and their complex calculus, geometry or analysis? What does that have to do with genetics—or ideals? You seem to be postulating that there is a structural analogy between a physical genome and a "spiritual" one. But how many people have time for spirituality or even know that there is such a thing as spirituality? Besides, spirituality differs from culture to culture. How then can we make a bridge between such cultures or let people base themselves on an alleged GEM method to fashion an interdisciplinary and interfaith method for a viable world ethics?

John: Okay, my realist friend, did you ever think about how even such basics numbers as 1, 2, 3 and 4 involve both ideals *and* reality? Applying AIRR loci and their potency-*form*-act *triad*ic conjugates can empower us both in our daily lives and in how we per*form* in the arts, sciences or philosophy. Just as Nirenberg discovered and applied the triplet-binding virtuosity of tRNA and mRNA and clarified how amino acid triads affect DNA's four nucleotides, so GEM's potency-*form*-act triad is relevant to explaining our minds' trans*form*ative AIRR *feedback* ability. As anticodon triplets are needed to end the coding roles of other amino acid triplets, so various kinds of triads specify or model the role of potency-*form*-act triads.

A GEM spiritual genome is postulated to account for the structural "4-3-5 mode of operating" in a physical genome as well as in a spiritual one. Since all humans have a fourfold set of knowing-doing operations and are, in principle, called to live a spiritual, ethical life, the burden falls on those who realize this to establish a viable "feedback" way that can implement the psychic, intellectual, moral and religious conversions which Lonergan and his GEM have outlined.

The next chapter contextualizes mathematicians' ideal use of the procedures of the AIRR-4-3-5 human mind so as to prepare for Part II's feedback method (fig. 4) that outlines how each person's 4-3-5 operations are reduplicative ones, that is they are susceptible to be transformed and employed in interdisciplinary ways so to allow experts in various fields to cooperate in furthering the bounds of knowledge and to take heed of the ethical implications of their work. Despite differences in language and culture, GEM enables us, by adverting to one's basic intentional operations, to become cooperators on a level more basic than any acquired language.

Chapter 3

Transform*ative* *Forms* in Mathematics

This book explores spiritual allelic loci so as to link them in ways able to face our social upheavals. Chapter 2 contextualized Deleuze and Guattari with a spiritual spindle's reason-faith alleles that trans*form* us from self-seeking to self-giving patterns. It suggested ways to ethically integrate our patterns of experience. If Galileo and Lavoisier fostered science by measuring and quantifying, I use allelic AIRR's in-between "qualia loci" to illustrate how 4-3-5 GEM can help us develop ideals, how it transcends amino acids' 4-3-5 trans*form*ational properties. It is concerned with the insights that occur in all fields of endeavor including those of ethics[1] and mathematics.

Delving into the 4-3-4 spacetime continuum, this chapter argues that within 4-dimensional spacetime we can seek East-West *ideals* in the face of inauthenticity. It contrasts common sense with the way mathematicians seek the general rather than existents. It examines how Cantor and Einstein used their AIRR loci in ways that illustrate this book's attempt to empower philosophy and science. Delving into the spacetime continuum, it argues that within 4-dimensional spacetime we can seek East-West *ideals* in the face of egotistic inauthenticity, as did Einstein. After some preliminary remarks on life's imponderables and infinity (1.1 to 1.7), it considers, 2) poetry and the in-betweens of numbers, 3) Einstein's use of tensors and 4) a spiritual topology. Inquiring into mathematical 4-3-4 invariants in group theory and in the theory of manifolds, it compares such invariants with our invariant AIRR *opera*tions. It does so with a view to implement GEM's allelic loci in Part Two through a feedback method that confronts the evils of sin with ideal loci discovered by mystics or even by some scientists.[2]

Logically, we can prove neither a basic law of physics nor ethical ideals. Mathematical and ethical models both use *ideal* terms and relations rooted in our AIRR *opera*tions, not unlike Lorentz-Einstein trans*form*ations grasped by our 4-3-5 structured spirits, where the "3" refers to potency-*form*-act triads mediated by judgments and the AIRR decisions we put in to practice.[3] Galilean trans*form*ations presupposed the absoluteness of time. Lorentz trans*form*ations use coordinates that trans*form* both space and time. Absolute truth (mediated in symbols and texts) cannot be named directly by language as an object is named; nor can it be dismissed in the direct exercise of critical reason as in Kant.[4] GEM's potency-*form*-act and body-mind-spirit triads, analogous to amino acid triplets, are not codes but "meta-catalysts" (analogous to enzymes) that trans*form* us as we use our freedom. AIRR feedback outlines some of the trans*form*ative 4-3-5 ideals that Einstein applied to the real world in defending ethical causes.

1.1 *Points of Departure for "4-3-5 Interpreting" Einstein*

GEM rejects positivist claims that only the senses are the source of scientific fact. I interpret Einstein's lifework in light of GEM's ability to relate our judgments of fact and of value. The latter involve a knowledge of humans and of reality, intentional responses to values and an initial thrust towards moral self-transcendence constituted by a judgment of value itself (*Method*, 38). Brain and mind do not interact in reductionist ways, but in enriching AIRR-4-3-5 brain-mind spiritual patterns. Einstein's mysticism lays a basis for a foundational 4-3-5 metaxy. Science and religion are distinct kinds of language games, each with its own inner logic. GEM links the two through the beliefs in*form*ing both science and religion. We appropriate our social, cultural and religious heritage because of beliefs. There is much that one finds out for self, that one knows in virtue of one's inner and outer experience, one's insights and judgments of fact and of value. But such an "immanently generated knowledge is but a small fraction of what any civilized man" in fact knows (*Method*, 41). The positivist imperative promoted a bias demanding not only that science "test its theories against observation ... but that every aspect of our theories must at every point refer to observable quantities."[5] This bias initially fought against atomic theory and still impedes theoretical physics. GEM rejects positivist claims that, since science is based on external evidence while religion is the realm of emotions and moral feelings, one cannot bridge the two. I bridge the two with a map of love that transcends language games by studying games' rules. If Chomsky's trans*forma*tional rules and notion of constituent (phrase) structure are analogous to bracketing in logic (enclosed terms are treated as single terms),[6] a 4-3-5 map of love does not "bracket." It transposes, converts our psyches' deeper structures into ones of interrelated love.

Figures 1-4's shorthand (4-3-5 "linking" spirituality with AIRR *opera*tions) develops GEM's "radically" trans*form*ative philosophico-theological allelic loci. Rather than parrot all of GEM, my AIRR shorthand lets the various perspectives of scientists, philosophers, mystics and poets/artists "converge" in integrating our allelic feelings and thoughts. GEM's "mystic poet-artists" lay out a transcendental field that respects the rights of immanence. Figures 2 sought to contextualize ethics and spirituality with the analogy of spindles *opera*tive in our physical and spiritual genomes. Figures 3 focuses on three of the trans*form*ative triadic models I have been exploring, two of which involve 4-3-5 structures. Deleuze and Guattari's model forfeits a spiritual-ethical potential because of its conceptualist nature, even while it tries to recover Spinoza's deep sensitivity to feelings. While Spinoza's pantheism dilutes our 4-3-5-structured cognitional freedom, GEM's ethical AIRR ideals replace his pantheism with a flexible trans*form*ative cognitional structure that "4-3-5 transposes" science's idealizations. Scientific idealizations 4-2 misrepresent reality in their use of a mediating mathematical tractability.[7] In figures 3, GEM's triadic 4-3-5 model includes both potency-*form*-act and body-mind-spirit triads whose ideal trans*form*ative AIRR feedback is to be explored in Part Two.

FIG. 3 AIR-4-3-5 TRANSFORMATIVE LOCI THAT TRANSCEND GENETICS
OR 4-3-4 CONCEPTUAL PHILOSOPHIES

Genetic 4-3-5 Triad	Deleuze-Guattari's 4-3-4 Triad	GEM's 4-3-5 Triadic Feedback Spindle
Trans*form*ative DNA	Conceptual - Personae	Conjugate Potencies (including Feelings)
RNA-Uracil	Concepts	Trans*form*ative AIRR *Form*s' Conjugates
Codon-amino acids	Plane of Immanence	Ideal 4-3-5 Ethical Actions' Conjugates

GEM's 4-3-5 feedback spindle (illustrated on pg. 20) maps, transposes feedback contextual alleles of reality and of thought. Such a feedback spindle (sublated within 4-3-5 ethical alleles) suggests how transformative 4-3-5 loci differ from genetic or conceptual triads while integrating both of these and their otherwise coincidental manifolds within GEM conversions open to love and ethics.

Figure 2 suggested a *cooper*ative feedback spindle analogous to the spindle mediating DNA-RNA trans*form*ations. Geneticists have proposed a spindle matrix that organizes and stablilizes the microtubule spindle during mitosis.[8] Figures 3 suggests that a trans*form*ative feedback spindle can foster ethical co*opera*tion; it extends a physical-spiritual genomes analogy by transposing our cognitional AIRR per*form*ance into a 4-3-5 trans*form*ative ethics that sublates enzymes' catalyst action. What is wanted is not a conceptual foundation, but one that gives full scope to reflective judgments, one that maps and interrelates East-West ways of thinking based on a 4-3-5 mutually trans*form*ative foundation. I remap a rhizome's multiple entry points with GEM trans*form*ative insights so as apply its love-mapping ability to ethico-spiritual realms (Part Two). Let us probe into how 4-3-4 analysis and 4-2 reductionism overlook 4-3-5 philosophical, spiritual and ethical issues.

1.2 GEM and AIRR Operators' Infinite Number of Creative Possibilities

The word *symmetry* (well-proportioned, well-ordered) originally designated properties of paintings or sculptures; it implies an infinite number of creative possibilities. In science, however, symmetry is associated with *opera*tions on a system that trans*form* it into itself in such way that a trans*form*ed system is indistinguishable from its initial state. In science, symmetry and invariance are closely interrelated; these are also a basic feature of AIRR *opera*tors but in a transposed way that reflects AIRR acts' creative possibilities. Within AIRR invariance, AIRR *opera*tors paradoxically allow subjects to be trans*form*ed in their ever trans*form*ing worlds; they map one set into another, but also help us discern a 4-3-5 good from allelic evils. I now illustrate this by surveying *opera*tor theory, matrices, group theory and "complex numbers as vectors" that all hint at how our AIRR invariant structure clarifies 4-3-4 procedures and grounds the possibilities of a 4-3-5 world ethics.

*Operator Theory and Matrices. Opera*tor theory emerged in the 1850's with William R. Hamilton's discovery of quaternions (an element of a system of four dimensional vectors obeying laws similar to those of complex numbers)[9] and with Hermann Grassman's exterior algebra. It was influenced by James Sylvester's study of matrices, by Cauchy's proofs of the spectral theorem for self-adjoint matrices[10] and of the diagonalizibilty of every symmetric, real matrix. It studies structures rather than particular realizations of those structures. Matrices help us study problems in which the *relation* between elements is fundamental; unlike determinants, they omit quantitative value.[11] They can be *form*ally extended to infinite matrices as the *opera*tor is trans*form*ed. While analysts are concerned with what can be added and multiplied, linear algebraists study matrices as fun objects that can be added and multiplied in flagrant disregard of the law of commutativity. If every matrix satisfies its characteristic equation, and if the Cayley theorem states that any group is iso*morph*ic to a group of trans*for*mations, GEM studies our more basic, consciously poly*morph*ic-trans*form*ative AIRR ideals that allow us to interrelate various thought *form*s. If in *opera*tor theory, *opera*tors act like matrices, GEM *opera*tors map structural relations. I use insights into *opera*tor theory[12] and matrices to study our AIRR structured, yet free *opera*tional motives. Neo-Platonists argued that rational knowledge depends upon direct contact with immaterial *form*s of knowledge that emanate from the One. For GEM, human wonder gives rise to 4-3-5 poetry and mathematics. If the West failed to invent zero and if it is often non-plused by a *sunya*-void, the study of real and complex numbers reaches an analytical limit that we transcend when grasped by a "4-3-5 void" of mystic unknowing or that we actualize in new discoveries such as of diagonalizable matrices.[13]

Group Theory. In the nineteenth century, algebraic *form*s were generalized to quadratic *form*s of degrees 3 or more (quintics). Ruffini and Abel showed that solving the general quintic cannot be written as a finite *form*ula using only the four arithmetic *opera*tions and the extraction of roots. Galois groups made it possible to determine which polynomical equations are solvable.

Galois classified the ways a little thing can sit in a bigger thing. He realized that you can pick out a point or line in the plane by keeping track of which symmetries of the plane map this point to itself. Topology is about our concept of space; group theory is about our concept of symmetry; the two are, in fact, two aspects of the same thing. Felix Klein's Erlangen program used group theory to synthesize geometry as the study of the properties of space invariant under a group of trans*form*ations. Sophius Lie used it to clarify algebraic invariants. Mathematically, the set of all symmetries of a system *form*s a group structure that can be described by Lie groups.[14] In Iwasasa theory, one seeks analogues for algebraic varieties defined over a number field using techniques applied to varieties defined over finite fields. Hasse's "local-global" principle is that the quadratic *form* (general expression with terms of second order) can be used to decide whether a number represented by a given *form* is equivalent to other *form*s. The work of Hasse, Grothendieck and Weyl provide unifiying themes in geometry, number theory, topology[15] and complex analogy; but they remain on analytical levels. My interest is in how GEM helps us solve problems involving the in-between logics of both 4-3-4 analysis and a lived 4-3-5 ethics. If algebraic topology reduces topology to 4-3-4 group theory, thus providing a bridge between the two, a spiritual topology provides us with a 4-3-5 world bridge that extends Piaget's group theory to spiritual, ethical areas.

Instead of classical theory's study of algebraic *form*s (symmetric tensors), mathematicians now use Abelian groups' permutations and transpositions that exchange two elements within symmetric groups. Instead of the action of linear trans*form*ations, I use existential contexts to transpose the feelings of the heart as these influence persons and history. If Galois was the first to understand that the algebraic solution of an equation depends on the structure of a group of permutations related to the equation, I apply GEM notions of group *opera*tions to help us realize how 4-3-4 and 4-3-5 ethical views of infinity differ.[16] GEM uses group theory's unifying potential to remap relations between sets while preserving invariant AIRR relations between elements.

If Poincare used auto*morph*ic functions (invariant under group trans*form*ations), or if group theory depends on numbers' invariant symmetry, I "4-3-5 remap" AIRR invariant group relations on the analogy of how these relations are applied in various fields. If abstract category theory deals with *morph*isms between objects, GEM transposes mathematics' iso*morph*isms into the trans*form*ative maps of a 4-3-4 physics or a 4-3-5 ethics; it transposes its homo*mor*-

*ph*isms as a map that sublates group structure by adding such an ethics. If our immune system protects our cells against viral highjacking, AIRR-4-3-5 ideals restore our highjacked freedom through self-transcending action.[17]

GEM derives the contexts of judgments for evaluating the limits of *axi*oms or of genetics. Fourier series help illustrate my argument that AIRR *opera*tors are analogical to Newtonian ordered *opera*tors; as Fourier series and group theory depend on invariants under trans*form*ations, but also give rise to different expressions that are only subject to very general conditions, so our invariant AIRR structure gives rise to innumerable types of expressions and (as illustrated in figures 1, 4) to a foundational ethics. While Fourier's series are the main tool in the analysis of periodic functions, GEM analyzes not physical vibrations or sounds but a heart's spiritual tones. It studies the ways in which enriching abstraction confers "intelligibility upon any materials resembling the empirical residue" (*Insight*, 313); it probes the mysteries of human hearts we are called to 4-3-5 discern and ethically apply. It implies that *axi*oms and *axi*ology derive from the groups of AIRR *opera*tions that devise both *axi*oms and problematical *axi*ologies. Its functional specialties are a group (unified set of elements and relations) of eight avenues for trans*form*ing minds and hearts.

Debates on the nature of quantum probabilities have led to an *opera*tional epistemic theory that involves extraneous non-epistemic factors based on Hilbert spaces; such logico-mathematical efforts rely on an equivalence of *opera*tors in expressions. Mathematicians "4-3-4 postulate" abstract spaces, but the process enabling these is enriching abstraction. Whether it be deriving the Pythagorean theorem, the cosine law, Fourier trans*form*s (expressing data as component frequencies), Hilbert spaces or group theory, enriching abstraction is pivotal in that it "4-3-5 exceeds" DNA-RNA and mathematical loci's limits as it AIRR trans*form*s human minds and spirits.

Complex Numbers as Vectors. Before 1900, mathematics could be directly related to our world. In arithmetic, one would count; geometry referred to the sizes or shapes of objects; algebra studied general truths about calculations. Since 1900, mathematics tends not to have immediate contact with reality. Mathematicians now study common ingredients in the various branches of mathematics, reminiscent of how chemists identify the same vitamin in various foods. The study of vectors began with Galileo's parallelogram law that combined forces; a vector was represented by a line segment AB in 2 or 3 dimensions as it was applied to forces, velocities or displacements.

A vector now means anything with such properties. It does not indicate just a particular type of object, but can refer to aspects of many situations. It can be multiplied by a number; two vectors can be added. Any collection of mathematical objects, in which these two *opera*tions can be defined, is a *"vector space."*[18] Mathematicians realize that vector analyses differ from other types of analyses for they concern mappings from one collection of vectors to another. A mapping of abstract correspondences between numbers helps us understand reality. Some algebraic methods deal with topologies of abstract vector spaces where addition and multiplication take on *axio*matic meanings. A spiritual topology explores AIRR-4-3-5 loci inasmuch as they have imaginary, real and transcendent facets. Our AIRR *opera*tions are invariant, but they work in trans*form*ative ways.

1.3 Limitations of 4-3-4 Analyses[19] Versus Dirac's "Irrelevancies"

Schrödinger's *psi*, a state vector evolving in time, implies active unitary trans*form*ations. The emissions of a spectral line of a certain frequency are co*opera*tive results of two vibration functions. The state vector is trans*form*ed but all *opera*tors are constant in time unless they contain time explicitly. Basis vectors do not change, but the *opera*tors are defined through their action on the basis vectors. That Heisenberg's infinite matrix of noncommutative algebra was compatible with Schrödinger's wave theory seemed strange. Heisenberg's equations imply an equivalent passive unitary trans*form*ation where the state vector is constant, but one can switch between changing vectors' representations. The same spectral line is emitted by an individual vibrator. By introducing special relativity into Schrödinger's wave equations, Dirac reconciled seeming contradictions between quantum and relativity theories. His trans*form*ation theory of quantum mechanics, using the Klein-Gordon equation as a way to multiply complex conjugates, was able to calculate certain variables' statistical distribution when others are specified. Though a wave mechanical equation should contain the same derivatives in all four coordinates, the wave equation of Schrödinger did not do so for it was derived from one of Newton's equations.

Dirac theorized that if he could not obtain a good result using the second derivatives on the time coordinates in the relativistic wave equation, "why not use the first derivatives on space coordinates in it?"[20] Introducing more imaginary units i, he made the wave equation symmetrical in space and time. His linear equation uses only first derivatives and is unstable, but it represents the creation and annihilation of virtual particles from essentially empty space and clarifies the problem of spectral lines in hydrogen. He argued that an electron spins on its axis and there must be states of negative energy. This seemed to contradict reality, so he predicted the existence of a short-lived positively charged particle, later confirmed in the positron. Arguing that the electron can be described by four wave functions that satisfy four simultaneous differential equations, he applied quantum mechanics to special relativity to attain a notion of quantum statistics that complements relativity. Dirac avoided using any mental picture of the phenomena described by mathematical symbols. I argue that there are analogies between the way he trans*form*ed quantum mechanics and the imponderables of life. For him, the basic laws of nature control a substratum that we cannot explain without introducing irrelevancies. I argue that the 4-3-5 metaxies of Jesus, Buddha, Pythagoras or Plato contain "irrelevant," but important equivalence trans*form*ations of a sort that involve, not the symmetry of Schrödinger's equation, but asymmetries of a lived love.

1.4 *Insufficiency of Dewey's 4-2 "Irrelevancies"*

In mapping ethical ideals and a world-encounter bridge that can cope with postmodern crises, GEM cautions us on the limitations of mental pictures, but it trusts the "irrelevancies" of the heart and its trans*form*ative AIRR loci. While John Dewey reproached the past for having put more emphasis on the "purely cognitive" rather than on doing, Husserl and Lonergan both studied acts of consciousness. By demeaning spirituality, Dewey, the pragmatist, introduced more (4-2) problems into society than he solved. Seeking to make the value of objects "more secure,"[21] he rejected as "irrelevant" what did not originate in nature nor "serve" human needs and goals. The education he helped democratize has floundered on the "subjectlessness" of postmodernism. To empower persons, we must see the relevancy of what Dewey deemed "irrelevant." We must learn to link reason-faith allelic in-betweens' "interplay" in 4-3-5 ethical trans*form*ative ways; otherwise, we distort the complexity of our 4-3-5 AIRR structure by resorting to 4-2 reductionist brain-mind theories that cast doubt on the reality of our body-mind-spirit structure. Such theories confuse descriptive and explanatory accounts of human AIRR-4-3-5 consciousness. Just as Dirac trusted in irrelevancies and avoided using mental pictures of the phenomena described by his mathematical symbols, so GEM does not ignore "irrelevancies." Common sense, too, depends on irrelevancies, but it is unable to synthesize the different analytical elements that go into knowledge. Our minds' synthetico-analytic abilities can conceive transcendental numbers or abstract spaces. GEM's open, iso*morph*ic feedback ability relates the world of matter to spirit. Its generalized *opera*tions use the in-betweens of analysis and synthesis to arrive at a 4-3-5 trans*form*ational spiritual topology that consciously addresses the handicaps faced by youth who are programmed away from the spiritual.

Gauss, Bolyai and Lobachevsky moved beyond Kant's transcendentalism which held that space, time and extension are an priori of our minds imposing order on sense experience. With GEM, I let 4-3-5 structures prevail in the cognitive realm. A non-reductive 4-3-5 metaxy respects Dewey's valid insights into education, but not his failure to train students in such core subjects as religion and discipline. To that failure, I oppose an ethical "ego ideal." In psychoanalysis, the ego ideal is the entirety of an individual's identifications with reassuring, loving parents or parental substitutes, regarded as a differentiated component of the mature ego. For GEM, such an ideal is reached by using one's AIRR *opera*tions wisely and by letting one's ego co*opera*te with the ideals of others. This involves the body-mind-spirit trans*form*ative triad which modernists like Freud[22] and Dewey shortcircuit by reducing it to 4-2 brain-mind interactions. In the face of reigning secular ideologies, parents and pastors know that theirs is a thankless task, one that educators are called upon to supplement with 4-3-5 loving care, with a wisdom that spans the ages. Science has its "4-3-4 equivalence" trans*form*ations, but an AIRR-4-3-5 philosophy has trans*form*ative wisdom.

1.5 *Dedekind and Cantor:*
4-3-4 Transfinite Numbers and 4-3-4 Set Theory

Since 4-3-5 in-betweens include reading between the lines of how persons per*form* in their professional, personal and community life, I study (*axi*ological) values in ethics and implications of mathematical *axi*oms (Hilbert) so as to foster respect for "irrelevants" grounded in a 4-3-5 topology. There is the fact of a 4-3-5 physical genome and a claim of a 4-3-5 spiritual genome. I seek to show how GEM, as spirit philosophy, deals with irrationalities. Pythagoreans' discovery of irrational numbers in their exploration of right-angled triangles illustrates my argument for 4-3-5 structures; if an irrational-number hypotenuse illustrates the wonders of mathematics, AIRR ideals should not be reduced to a 4-2 brain-mind structure. AIRR acts, probing into irrationality, function as they should when they fathom potency-*form*-act or body-mind spirit triads. My trans*form*ative feedback approach reflects on mathematicians' AIRR per*form*ance; it asks why 4-2 de*form*ations occur and how these can be "4-3-5 remedied." Values are in crisis today, as they were when Pythagoreans discovered irrationals. GEM focuses on sets of terms and relations in a completely general way; it stresses such in-betweens as a spiritual respect for others because it is geneticists or philosophers *as persons* who make judgments of fact or of value using their respective genetic and philosophic triadic models. My 4-3-5 in-between approach to trans*forma*tions (figures 1-4) uses foundational AIRR loci to compare genetic and philosophical triads. GEM's heuristic structure integrates all the in-betweens of feedback judgments, including those of academics who ratify or reject physicists' theories that use 4-3-4 mathematical models to predict objects' behavior.

The 19th century's critical spirit led to an ever greater arithmetization of mathematics, to ever more complex analysis and to group theory, as these were influenced by the work of Gauss, Cauchy, Monge and Poncelet). In 1831, Gauss published his interpretation of complex numbers (linked real and imaginary numbers)[23] and Cauchy showed that an analytic function of a complex variable can be expanded about a point in a power series in the neighborhood of a singularity.[24] In sum, they *form*ulated a rigorous algebra of complex numbers based on the geometry of the complex plane. In the 1860's, many thinkers thought of an infinity as an unending progression of definite things that we can imagine, such as the sequence of whole numbers 1, 2, 3, *n*. Gauss and Riemann's *real numbers* (rational and irrational numbers whose square is a positive number) as well as complex numbers helped revolutionize mathematics. This led to an acceptable definition of irrational numbers such as *pi* (a ratio of non-repetitive numbers). In 1872, Richard Dedekind proposed his Dedekind cut that *theoretically* defines the system of real numbers. Perceiving that the character of the continuum need not depend on the quantity of points on a line segment but rather on how we can divide the line, he separated all the real numbers in a series into two parts.

Dedekind subdivided the rational numbers into two nonempty sets that satisfy the condition that any number of the first set is less than any member of the second and the condition that the first set has no largest member. The square root of 2 is the unique number that divides the continuum into two collections of numbers such that all the members of one collection are greater than those of the other. Such a cut separates a series of numbers into two parts whereby one collection contains all the numbers whose squares are larger than 2 and the other contains all the numbers whose squares are less than 2. This gave us a new model of continuity that includes rational *and* irrational numbers whose square is a positive number. Dedekind's work, ignored by most mathematicians, was first espoused by Georg Cantor. Wanting to invent an arithmetical foundation for mathematics, Cantor began to explore the idea of a finite set that could refer to numbers, people, objects or whatever. In 1873, he proved that the rational numbers are infinite but countable because they can be placed in a one-to-one correspondence with the integers 1, 2, 3 ... (natural numbers).

When Cantor applied the device of one-to-one correspondence to study the characteristics of sets, [25] he realized that finite and infinite sets differed in the extent of their membership. The set of real numbers is infinite and uncountable. Such a set is *equivalent* (in size) to another if the elements of one can be paired numerically with those of the other. Cantor's transfinite numbers are a cardinal or ordinal number that is not an integer; they allow an infinite set to be placed in a one-to-one correspondence with one of its subsets. The smallest transfinite number, aleph-null symbolizes the cardinality of any set that can be matched with the integers; it can be placed in a one-to-one correspondence with the integers. Aleph-one and aleph-two indicate sets that correspond to the real numbers and functions, respectively. Any finite set can be used as a *stepping stone* to define other finite sets ad infinitum. Cantor's approach allows us to compare extremely large numbers and to discriminate between sets of infinitely large populations but it does not require us to count or even know the population of two sets in order to assess their equivalence. Cantor proved that the set of all algebraic numbers contains as many components as the set of all integers and that transcendental numbers (non-algebraic numbers such as *pi*) which are a subset of the irrationals, are uncountable and are therefore more numerous than infinite integers. Cantor's sets (based on a definite whole) decompose concepts of continuity into more primitive set-theory notions, showing that 4-3-4 analysis can be based on a few basic principles.[26]

Cantor's opponents rejected transfinite numbers on the ground that only integers exist. To be consistent, they argued, he should have treated the sequence of transfinite numbers as he had the sequence of whole numbers, which would have led to other unending series. Cantor replied by positing an "Absolute Infinite" denoted by *omega*, the largest conceivable infinity; *omega* is, by definition, a non-vizualizable infinity, the reality of God. Cantor first appealed to Aristotle's actual and potential infinite to explain his ideas so as to let numbers function as verbs. He later rejected such a potentially infinite as being a borrowed reality since a potentially infinite concept "always points towards a logically prior actually infinite whose existence it depends on." He settled upon a Platonic notion that sees numbers as "nouns," as transfinite, *ordinal* numbers that are not integers but include the cardinal number property of a set (its potency). For him, infinite numbers had an actual existence and were to be treated *not* as an interminable sequence, a verb, but as an actual infinite set, a noun, that is as if "existing" in a world of eternal *forms* as opposed to the transient world of experience. It was like playing God and "realizing" Blake's telling image of "holding infinity in the palm of your hand."[27] If Cantor *imagines* that numbers function as nouns, I argue that Blake's poetic notion of holding the universe in the hand functions as a *verb*, not as a noun, but at several removes. One cannot square the circle using only a finite number of Euclidean *opera*tions. Yet, historically, attempts to construct an ideal square led to important achievements. Kepler used Apollonius' study on conics to derive his laws of planetary motion from Brahe's data. Newton used Kepler's studies on the hyperbola, ellipse and parabola to identify centripetal forces.

Such examples illustrate our pure unrestricted desire to know, initiating us into our finite realization of our impotence in relation to "intimations of immortality" and of irrationality.[28] An awareness of our inadequacies and intelligent aspirations leads to dilemmas best solved with faith-reason's allelic trans*forma*tive in-betweens. Gauss rigorized 4-3-4 analysis; GEM empowers us by sublating dualisms. Contextualizing the complexity of AIRR *opera*tors, I compare mathematicians' *analytic* notions with a poetic approach to the in-betweens of numbers. If Dedekind showed that the character of the continuum does not depend on the quantity of points on a line segment but on how we can divide the line, AIRR *opera*tional loci pivot on our minds' quasi-infinite, poet-like plasticity. Things are not mere numbers. Our minds' AIRR loci appraise numbers' 4-3-4 status, but also help us realize that we can transcend such a status with a 4-3-5 genomic analogy. Love acts as a fifth trans*forma*tive precept. While one can plot real numbers on a real axis (using an Argand diagram with axes representing both real and complex numbers), I map our trans*forma*tive AIRR-4-3-5 loci and the refractory *or* good aspects of our human nature, even if it remains problematic whether our alpha, beta, theta and delta brainwaves will ever help us "locate" brain actions that would identify how love's higher spiritual realm affects ordinary brain patterns.

For GEM, our unrestricted desire to know leads to a notion of being. Categories are determinations with limited denotation; transcendental modes of intending "are comprehensive in connotation, unrestricted in denotation, invariant over cultural change."[29] We objectify the content of that intending to *form* the transcendental concepts of the intelligible, the real, the truly good. Distinct from any concept, there are prior (4-3-5) transcendental notions that constitute the very dynamism of our conscious intending and promote us through AIRR stages. That dynamism is not the product of cultural advance but the condition of its possibility. I seek to locate GEM's fifth ideal and faith-reason's trans*form*ative allelic in-betweens that can move us from mere reason to a 4-3-5-based world ethics. Two excursi shall outline how Lonergan arrived at his trans*form*ative view of insights and the transcendental notions so as to evaluate Cantor's 4-3-4 transfinite nouns in an AIRR-4-3-5 light.

1.6 *Excursus: GEM's Inner Word: Creative Insight or "4-3-5 Verbs"*

GEM began with Lonergan's study of *inner word* in his early *Verbum* articles in which he strove to integrate Augustine's phenomenology of the subject with Aristotle's psychology of the soul. Aquinas had retrieved Aristotle's theory of intellect that involves the procession of an inner word, but sublated his theory on the process of abstraction. GEM revises Aristotle and Aquinas with a system equal in comprehensiveness but careful to con*form* to fact. Lonergan shows how our inner words arrive at the two *forms* of insight, namely insights that lead to 1) *form*ulating concepts and theories and 2) reflective processes that result in correct judgments. The intellect returns to a sensible data that initially had provided the material for an intelligible synthesis that constitutes the object it contemplates. Understanding grasps how the data of consciousness and of sense are related. It adds to the manifold of presentations a correlation, a meaning, that unifies the data into an intelligible unity. This involves objective abstraction (the illumination of a phantasm that constitutes an imagined object as something to be understood) which is then understood through apprehensive abstraction or insight into phantasm. "Between the activities of sense and, on the other hand, the concepts, judgments, and inferences that constitute thought, there stands the intellect itself."(*Verbum*, 185). Intellectual habits of understanding are not judgment; they lead to it. Intelligibility is passive and potential; it is not understanding as such; it is a *potential* object of the intellect. To understand the law of inverse squares, for example, one is dealing with a specific natural law but not with the intelligibility (*form*) of the very idea of intelligible law. This is because the intelligibility of natural process is imposed from without: natures act intelligibly, *not* because they are intelligent, but because they are concretions of divine ideas, of a divine plan. The intelligibility of the procession of an inner word, however, is not passive nor potential; it is active and actual; it is intelligible for it is the activity of intelligence in act. The light of our souls enters within the range of introspective observation, when, for example, one grasps first principles. Scientific conclusions are accepted because they are implied by first principles; but assent to first principles "has to have its motive too, for assent is rational; and that motive is the light that naturally is within us."[30] The inner word (*verbum*) names the light of our souls grasping intelligibility (*form*) in potencies to which intelligibility then assents. Lonergan alludes to the efficacy of God's *prima lux*, a hint of AIRR-4-3-5 graced verbs that allow divine and human teachers to lovingly co*operate*.

If Cantor went beyond Galileo in proving that one infinite number can be greater than another, the inner word of insight (*verbum*) lets our minds grasp intelligibility (*form*s) in *potencies* and lets our reason be in tune with alleles of faith. We can never visualize God, but the theologies we use to speak of God are "4-3-5 verbs" grasping, assenting to intelligibility. Cantor's "nouns" are, in fact, rooted in our 4-3-5 *opera*tional verbs able to unite humans by being open, or to *divide* them, when closed. Unlike Cantor, GEM sublates Aristotle's potency-*form*-act triad by distinguishing theory's necessary relations from the contingent views of common sense. "In Aristotle, there are not two sets of objects but two approaches to one set. Theory is concerned with what is prior in itself but posterior for us, but everyday human knowledge is concerned with what is prior for us though posterior in itself.³¹ Our AIRR *opera*tions are a trans*form*ative ballast that gives rise to all philosophic, mathematical or poetic insights.

This may be illustrated with the examples of Blake and Henri Poincare, both renowned for their minds' eidetic ability. Blake's eidetic ability enabled him to draw imaginary persons at will or to visualize one who holds infinity in one's hand. Poincare recounted his flash of insight that enabled him to solve Fuchsan functions when thinking of something else. These men's eidetic feats illustrate the paradoxical role of images in mathematics and in teaching. A great merit of Cantor's notions of set and equivalence is that they enable us to compare and distinguish various types of infinities. Focusing on infinity as a verb can help us correct absolute idealisms with viable, in-between allelic ideals.

Kronecker's realism and Cantor's idealism, being complementary, can be contextualized with the in-betweens of a self-interest serving the common good. Using AIRR 4-3-5 verbs as a set of in-betweens or as a "cut" that implements the trans*form*ational plasticity of our minds but avoids 4-2 reductionisms, I dialectically transpose realist-idealist *différances* into complementarities facilitating co*opera*tion.

1.7 *Further Excursus: GEM and the History of Western Philosophy*

GEM helps us trace the history of philosophy that led to Descartes' 4-2 dualism. After Descartes, philosophy went into opposed rationalist and empiricist modes that were only partly reconciled by Kant. Humean-Kantian views on causation have roots in Scotus' rejection of Aristotle's notion that intellect apprehends the intelligible in the sensible and grasps the universal in the particular. Opposing Aquinas' notion of enriching abstraction, Scotus developed a theory of intuitive cognition that shortcircuits our potency-*form*-act (experience, understanding, judgment) triadic process of abstraction. We should not separate (a la Kant) the givens of experience and of data from the *form*s allowing access to the 4-3-5 allelic in-betweens of spirituality. Attempting to overcome Humean skepticism rooted in Locke's treatment of ideas, Kant's synthetic a priori that transcends experience set philosophy on a new course. Unlike his categorical imperative, AIRR imperatives integrate pure and practical reason's judgments. Refusing to focus on concepts, GEM distances itself from Kant. Yet, the later Kant's study of judgment places him closer to GEM.[32]

Analytic philosophers use their own AIRR *opera*tions in overlooking the process on which their judgments are based. Analytic philosophy, which began with Frege and Russell, has outgrown logical positivism.[33] In fact, we know more than what language mediates to us. Using our data of consciousness and guided by a transcendent exigence for an unconditioned, we are led to the realm in which God is known and loved; our AIRR sources of meaning surmount postmodernist misunderstandings of enriching insights which are a basis for ever new discoveries such as those that enabled creative men like Cantor and Cezanne to be original in their own field. For Cezanne, everything in nature "adheres"[34] to the cone cylinder or cube, an insight that influenced Cubists' efforts to realize infinite, *form*al possibilities. What are the in-betweens of judgments of fact and of self-transcendent judgments of value that can 4-3-5 empower philosophy, artists and science?

Lonergan's *Insight* consists of two parts; part I, "Insight as Activity," studies the process of judging; it ends with a crucial distinction between analytic propositions and analytic principles that differ in how they link and fulfill conditions. In analytic propositions, the link lies in rules of meaning that generate *propositions* out of partial terms of meaning; the fulfillment is supplied by the meanings or definitions of the terms. Such propositions become analytic principles when their terms are existential. Terms are existential when they occur in definitive factual judgments. In judgments of fact, we ascertain whether one correctly interprets the data of consciousness and of sense.

Judgments of value[35] enable us to live up to our consciences' quest for self-transcendence. Part Two of *Insight*, "Insight as Knowledge," opens with "It is time to turn from theory to practice." It asks whether correct judgments *do* occur. The answer is the *act* of making one in a judgment of self-affirmation: the self affirms itself in a judgment that says *in fact* I do exist. On this judgment, GEM stands or falls. Each must make that judgment *one's self*; it results from the per*form*ance of AIRR acts of sensing, thinking, grasping the unconditioned; it involves the elements of any other judgment. The relevant conditioned is the statement "I am a knower;" the link is a *proposition* such as "I am a knower, if I am a concrete, intelligible unity-identity-whole" who understands, judges. The problematical element of fulfilling the conditions of consciousness is solved when a person in fact affirms his/her own self, thus *fulfilling* the conditions for true judgments. I presuppose consciousness as the data of inquiry, but by a reverse shift from the perceived and understood to the merely perceived, I verify that an experiential *is given*, not merely postulated. Affirming my concrete, recurring AIRR structure means that I explanatorily unite the data of my experience, understanding, judging in patterns of intelligible relations. Positing a synthesis at the end of reflective activity enables a mind to return from a prior synthesis achieved through insight into images (phantasms); judgments' virtually unconditioned posit or reject synthesis; they are not a synthesis. GEM moves beyond 4-2 structured views of reality that limit cognition to brain-mind activities shorn of spirit. It authentically links traditions with modernity with the in-betweens of judgments of fact and of empowering judgments of value. If at each turn of the wheel of insight, proposal, action and new situation, group bias tends to exclude some fruitful ideas and to mutilate others, the data of sense questioned in reflection enable one to move from *thinking* an object to *affirming* it and knowing it as being. In their judgments of fact and of value. GEM artists and mystics realize their dependence on all else. All of creation is interrelated. Mathematicians cannot explain such interrelatedness. If Einstein helped us understand our universe, attempts at a Grand Unified Theory[36] have so far failed. Einstein did live out AIRR ideals that imply loving judgments. Latent AIRR-4-3-5 foundations challenge us to understand how we can transcend 4-3-4 spacetime.

These two excursi help us evaluate Cantor's focus on infinity as a noun in an "AIRR-4-3-5 light." GEM's dynamic verbs recover what is AIRR common to all of us, even our irrationalities.

2a *Mathematics, Poetry and a Trans*form*ative AIRR Matrix Generating Verbs' In-betweens*

If, as A. Church observed, Frege erred in confusing the use of names with the things themselves (thereby misinterpreting Leibniz' notion of identity)[37] GEM goes beyond 4-3-4 *axio*matizations of logic by adverting to and applying 4-3-5 ethical verbs as an "irrelevant" *poetry*.

While Heidegger proposes "ontological difference" to counter the effects of technology, GEM derives its basic AIRR intentional acts that it then uses to 4-3-5 trans*form* metaphysics and theology. If 4-3-5 RNA is the mediating matrix for DNA and for evolution as catalyst of critical chemical reactions, mathematicians' creative insights have developed analogical 4-3-4 matrices and *opera*tors. I explore such matrices and *opera*tors to help us grasp how GEM's insights into a potency-*form*-act triadic matrix (as key to knowing) can help us live a 4-3-5 love ethics. Just as GEM speaks of conjugates rather than of an Aristotelian, Lockean or Spinozan substance, so I argue that poetry and art (as creative verbs, not nouns) illustrate and underlie notions of "GEM artist," that is, loving persons able to authentically live out 4-3-5 ideal loci. Cantor and Einstein's lives exemplify these trans*form*ative loci. If in Cantor's scheme, the Absolute Infinite, God, is the unattainable "Noun-limit," source of transfinite numbers, in GEM, God is the Absolute enabling us to implement "4-3-5 love verbs."[38] The difference is that AIRR verbs function as dynamic in-between trans*form*ative loci enabling creative geniuses or ordinary mortals to act, per*form* in self-transcendent AIRR ways despite the rampant irrationalities besetting us. If a trans*form*ation matrix trans*form*s one vector from one reference frame to another (changing the perspective), or if transfinite numbers allow for many intermediate levels between the finite and Absolute Infinite, a 4-3-5 ethical trans*form*ative matrix transposes in-betweens affecting East-West orientations.

Curvilinear measurings led to disagreements as to the existence of Platonic numbers and sets. Are their *loci* ideal or real? Seeing real numbers as inhabiting a line and complex numbers, a plane, the classical approach could not give a geometrical picture of the multitude of possible functions from which to choose a given function. Seeking to obtain such a picture (1906) Maurice Frechet founded the theory of abstract spaces. Generalizing the traditional definition of space as a locus for the comparison of figures, his fully metrizable space is a topology of infinite loci (one in which space is defined as a set of points so that the space is a metric space of open sets). By doing so, he changed the calculus of variations into one that resembles ordinary calculus for it involves a maximum or a minimum, but differs from it in that the unknown is not a number but a function.

He asked how $y = f(x)$ might express the securing of a chain's ends so that its center of gravity be as low as possible; he observed that distance plays a decisive role. Analysis is concerned with limits. For both real and complex numbers, a sequence of numbers zn is tending to a limit L if the distance of zn from L is tending to zero. Frechet sought to adequately define the distance between any two mathematical objects that would yield theorems about these objects analogous to the theorems about complex or real numbers. After studying the properties of distance measured by non-negative real numbers and using an integral representation theorem for functionals on the space of quadratic Lebesgue integrable functions, he was able to define distance between two matrices, two trans*form*ations, two *opera*tions, two functions that involve differentiation and integration. One specifies a point's position by the vector coming from the origin to it; we can speak of a point u which stands for a vector (the point at the end of the vector u, originating at the origin). In a non-Euclidean vector space, a parallelogram's diagonals bisect each other. In ordinary physical space, the numbers 2 and 3 have special significance but, in the patterns of 2 or 3 dimensional vector spaces, we are not constrained to the particular numbers 2 and 3. We are free to define a vector in space of *n* dimensions specified by numbers. To multiply such a vector by k, we multiply each of the numbers specifying it by k. We add two such vectors by adding the corresponding numbers, specified in applicable brackets. Such procedures can be extended to functions treated as vector spaces in that the latter are similar to *n*-dimensional vector spaces.

Using a geometry that expresses the dot product u • v, where u • v = 0, Frechet specified the condition for u being perpendicular to v. The Pythagorean hypotenuse in right angles allowed him to establish Euclidean spaces[39] of infinite dimensions analogous to function spaces. By defining a dot product for function spaces, he found a meaning for one function orthogonal (perpendicular) to one another. This follows the same pattern as before, but with integrals instead of sums.

A Frechet space generalizes Euclidean spaces so that closeness or limits are described in terms of relationships rather than of distance. Such a space, helping us "map" infinity, are *results* of ideal AIRR verbs' implicit loci, loci that also permit us to "parse" irrational numbers or to posit transfinite numbers. By mediating the ambiguous allelic in-betweens of feelings and reason, of being and a void, GEM helps us "4-3-5 discern" the rational-irrational and benevolent-malevolent sides of our human nature. Such discerning includes spiritual conjugates that do not eliminate *evil resistance* to God, but may help us become instruments of peace. GEM's pure, experiential and spiritual conjugates reunite pure and practical reason. They help us promote human co*opera*tion by repairing the ambiguous in-between 4-2 phase *boundaries* that shortcircuit or *exclude* our access to God or *falsify* such an access; a 4-3-5 spiritual topology (an *open set* for trans*form*ative notions such as being-emptiness) parallels Frechet's rethinking the study of the *axio*ms underlying set theory.[40] From Zeno to Russell, thinkers have proposed paradoxical arguments in which it appears that an obvious untruth has been proved. If Russell or Zermelo overlooked basic 4-3-4 paradoxes in their set theory assumptions, GEM, a generalized method, studies the brilliance *and* limitations of *homo viator* within a time-eternity context. It maps mathematical notions such as asymptote, chaos, limit and convergence with the AIRR *opera*tions giving rise to such notions. If a Hermitian transposes a complex conjugate, I map AIRR acts that create mathematical and other matrices' complex conjugates.

In quantum mechanics, the Hermitian conjugate is the "adjoint of the matrix" (spin and position are self-adjoint *opera*tors on a Hilbert space, scalar product space complete with respect to the norm defined by the inner product). If Frechet's abstract space is a completely metrizable topology of infinite loci, I seek to "locate" a 4-3-5 foundational space for mental-spiritual-ethical trans*for*mations. As a zygote is a cell *form*ed of two gametes (or a conjugated organism from such a cell), or as Frechet generalizes the definition of space as a locus for comparing figures, so GEM conjugates map humans' AIRR-4-3-5 trans*form*ative matrices for self-transcendent growth. Eilenberg and Mac Lane's purely abstract definition of category leads to studying a universe of sets and functions without saying what is in any set. Only the patterns of functions occurring between sets matter. If such mathematical categories concern only structures and trans*forma*tions, AIRR conjugates integrate trans*form*ative genetic, mathematical and spirit loci; such an integration leads to a higher-dimensional AIRR matrix that explores and reconciles a 4-3-5 East-West ethics on the analogy of Lawvere's postulated higher dimensional categories and algebraic structures.[41] Part Two will explicitate a trans*form*ative AIRR matrix generating "4-3-5 in-betweens" that take seriously the ethics of Jesus' Kingdom ideals and of Buddha's Noble Truths.

2b *Exercising 4-3-5 Liberty within an AIRR Matrix of Personal Relations*

For GEM, we exercise liberty within "a matrix of personal relations"[42] that I map as a love metaxy. If extensive genomic variations occur over the span of a single generation, and if Frechet changed the calculus of variations into one resembling ordinary calculus, I contextualize mathematical judgments. I map a 4-3-5 spiritual topology as invariant foundation for a free, trans*form*ative ethic that transposes Spinozist ideals wedged in a monist Substance, an ethic that credibly offers an alternative to Hume's naturalist approach based on sentiments and 4-2 reason.

If the 4-3-5 RNA template is an in-between used by amino acids during protein synthesis to trans*form* DNA, AIRR verbs have a set of 4-3-5 in-betweens in*form*ing our minds' plastic ability to link the mundane and spiritual aspects of our lives. 4-2 reductionists sabotage our freedom, but mathematicians reach for the infinite. Scientists' insights can lead to breakthroughs, as when de Broglie's interest in music led him to introduce "pilot waves" of such a nature that 1, 2, 3, etc. of them would fit exactly into the 1st, 2nd, 3rd of Bohr's quantum orbits. Influenced by the wave model in*form*ing Euler's studies into the vibration of musical strings and by Hamilton-Jacobi theory that pointed to a duality in material particles, his approach points to some 4-3-4 analogies between waves and complex numbers. For him, this represented a geometrical optics; it led him to associate wavelength with mass and so to obtain quantum numbers rarely found in mechanics but occurring frequently in wave phenomena and particles dealing with wave motion. Our minds have breakthrough insights. I argue that the human spirit, too, has spiritual insights that can lead to collaborative breakthroughs in societal structures if we integrate Buddhist-Christian 4-3-5 ideals. Gamow and Schrödinger's insights into the codes of our physical genome inspired Watson and Crick to study DNA.

My analogy of our two genomes calls attention to variations within 4-3-5 invariance in both genomes. Thinkers make and revise judgments of fact and of value to attain their life goals. GEM differentiates yet interlinks such judgments. Its 4-3-5 structure can lead to a new appreciation of how spirituality can empower philosophers or scientists. Comparing Pythagorean ideas (e. g. its sacred decad of $1 + 2 + 3 + 4 = 10$ implying a perfect triangle) with the functioning of physical and spiritual alleles can help us better grasp the trans*form*ations occurring in our lives. Pythagoreans' mysticism led to their being irrationally persecuted. Humans fall victim to cancer or to terrorism. As with the zeta trans*form*ative function[43] in mathematics or uracil's trans*form*ative function in genetics, so GEM uses AIRR ideals to trans*form* us. Both DNA and in*form*ation theory encode in*form*ation; trans*form*ative AIRR loci "4-3-5 mediate in*form*ation." If in in*form*ation theory, "in*form*ation" has nothing to do with inherent meaning in a message, but only refers to a degree of order or non-randomness that can be mathematically ordered, GEM maps meaning and values and how these can be trans*form*ed in ways that respect traditions and the people who originated a body of meaning or values. If Turing obtained a complete-ness result for the class of true statements of the *form* that all natural numbers have a given, effectively decidable property, and if he showed that any ordinal logic that strictly increases with increasing ordinal representation cannot have the property of invariance, GEM grounds the invariance of our AIRR *opera*tions which I transpose with its feedback ability to interrelate 4-3-4 disciplines.

In physics and mathematics, the concept of potential is very extensive and well-developed. It refers to the work done against a conservative field or its negative (depending on conventions) in bringing a unit of the proper sort from infinity to the point in question, or the value at the given point of a function whose directional derivative is equal in magnitude to the component of the field intensity in that direction at the given point. For GEM, the mind is a universal potency which it links to faith-feelings and being-relatedness alleles. I approach a "poetry" of numbers with a study of their in-betweens or what is lacking in them. One can be inspired by images of infinity or write poetry about holding infinity in one's hand. Such a "holding" is a verb with a possibly mystic dimension. Poetry and mysticism lead us beyond tautological analyses to reach feeling and reason's in-between alleles. *Opera*tor theory analyzes trans-*form*ations between vector spaces of infinite dimensions; my 4-3-5 poetic approach to numbers and life complements 4-3-4 trans*form*ations. If von Neumann foresaw that the geometry of vectors in infinite-dimensional space has the same mathematical characteristics as the structure of the states of a quantum-mechanical system, I see GEM as enabling us to relate such structures to an infinitely dimensional Buddhist-Christian love.

God is a non-pantheist Totally Other; in grace, God shares Self with creation. GEM's philosophy of interrelated beings amends Spinoza's monism and Nietzsche's reevaluation of values. It reinterprets Husserl's acts with 4-3-5 grace-reason alleles interacting in feedback ways. Yet, it leaves philosophy free to accept only reason's alleles in facing the realities of an atheist secularism. Despite today's hybrids of Frego-Husserlianism or Wittgensteino-Heideggerianism, I seek to show how GEM's AIRR-4-3-5 *opera*tional loci enable us to transcend concepts and words and to live ethically. As amino acid triplets and mathematics' three dimensional analyses lead to infinite combinations,[44] so GEM potency-*form*-act triads (central and conjugate *form*s) correct 4-2 Cartesian ontologies. Aristotle's "first philosophy" was an ontology (later called metaphysics). GEM parallels Husserl's attempt to use a pre-abstractive epoche to confront philosophy's crises. In philosophy, ontology is a systematic account of existence, but in AI circles it is often confused with epistemology.

GEM first specifies the metaphysical elements as "the yet unspecified U, V, W, and X, Y, Z that are to be specified if proportionate being is to be explained."[45] It develops an integral heuristic structure for specifying U, V, W, and X, Y, Z. It explains how knowing and reality are interrelated by heuristically defining central and conjugate potency-*form*-act triads in terms of AIRR acts. Only then does it address a Cartesian ontology. What counts are differences in how we know rather than differences in the to-be-knowns. Insight is a knowledge matrix that can 4-3-5 ethically mediate various kinds of AIRR differences in feedback ways. This includes a cycle of daily life and a greater cycle of 4-3-5 grace or of a self-transcending secular ethics. The many self-transcendent in-betweens mediating such cycles are this book's main East-West 4-3-5 focus.

3) Einstein's 4-3-4 Tensor Field Equations and his 4-3-5 Ethics

So as to broach ethical ideals, Part One has delved into philosophy, mathematical and genetic trans*form*ations. This section furthers a AIRR 4-3-5 shorthand that remaps GEM's ideal *opera*tions. It transposes tensors' trans*form*ative forte to one that remaps GEM's unique feedback ability to empower scientists and philosophers with a virtuous eye of love spindle, a "we-thinking" ability.

3a *Einstein's Theories of Special Relativity (STR) and of General Relativity (GTR)*

In his theories of relativity, Einstein used tensors invented to enable scientists to *form*alize the manipulation of geometric entities arising in the study of mathematical manifolds. I seek to ground 4-3-5 foundational loci, partly by relating Einstein's locus of points equation (squaring spacetime dimensions in the frames of reference $x + y + z = ct$ and $X + Y + Z = cT$) with how he used 4-3-5 loci in his pacifist life. His trans*form*ative use of tensors can help us adjudicate our professional, personal and ethical conflicts. I focus on spiritual loci opposing the irrational surds of evil or injustice with virtuous in-betweens. Such loci are not systems of points but AIRR sets of potential 4-3-5 self-transcendence. GEM explores the allelic in-between loci of self-centeredness and self-transcendence; it relates being to the holistic aspects of Eastern philosophies. Like the latter, it does not arbitrarily divide what is essentially one. It moves beyond rhetoric or a 4-3-4 mathematics to spiritual realities, to the dreams of poetic creativity. It avoids pantheist dangers by showing that our transcendental *opera*tions open us to a transcendent God, from whom we are distinct, yet to whom we are related through our reason-faith alleles.

A tensor is a single point or collection of isolated points of spacetime, or a continuum of points. In the latter case, a tensor's elements are functions of position and the tensor makes up a tensor field (where the tensor is defined at every point within a region of spacetime rather than a just a point). As tensors enable us to isolate intrinsic geometrico-physical properties from those depending on coordinates, so AIRR-4-3-5 loci isolate intrinsic human trans*form*ations from mere verbalisms. Using the language of Cartesian analytic geometry and its coordinate definition of dimension, Riemann had explored the implications of a mathematical fourth dimension and had discovered non-Euclidian geometries that describe worlds of every whole-numbered dimension from zero to infinity, some of which refer to worlds that are not spatial in the ordinary sense. For him, the term "manifold" referred to purely conceptual spaces.

"Manifold" no longer need refer only to sensible space nor to a realm filled with galaxies, stars and planets. In this sense, a manifold can refer to any multidimensional realm, be it the economy or human beings, to the dimensions of a lived, 4-3-5 ethics. Riemann's imaginative leap toward abstraction liberated geometry from Euclid even more than Descartes had liberated it from its dependence on the physical notions of length, width and depth. If we imagine for a "moment that the stock market depends on but one factor, the hemlines of women's skirts, say, then we would represent it mathematically by a 1-D manifold, a line."[46] This means that the status of the stock market at any time or the height of the hemlines could be described by a single number and illustrated as a point somewhere along the 1-D manifold. Thought of in this way, humans are "manifolds" of nearly countless dimensions. If philosophers and social scientists are have the unenviable task of explaining so many dimensions, GEM uses the patterns of experience to AIRR-interrelate human dimensions' dynamic manifolds. Its metaphysics integrates East-West philosophies through AIRR-4-3-5 faith-reason alleles and their mutually trans*form*ative properties.

The fact that GEM (like Riemann and Einstein) appeals to dynamic manifolds, augurs well for a spiritual topology that addresses the complexity of human beings by invoking an invariance within their trans*form*ational AIRR *opera*tions. There is permanence within processes of continuous change, a fact much discussed since the Eleatics, Heraclitus and the Buddha. I focus on our AIRR loci as dynamic *opera*tional verbs, trans*form*ed by love just as DNA is trans*form*ed by uracil.

Awkward situations cut us down to size; they embarrass us. Saintly, wise diplomats defuse embarrassments. Focusing on such ambiguities as Einstein's compromise in supporting the making of an atom bomb before the Nazis could do so, I seek to bridge the asymptotic character of being-nothingness or 4-3-5 faith-belief imponderables by applying an ethics such as motivated Einstein who realized that ideals can be trans*form*ed *or* de*form*ed. As he revolutionized our understanding of spacetime, so his ethics was based on principled ideals repressed by militant ideologues. GEM re*form*s 4-2 de*form*ations; it links the poetry of verbs with rigorous analytical-synthetic *form*s. If Einstein reconciled irrational numbers with complex numbers, or if he generalized the notion of tensors as objective entities with trans*form*ative properties, I generalize AIRR ideals. AIRR ideals motivated the professional lifework of Dedekind, Cantor and Einstein as well as the courage they showed in the face of opposition. If a point with the same eigenvalues in a tensor field[47] behaves like a singular point in a vector field where the magnitude vanishes, or if Riemann's tensors helped Einstein redescribe reality in terms of a geometry using four by four tensors, our AIRR structure relates the in-between loci that in*form* our daily lives to the way mathematicians do their work.

As critical points in vector fields are important, or as a point with the same eigenvalues in a tensor field behaves as a singular point in a vector field, so I seek to explain how GEM 4-3-5 trans*form*atively links AIRR's ethical principles our lives with the sciences we invent. Ernst Mach realized that Newton's inertia law required a means to link the inertial behavior of each body with all matter (stars) of our universe. Mach's principle states that inertia results from a relationship of an object with all the rest of the matter in the universe. Inertia is a function of the interaction between one body and other bodies in the universe even at enormous distances. Einstein used Mach's principle; he abandoned it when he realized that inertia is implicit in the geodesic equation of motion and need not depend on the existence of matter elsewhere in the universe. Einstein's two theories of relativity use tensors differently. His Special Theory of Relativity (STR) speaks only of *relative* velocities, not absolute velocities. It only asks if a particle is at rest relative to another one, velocities being described as vectors in 4-D spacetime. Switching to a different coordinate system can change the way these vectors point but not whether two of them point the same way. In 1907, Einstein realized that if one were to fall freely in an elevator or gravitational field, one would be unable to feel one's own weight. He began to use a principle of equivalence to parlay STR into General Theory of Relativity (GTR). STR is partly a hyperbolic Pythagorean theorem, $c = a + b - ab$. For any local (sufficiently small spacetime) region, it *form*ulates equations governing physical laws such that the effect of gravitation can be neglected, since gravitational acceleration cannot be distinguished from acceleration caused by mechanical forces.

STR speaks of finite Galilean regions, where, with respect to a suitably chosen space of reference, material particles move in unaccelerated ways; after 1907, Einstein insisted that the principle of equivalence demands that in dealing with *Galilean regions*, we may just as well use non-inertial systems, that is, coordinate "systems that relatively to inertial systems, are not free from acceleration and rotation."[48] In STR, physical experiments cannot distinguish one state of uni*form* velocity from another, but since it is valid for local situations, one deduces that light travelling across a freely falling elevator follows a curved path in a gravitational field and that light travelling upwards in such an elevator is redshifted in that field. In GTR, we only talk about *relative* velocities *if* two particles are at the same place at the same instant in spacetime; we cannot speak of clocks as being at rest relative to each other or of unaccelerated trans*forma*tions, since we can only unambiguously define the relative velocity of two clocks if they are at the same location. The concept of an inertial frame of reference (non-accelerating system of constant velocity where inertia laws hold) so important, in STR, is *banned* from GTR since GTR takes seriously the notion that a vector is a little arrow sitting at a particular point in spacetime. To compare vectors at different points of spacetime, we must carry one over to the other. To do so along a path, without turning or stretching it, is called 'parallel transport'. The definition of *curved spacetime* depends on parallel transport from one point to another (on the path taken). It is ambiguous to ask whether two particles have the same velocity vector unless they are at the same spacetime point.[49] Tensor analysis studies relations or laws remaining valid regardless of the system of coordinates specifying the quantities. Such relations are "covariant."[50] In using tensors that permit the use of arbitrarily moving systems of coordinates despite the difficulty of geometrically expressing the laws of configuration of ideal bodies, Einstein used the work of Riemann, Ricci and Levi-Citta who had extended Gauss' views to continua of infinite dimensions.

Important points of contact between Gauss' theory of surfaces and GTR, lie in the metrical properties used in both theories. Gauss' plane geometry was based upon the concept of the distance *ds* between two infinitely near points. Einstein extends this view to continuously curved surfaces. "An infinitesimally small portion of the surface may be regarded as plane, to within relatively infinitesimal quantities."[51] GTR's curvature of spacetime is described by the Riemann curvature tensor of order four with 4 x 4 x 4 x 4 = 256 components. Permutations occur in Riemann tensors, in genetics and in AIRR ideals. One may compare the genetic code's 4-3-5 structure with spacetime's 4-3-4 structured permutations and with AIRR *opera*tions. As in amino acids, so, too, in spacetime, there are 20 mathematically independent components. If the genetic code uses 20 amino acid triplets involving permutations of 4 x 4 x 4 = 64, Einstein helps us grasp that we use our AIRR ideals to understand 4-3-4 spacetime.[52]

Riemann tensors involve 256 permutations, but GEM's scientific and ethical ideals depend on judgments of fact or value. Faced with evil and deception, I map an in-between demarcation line between physics and ethical or unethical loci. As figures 2 illustrates the interrelatedness triads at work in our two genomes and suggests an AIRR spindle of trans*form*ative feedback *opera*tions that enable GEM artists to be authentic, so I contextualize demarcations used in "synthesizing" artistic, mathematical or ethical ideal loci. GEM grounds concepts with acts of direct and reflective understanding; it can help us "live out" trans*form*ing ethical ideals. Gamow realized the need for a fifth nucleotide serving as template for nucleic acids to transmit life. Einstein moved beyond his STR inertial frames. I use GEM's 4-3-5 trans*form*ative ideals to transpose a mere geophilosophy into a spirit philosophy.

3b *Transposing 4-3-4 Mathematical Loci with "Ethico-Spiritual" 4-3-5 Loci*

Penrose and Hawking developed mathematical techniques for analyzing the way points in spacetime are related to one another. Highlighting space's significance, they "did away with the confusion of the messy interactions bet-ween material particles"[53] If, like Einstein, they pioneered new techniques, GEM explores specialized and generalized geometries' mathematical expres-sions. Mathematical expressions' meaning lies in their *form*. Previous notions of measurement failed to realize that relativity enters into the very notion of a determinate measurement. Invariant theory studies quantities associated with polynomial equations that are left invariant under variables' trans*form*ations. But as long as we remain on a level of invariant expressions, we ignore concrete extensions and durations since each person views them in their own way. Because mathematical expressions of the principles and laws of a geo-metry are invariant under that geometry's allowed trans*form*ations, Lonergan clarifies Riemannian manifolds by differentiating between Euclidean, projective, topological, affine geometries. He outlines a generalized geometry and examines the equations for trans*form*ing from the frame K, to a frame K'.

The coordinate systems, K and K', have the same meaning and stand for the same propositions if they have the same symbolic *form*. To avoid ambiguities, trans*form*ations from one frame of reference to another must belong to higher-order statements: "the relations between different universes of discourse regard, not the things specified in those universes, but the specifications employed to denote the things."[54]

If invariance (preserved in QED) was later applied to the strong reaction, I study 4-3-5 ethico-spiritual trans*form*ations that can effect variable changes by way of our AIRR iso*morph*ic knowing. Our AIRR oper*a*tions are an invariant manifold within change. As Lonergan uses group theory's invariant facets to characterize GEM, so I study invariant structures in our genetic and spiritual genomes for their 4-3-5 trans*form*ative abilities. If in quantum field theory, a scalar field is associated with spin 0 particles (such as mesons), or if gauge trans*form*ations[55] consist of alterations in the values of those potentials that do not result in a change of electric and magnetic fields, our invariant GEM cognitional structure is "AIRR source" of all trans*form*ations we effect.

GEM links abstract thought to its AIRR roots. As Galois F* field theory helps us grasp that irreducible (non-factorable) polynomials have roots adjoined to the rational numbers but *form* an algebraic number field (a field F* can be extended if it contains a field F), with GEM, I transpose logical oper*a*tions with 4-3-5 loci. If Minkowski introduced a four dimensional manifold so as to systematize timespace, or as the relations between different universes of discourse regard not things specified in such universes, but the specifications employed to denote the things, I shall give two examples of how AIRR ideals move from abstract to concrete realms in transposing 4-3-4 analyses to AIRR-4-3-5 structured ethico-foundational loci. A first example is Patrick Heelan's interpretation of quantum mechanics in the light of GEM; the second, on "GEM 4-3-5 artists," complements the first. Both examples rely on invariant AIRR oper*a*tions to transcend expressions.

Heelan develops the meta-context language of quantum mechanics that uses a language of exact position and exact momentum as their necessary and sufficient conditions. Precise position language requires that a quantum system be in contact with a position-measuring environment such as an instrument plus suitable boundary conditions. Precise momentum language, measuring another pertinent context, requires that the quantum system be in contact with a momentum-measuring environment. These two languages are subsets of a broader, more inclusive quantum mechanical language in which the spacetime description of a quantum system can be *form*ulated, even if the environment excludes possibilities of a precise position or momentum measurements.

A higher-viewpoint language that integrates precise languages constitutes (with suitably defined complements) "a non-uniquely complemented lattice of languages."[56] Lower and upper bounds affecting non-distributive lattices differ from Boolean lattices in which the oper*a*tions of sum and product are distributive. Heelan develops framework transpositions that allow a quantum system to be in contact with a momentum-measuring environment. He illustrates non-Boolean structural relationships by instancing biological populations of the same species where genotype distributions play a role analogous to descriptive languages. If two stable populations, A and B of the same species, exist in different environments isolated from one another by a broad impassable river or such, then each population has the same set of genotype distributed according to different statistical curves. The isolated species clarifies what is a set of distributive Boolean union of the two populations; but it has a minimal scientific interest since it refers to geographically separated populations.

What *is* of interest is when two such populations are connected by a bridge enabling them to produce hybrid-producing genes. In this case, the distribution of the two statistical curves is non-Boolean. It constitutes a least upper bound in a non-distributive lattice involving relevant statistical curves as elements of the partial ordering. Another instance of non-Boolean lattices is found in how Aquinas synthesized Platonic-Augustinian and Aristotelian traditions by creating a philosophic language that respects the earlier traditions but integrates them in an original way.

AIRR-love and AIRR-4-3-5 loci are equivalent implicit definitions that, using Heelan's non-distributive lattice, can, for example, transpose static models of distributive justice focused on material goods to dynamic one[57] that address the processes of decision-making. Part Two continues the transposition by way of an AIRR-4-3-5 feedback spindle or virtue matrix of "AIRR-void ideals," thus illustrating that an AIRR shorthand approach to GEM can confront both today's hyperreality and its tendency to distort the icons of spirituality with banal ones that neglect deeper ethical realities.

Heelan integrates incommensurate theoretical languages with non-distributive lattices that relate languages rather than sentences. In his context logic, each language has its unique context, namely, the set of necessary and sufficient conditions for its valid use; a logic of languages is also a meta-context logic. This can be illustrated in how QED insights into atoms have helped resolve a Bohr-Einstein controversy. Einstein could not reconcile gravity with quantum theory since the laws of geometry fail at very short ranges. What counts is an understanding of the movement from the polarity between wave and particle (of pre-quantum mechanics days) to a *loss* of polarity in quantum mechanics.

The correct locus of quantum mechanics' non-classical logic lies, contrary to the received view, not in a quantum mechanical object language (probably subject to classical logic), but in the "meta-context language of quantum mechanics."[58] Quark and gauge theories vie in describing global changes that cannot be observed since quantum waves have no mass and are without time or space. Gell-Mann calls his quark-octet model that groups subatomic particles an "eightfold Buddhist Path." If his path is now the orthodox quark model for explaining the basic units of matter, in Part Two, I develop GEM's "eightfold path," an ideal eightfold ability to verify or *revise* all theories. Scientific and philosophical developments in language occur in meta-language AIRR loci that furnish in-betweens for interrelating linguistic terms within or among traditions in a meta-linguistic, "hypergeometric" language of clear thinking and/or 4-3-5 virtuous conduct.

3c *Cantor and Einstein as GEM Artists or 4-3-5 Thinkers*

A second example focuses on Cantor and Einstein's efforts to "transpose" mathematics' limits. Both their lifeworks illustrate how one moves from a SAS-focused GEM to one able to integrate spirituality and science. Cantor's notion of a whole, identical to its parts led to debates on the principle of identity. Traditionalists did not believe that a single mathematician could handle transfinite numbers' infinities. This seemed to require a type of person with a non-simple identity, one with multiple selves.[59] Cantor replied that one's unconscious or spiritual aspect is somehow involved in transfinite sets. Einstein made us reconsider spacetime relations and the notion of force. His three papers, published in 1905, on the Brownian motion, on the theory of STR, and on photons made him famous. Until 1914, as a member of a small international group who sought to discover the nature of the physical world, he conversed with Lorentz, Madame Curie and Mach. Contrasting sets' static nature with tensors' trans*form*ative[60] properties gives us contexts to evaluate Einstein's conviction that scientists should not hide behind ivory towers.

In mathematics' universal language, the group of such interrelated concepts as *property*, *define* and *rules of construction* have not been fully grasped with regard to time and the questions of "existence."[61] We can only mediate such immanental events or states of affairs in systems of reference (where *form*s are implicitly defined conjugates) when one contextualizes mathematical potentialities in ways that transcend utilitarianism and respect AIRR ideals. Mathematics' different yet equivalent conceptualizations (*Insight*, 734) offer an analogy, but do not exhaust the gamut of human experience. I extend that analogy to include a relational "void" within potency-*form*-act.

Hausdorff's paradox states that we can represent the surface S of a sphere as the union of *four* disjoint sets A, B, C and D such that D is a countable set and A is congruent to each of the three sets B, C and B ∪ C; except for the countable set D. A is both a half and a third of S. I transpose such a 4-3-4 feat with GEM's retrieval of reason-faith allelic in-betweens. GEM equips us with a feedback method that addresses our finitude and the limitations of infinity as grasped in calculus' infinitesimals or as intimated in our attempts to reach for the infinite. *Pi* illustrates how our spirits find solutions to life's irrationalities. It symbolizes the mysterious harmony studied in science, the puzzling roots of a void or of irrational numbers. 4-3-4 *form*ulations, essential to our mechanized world, depend on theories of harmonic analysis that originated with Pythagoras' *pi* and his studies of musical notes' periodicity.

If writing came only after the development of speech or as human ability to graphically represent numbers depended on counting, I study the implications of the irrationals and of a GEM knowing-known iso*morph*ism that allows us to address all irrationalities. Or again, as Fourier taught us to use the simplifications that occur when a complicated function or curve is represented as the sum of a number of simple harmonic or sinusoidal components, I rely, in part, on GEM's insights into statistical probabilities to *form*ulate a 4-3-5 reflective spirituality.

Cantor's bridge to infinity is set within Platonic limits that do not indicate how science and philosophy differ. My analogy between the roles of spindles in our two genomes considers our ability to use transcendental numbers. If the latter are a subset of irrational numbers, humans deal with various irrationalities beyond those of a 1.41421 hypotenuse's relevance to QED theory. Whereas real numbers can be found on the number line (numbers naming the distance of any point from 0), a 4-3-5 metaxy addresses our irrationalities in self-transcendent ways. Statistical and classical rules are complementary. This fact helps us grasp how QED can incorporate Maxwell's electromagnetic theory and quantum rules or how Einstein's STR and GTR that resolved a clash between views of space and the universe as continua (space and the universe can be measured in units as small as you wish)[62] has to be complemented by QED's discontinuities.

An AIRR approach to GEM helps generalize GEM itself. It instantiates GEM's transposition of Hilbert's implicit definition. For GEM, *implicit definition* is important due to its *complete* generality (explanation without nominal definition where terms and relations define one another. One is *not* restricted to the *objects* one is thinking about; one can concentrate upon the sets of terms and relations in which the scientific significance lies. The trick is to obtain the rules that fix the *opera*tions which fix the numbers, using the large, dynamic, virtual images" of mathematicians to transpose these so as to grasp a new set of rules governing the *opera*tions in a more general way. For every basic insight there is a circle of terms and relations, such that the terms fix the relations, the relations fix the terms, and the insight fixes both. Patrick Byrne stresses[63] that GEM transposed Hilbert's conceptual approach into one based on concrete *opera*tions. I further that transposition with a generalized AIRR-ATGC analogy transposing not rules, *opera*tions, numbers but ideal AIRR matrices. The traditional potency-*form*-act metaphysical terms are heuristically redefined into such matrices whereby insights into the in-betweens of situations and/or events yield (4-3-5) courses of action.

Without implicit definition, GEM appears as *form*ally abstract, irrelevant. GEM's account of inverse insight helps us grasp how Einstein arrived at the STR postulate that the mathematical expression of physical laws is invariant under inertial trans*form*ations. Byrne rightly stresses that a focus on the SAS (subject as subject intentionally conscious and aware of others) can also serve as a foundation for GTR because insights presuppose a SAS's existence, a concrete, conscious, unity, identity whole. Still, an SAS view leaves out important implications for applying GEM and Einstein's work to our world's needs. It risks overlooking some of the ways in which a SAS is related to the rest of reality. SAS views do not delve sufficiently into the roots of evil, into how an East-West bridge can help combat egoism, or into how Einstein lived out AIRR *ideals*. My focus is, rather, on GEM's ability to link traditions despite language problems.

GEM dialectic interrelates linked but opposed principles by appealing to the conscious AIRR activities of *many* subjects. My metaxic-love focus transposes a "SAS" view to a "meta-SAS" one. A mere SAS view can remain in "splendid" isolation. "SAS" in GEM implies *interrelated* subjects. A holistic, meta-SAS world perspective that relates our invariant, yet trans*form*ative AIRR loci with the analogical allelic loci of biology, with the matrices and group structures of mathematics, with our 4-dimensional manifold. Unless enough persons are converted and begin to use their allelic *opera*tions co*opera*tively, all is for nought, in that we undercut SAS's AIRR trans*form*ative abilities to transcend reductionist 4-2 brain-mind views on cognition.

The relations between different universes of discourse regard not things specified in such universes, but the specifications employed to denote the things. I stress that potency-*form*-acts are general concepts and names. The ground of this "generality without abstractness" is that the metaphysical elements are defined heuristically. "*Form*" does not refer immediately to reality, as does the definition of man or of hydrogen. Its immediate reference is to a type of cognitional activity; "only through the occurrence, which is usually hypothetical, of such activity does it refer to being" (*Insight*, 503). I transpose potency-*form*-act in ways that impinge on a meta-SAS implications as lived out by Einstein.

By tracing the sources of disparate Buddhist and Christian traditions to the teachings of their founders, one can arrive at the AIRR-loci that inspired their love-void metaxies. One must explicitate the implications of "SAS conversion" by re*form*ulating such core terms in ways "4-3-5 able" to engage all disciplines. Figures 2 (on proteins and enzymes' biochemistry and on how sensitive or imaginary presentations are organized into patterns of experience) proposed ways to relate the components of our physical and spiritual genomes. Heelan is on the right track. He identifies the similarity-within-difference between SAS and "meta-SAS" GEM approaches; he sublates, AIRR-grounds physical notions of correspondence.

The two above examples of loci transpositions illustrate how a 4-3-5 topology's meta-SAS loci imply a trans*form*ation-enabling feedback that links psyche and spirit through our AIRR ideals. Such a topology (analogical to Bion's grid) takes into account the contradictions that dog human endeavors. It helps us "rebut" postmodernist critiques by having us assert anew our AIRR ethical ideals. If Einstein's GTR field equations depend on symmetry in instantaneous rest frames, or if the distinct autonomous sciences are related as higher viewpoints emerging through insights arising according to the *opera*tions of former rules expressed in newly emerging rules, GEM's ethics is reinforced by its genetic intelligibility, by what is possible when we ask how new things emerge out of the old. Emergence (process in which otherwise coincidental manifolds of lower conjugate acts invite the higher integration effected by higher conjugate *form*s) needs conversions.

3d *Conversion and GEM Artists Striving for a Just, Politically Viable Society*

A gamma function generalizes the factorial function to non-integral values; it enables us to precisely define and calculate intermediate points on curves. As this function is useful in orienting other functions more than as a solution by itself (as seen in a psi function[64] or in Einstein's use of tensors) so I use GEM insights into the relational nature of reality to ground shared AIRR-love ideals that reach for the infinite. If Buddhist detachment is ambivalent on love, still, responding to infinite love enriches life, as Jesus taught. GEM helps us understand the ambiguities we face in balancing judgments of fact and value. It offers a solution to the problem of evil by appealing to habits that can enrich our sensitivities. I argue with Nietzsche that in every adult person there is an element of a twelve-year old at play. We are *related to all else*, as Eastern traditions insist. A proper grasp of Eastern insistence on the integral role of religion in life may help convert GEM purists to a better stance on faith as 4-3-5 eye of love that values mystics' "artistic" ability to link our outside with our inside; we keep these two in equilibrium by rooting judgments in the dynamic structure of rational self-consciousness. That structure is latent[65] and AIRR *opera*tive in everyone's choosing, but it takes some distantiation from self and our confusions to get us beyond verbalisms so as to reflect ethically. GEM's view on the integrative role of conversion in bringing about a just, politically viable society can help us erect a "world bridge." Some purists, focused on the Western thought, tend to wall off theology from philosophy. They, fail to grasp the analogical functions of physical and spiritual allelic loci. ATGC-U (genetic material in*form*ing living things) provide the chemical basis for storing and expressing genetic in*form*ation within cells and for transmitting life to future generations. These are *coded* transcriptive translations of physical life expressed in 20 amino acids. *Uncoded* GEM expresses how the human spirit works in meta-SAS ways. Heelan's non purist GEM transposition of trans*form*ative AIRR conjugate loci into a 4-3-5 process is analogous to how mathematicians and geneticists transpose their complex conjugates. If a gamma function generalizes other functions, GEM artists generalize love's powerful virtues.

With these preliminary notions of a trans*forma*tive holism, let us focus on Einstein as a "GEM artist" who never lost sight of his being related to the universe and to all humans. Just as he creatively used tensor fields, so I invoke some of the ethical ideals that guided his life. As a pacifist, in 1896, he gave up his German citizenship because of its intolerant militarism; he became a "stateless person." Keenly feeling his relative impotence in resisting militarism during the two world wars, his sense of humor helped him sustain his pursuit of peace. Yet, he endorsed a letter sent to President Roosevelt to urge the study of fission that led to the atom bomb. As tensors are entities whose components change according to a generalized vectorial trans*form*ation law, or as ATGC-uracil trans*form* a genome, so AIRR ideals are a generalizable trans*form*ing alternative to monism. In 1929, in reply to an inquiry from Rabbi Herbert Goldstein of New York as to whether he believed in God. Einstein replied "I believe in Spinoza's God who reveals himself in the orderly harmony of what exists, not in a God who concerns himself with fates and actions" of humans. In 1954, he said that the political pressures on scientists by ignoramuses who use their positions of power to tyrannize over "intellectuals must not be accepted" without a struggle. Spinoza followed this rule when, unlike Hegel, he turned down a professorship and "decided to earn his living in a way that would not force him to mortgage his freedom."[66] Einstein's Spinozism took "the form of a rapturous amazement at the harmony of natural law, which reveals an intelligence"[67] of such superiority that, compared with it, all our systematic thinking or acting is insignificant. GEM helps us to reassess our lives and to reorient philosophy and science lest we be left adrift in words or caught in a Dr. Jekyll-Mr. Hyde syndrome that would isolate disciplines. from one another. To oppose a social schizophrenia in which a non-moral will to power uses inhuman techniques,[68] I call attention to human per*form*ance.

Einstein is an example of how a (GEM) religiously in*form*ed ethical man reconciles reason-faith alleles, a personality whose mystico-ethical side opens us to the infinity of the universe. He was not a religious scholar, but if he had to make an in*form*ed choice between Spinoza and Buddhism, he might well have chosen the latter which is close to his beliefs. Buddhism philosophy is agnostic but it is not incompatible with Judaeo-Christian faith. GEM lets our emergent minds be ethically independent in ways that pantheism precludes. Just as Einstein appreciated the trans*form*ative power of our minds, so GEM resolves the imponderable in-between phase-boundaries of science, philosophy, religion and ethics by explaining how our various judgments of fact and of value are mutually mediated by persons' responsible decisions.

4a *A Spiritual, "In-between" Love Topology's 4-3-5 Trans*form*ative Abilities*[69]

I have been arguing that our mental processes can be likened to trans*forma*tive DNA (as mediated by triadic amino acids and by RNA). If empiricists cannot reconcile the mind's ineffable qualia with the brain's quantifiable matter, this subsection establishes a transition to Part Two's ethics based on 4-3-5 structures (with analogies in genetics or in a hypotenuse) rather than on reductionisms. Our AIRR trans*form*ative loci are interpersonal bridges; yet, the bridges are deficient if restricted to privatized "SAS's." A solution *may be* had by complementing such "SAS's" with a 4-3-5 spiritual *axio*logy that relates us with all reality by way of a spiritual topology's allelic loci.

Topology studies the properties of geometric configurations invariant under continuous mappings; the youngest but most sophisticated branch of geometry, it is closely related to modern algebra. It reached its status due to L. E. J. Brouwer's generalized method that rejected Hilbert's attempts to justify mathematics on the basis of combinatorial reasoning's elementary methods through strings of symbols in *form*al logical systems, an objection borne out by Gödel.[70] GEM moves us beyond *form*alisms by mapping the AIRR procedures of our minds and the ethical ideals that accompany authentic living. While a spiritual genome is a "structural" analogue of a physical genome, a 4-3-5 spiritual topology maps the in-betweens of 4-3-4 loci and of 4-3-5 ethical loci. All that Euclid could tell about straight lines, circles, spheres, conics or other such figures is lost under the figures' slightest de*form*ations. Mathematicians map de*form*ations, but not *why* these occur. In accounting for de*form*ations, GEM maps how we may objectify conscious intentionality in all fields of human endeavor. If maps work like functions, a spiritual topology transposes functions by mapping invariant AIRR *opera*tions' *free* trans*form*ations that Part Two will convert into an ethical feedback that can promote co*opera*tion. While the confluence of rivers requires a flat terrain and while Bion's grid interrelates all events in human interactions with horizontal and vertical axes, a spiritual topology links our immanent-transcendent encounters with allelic loci so as to move a spindle[71] analogy toward feedback patterns. If languages use words or symbolic conventions to say "gold" or "no smoke without fire," a GEM *axio*logy transposes conventions or mathematical mappings by way of AIRR-4-3-5 loci that reach beyond 4-2 and 4-3-4 limitations.

Lesniewski, a logician, criticized colleagues for neglecting people's basic insights into the way things work when resolving ambiguities. Arguing that a theory is to be judged with how it accords with reality, he mapped a *form*alism that did not interpret logic or mathematics as mere symbol games. GEM focuses on the potency-*form* act triads that underlie our mental acts and are common to both "naive" common sense and to mathematics, namely 1) experiencing the data of sensation or consciousness, 2) explaining such experienced data and 3) judging on explanations' validity (*Insight*, 431-57). It explains the in-betweens of how linguists or mathematicians per*form* their work or are able to love. All insights reflect dynamic intelligence. Mathematicians study loci, that is, systems of points, lines or curves that satisfy one or more given conditions. Their 4-3-4 *static* definitions change one function into another. *Opera*tors map one set into another, each having a structure defined by algebraic *opera*tions, a topology or a certain order. A 4-3-5 *axio*logy studies how we can trans*form* the *axiom*-foundational debates that are a grist for many academic mills.

RNA trans*form*s DNA, but I map how love trans*form*s GEM triads. As amino acid triplets enable trans*form*ations within physical genomes, so potencies and *form*s are subject to *form*ations and de*form*ations. Unlike classic control theory which studies open-loop and closed-loop systems, 4-3-5 GEM's AIRR loci are open to loving acts in defiance of ongoing evil de*form*ations. A 4-3-5 spiritual topology uses reason-faith allelic in-betweens to study and effect trans-*form*ations in our de*form*ed fields of knowledge or in social organizations. It transposes *form*alisms to underlying AIRR loci. It seeks to reconcile common sense with the complex findings of spirituality and of science so as to show underlying complementarities in these endeavors. Our minds function in 4-3-5 ideal ways when they go beyond language or mathematical *form*alisms to underlying mental acts. If mathematical loci's indefinite points move between infinity and nothingness, GEM maps *opera*tions researchers' AIRR loci, enabling us to link ethical values not restricted to systems.

As Gamow and other physicists helped us grasp RNA's trans*form*ational implications, so AIRR ideals motivate verbs' 4-3-5 in-betweens; they link persons' mystic and ethical abilities with scientific method by integrating our minds' analytico-synthetic properties in ways that transcend Kantian dichotomies. In GEM, questioning is not only about being but is itself being, being in its luminous openness to being, being that, realizing itself through inquiry and knowing, leads to an in-between metaxy of love. As Frege created his sequence of natural numbers out of nothing, or as John Conway's infinity of numbers show off the boundless potential of the null set and of the human mind itself, so mind is the real null set in Frege's and Conway's number theories. "The mathematical null set is but a subordinate entity created after the mind's self-image."[72] For GEM, our minds are open to and attain being. I argue that creativity in great mathematicians (who had some of their greatest insights when *not* thinking about the problems that beset them) illustrates how we recognize the telling difference between Buddhist nothingness and a null set's nothing. The former is a pregnant source for a 4-3-5 metaxy of interrelated love; the latter is a logical category. Both are to be distinguished from what does not exist. Perceiving nothing is not to be perceiving at all. Learning is not just sensation but it is to perceive, "to complete the hypothetical entity, the raw datum, with memories, associations, a structure, and one's emotive and expressive reactions."[73] It keeps us from having ocular illusions but can lead one to 4-3-5 love metaxies.

Feynman's diagrams show the successive trans*form*ations that occur in QED's complex numbers. Mathematicians can represent imaginary numbers on a plane along with real numbers. GEM helps us wrestle with nothingness-being's trans*form*ative in-betweens when nothingness is viewed as a creative dynamic interrelating all reality (Buddhism). If mathematicians disagree as to foundations, our AIRR *loci*, the real "nullset source" of mathematical nullsets, underlie *form*alists' judgments. *Form*alists "can do" without meaning; they *do* judge as to what is required for 4-3-4 *form*alizations! If the Lebesgue measure facilitates generalizations, [74] GEM generalizes AIRR loci's *inner* sources and *applies* them *outwardly*, subject to humans' ethical limitations. Pythagorean-genetic 4-3-5 analogies illustrate how GEM integrates immanence and transcendence in the face of mutagenic or irrational factors. Killings and rapes are facts; my analogy between AIRR and ATGC processes relies on facts of a different nature: Pythagorean harmony is an "ideal" inviting us to forego evil. AIRR and ATGC differ in the freedom they allow or fail to allow; AIRR ideals *"morph"* ATGC and RNA's codes. Their self-transcendent ability is due to psychic, intellectual, moral and religious conversions. To the extent that conversions occur, hope displaces despair.

4b A 4-3-5 Spiritual Topology and 4-3-4 Exponents of Singularities[75]

Logical positivism's claim that the only absolute truth is that there is no absolute truth has influenced postmodernists. A 4-3-5 map of love notes that string theory cuts totally against the positivist grain and has revolutionized nuclear physics by linking it with spacetime; its wave structure of matter describes reality in terms of the one reality that we all experience in common (space, affected by a wave medium). For string theorists, matter is *form*ed from spherical waves in space causing the 'particle' effect at their wave center. Time is due to the wave motion (activity in space). Since particle physics' interactions can occur at zero distance, while Einstein's theory of gravity is not viable at zero distance, string theorists replace the theory of hadron particles with one of quantum gravity involving a theoretical particle, the graviton with zero mass and two units of spin when energy strings are excited;[76] they interpret Mach's principle in non-determinist ways. Cognition is structured on supersymmetric genetico-functional axes. For GEM, the sensitive flow of our percepts and images is an underlying, otherwise coincidental manifold that allow for higher systematizations such as loving courses of action (*Insight*, 620). While a 4-3-5 structure is a given of physical genomes, a 4-3-5 metaxy actualizes our *ideal* AIRR loci with the ongoing conversions of our "lived out" spiritual insights that seem "irrelevant" to some, but not to a Socratic *daimon*.

Just as string theory traces all phenomena to vibrating loops, so our brainwaves subtly hint at how our 4-3-5 spiritual activities use, but are *not* exhausted by brainwaves. Rather than trying to give explanatory account of such realities, I outline insights into waves by Pythagoras, Kepler, Einstein, de Broglie, Schrödinger and string theorists in an attempt to arrive at a 4-3-5 spiritual mysticism that underlies and influences our dynamic human cognition. Just as Pythagoras was the "first wave theorist" who realized that vibrating lyre strings produce harmonic notes, or as string theory uses modern mathematics, so GEM enables us to relate mathematics to religious realities.

Eastern mystics focus on psychic-noetic development. Western mystics seek to master emotions and feelings. GEM does for cognition, what Feynman does for physics. Feynman used his pedagogic skills to explain physics' mysteries with trans*form*ational diagrams. In *QED*, he stresses that not only are we unable to check a quantum theory of gravitation, we even lack a reasonable theory to do so. GEM links the in-betweens of mysticism, poetry and science with its heuristic structures based on a subject's AIRR ope*ra*tions. In mathematics, topology is a central unifying notion that *form*alizes concepts such as convergence, connectedness and continuity. In architecture, topology is used to describe spatial effects that cannot be described by a topography of social or economic interactions. A spiritual topology links yet differentiates judgments of fact and of value made in organizing life and society. It addresses how the AIRR allelic in-betweens of faith and dreams complement our knowing-doing structures with a view to link East-West ethics. It integrates the religio-scientific views that guided the lives of such men as Cantor and Einstein.

In 1917, before the discovery of cosmological redshifts, Einstein proposed a cosmic model in which random galactic motions cancel out, yielding a static universe in which both the mean density of matter and the radius of the universe remain constant over time. He introduced a small repulsive force between material particles to keep the model from collapsing due to its own gravitation. In 1930, Eddington showed that Einstein's model is unstable; it should either expand or contract if perturbed. Upon rediscovering Friedmann's equations, Lemaitre offered a nonstatic model that began with the big bang and expands forever. Because of problems in GTR on which the Friedmann-Lemaitre model is based and because at the time of the big bang, the density of the universe and the curvature of spacetime would have been infinite, there is a point in the universe where the theory itself breaks down. Theories of science are *form*ulated on the assumption of a smooth, nearly flat spacetime, but they break down at the big bang singularity whose spacetime curvature is infinite.

Quantum mechanics makes it difficult to reconcile general relativity with the singularity. Like GEM, Feynman invokes statistical laws. Feynman used such laws to *form*ulate quantum theory in terms of a sum over histories. Particles do not have just a single history, as in classical laws; according to the uncertainty principle, they follow each possible spacetime path. In each particle's histories two numbers come into play, one representing the size of a wave, the other, its phase (position) in the cycle. One finds the probability that the particle passes through a particular point by adding up the waves associated with every possible history passing through that point. In fact, it is too difficult to actually per*form* such calculations. Stephen Hawking, using imaginary[77] time to avoid technical difficulties in the sum over histories, notes that the surface of the earth is two-dimensional; the position of a point is specified by coordinates of latitude and longitude. He uses spacetime diagrams to illustrate GTR's two other dimensions' need of intelligible contexts.

Comparing Hawking's skepticism with Einstein's faith in God illustrates reason-faith alleles. For Hawking, if the universe's rate of expansion "after the big bang had been smaller by even one part in a hundred thousand million million, the universe would have recollapsed before it ever reached its present size."[78] But ever the skeptic, he finds it difficult to accept the plausible conclusion that the universe is not due to chance. Still, he wonders why God gave us the power to understand physical laws. Is the universe due to chance or design? Is the micro-second between its survival or potential destruction fortuitous? Between the uncertainties of life or of the universe as modeled by Friedmann, the only certainties are our judgments. All acts of insights that reflect on physical, mathematical or ethical realties involve various in-betweens in our judgments of fact and of value. Using imaginary numbers (not just "real" ones) makes the distinction between time and space disappear, analogously to Einstein's use of tensors in working out his GTR. Unable to go into the technical details of a unified theory that combines quantum mechanics and gravity, this book proposes a 4-3-5 analogy between *opera*tional loci in biology, mathematics and GEM. It enlists such imponderables as character and love in guiding our lives. In mathematics, one can combine sets in subsets *without regard to order*. Using AIRR order to address ethical disorder can empower science, philosophy and art by combining imagination's might with the realities of how we arrive at knowledge or how we can live ethical lives in a "4-2 immanently secularized" world.

Empowering mathematicians means going beyond an analysis that investigates loci and points irrespective of possible application to the physical realm. Scientists test their insights so as to verify mathematical possibilities. Yet, one must explain what insights are. GEM and the physicist Fritjof Capra find common ground in reconciling scientific and mystical insights. This ground includes a non-Kantian a priori and the imaginative synthesis that leads to systematic unification of known contents. Just as mathematical theories must be tested experimentally, so religious ideals and legal systems have to be tested with the reality of how humans in fact behave.

Capra notes that the "splits" that rent Greek thought, beginning with the Eleatics, have continued to divide science and philosophy since Galileo. We treat the environment as if it consisted of separate exploitable parts. If scientists construct intellectual maps of reality, 4-2 reducing things to their general outlines, Heisenberg has shown the *limits* of a quantified knowledge. Because our representation of reality is easier to grasp than reality itself, "we take our concepts and symbols for reality...The concept of a distinct physical entity, like a particle, is an idealization which has no fundamental significance. It can only be defined in terms of its connections to the whole, and these connections are of a statistical nature, probabilities rather than certainties."[79] Likewise, a GEM bridge examines possible types of order amidst seeming chaos. The allelic in-betweens that order such possible types are open-ended, not closed. Even amidst the wondrous progress of scientific knowledge, there remain the quandaries of imponderable, allelic in-betweens in human character.

Societal situations can be integrated by linking the in-betweens of ethico-mystical realms. GEM's 4-3-5 structure offers us (through the agency of {partly} converted GEM artists) viable allelic in-betweens to reconcile our 4-3-5 ethico-mystical commitments. The quark-octet model includes indeterminacy and uncertainty that only statistics can interpret. Our universe is constituted by untold numbers of proton collisions and their resulting quarks and muons.[80] A 4-3-5 spiritual topology risks a Pascal like wager to say that an unknowable God may be the source of it all.

Capra realizes that our representations *fail* to attain reality. GEM's four methods (classical, statistical, genetic, dialectical) and its integral heuristic structure (metaphysics) explain the limits of representation. Instead of reductionists' 4-2 descriptive accounts of consciousness, GEM explains that by asking "what?, why?" classical methods specify conjugates that can be verified in events. Since in the empirical residue, there is nothing to be understood, statistical methods study the non-systematic. Asking "how often?", they study events that are defined only by conjugates. Both these heuristic methods involve inverse insights, a negative moment when one realizes that there is nothing to be understood. As with conjugates and events, they complement one another in their heuristic structures, modes of abstraction and verification.[81] Mentally separating the non-systematic in data lets one concentrate on the systematic in classical laws. Statistics stands to conjugates as questions for reflection stand to questions for intelligence. Statistical notions of quantum mechanics open the way to transposed developments of classical thought. Physics has radically revised mechanistic worldviews based on the notion of solid, indestructible particles. "Field theories have trans*form*ed the concept of the void. This began when Einstein associated the gravitational field with the geometry of space; it became more pronounced when "quantum theory and relativity theory were combined to describe the force fields of subatomic particles."[82] GEM concedes the field of physics to physicists, but it confronts simplistic notions that overlook deeper issues. It explains how various methods use insights to supply necessary links with imaginative presentations. It then transposes its study of insight to ethical applications (evil and conversion).

If classical methods anticipate an unspecified correlation to be specified, genetic method finds its heuristic notion in development; it proceeds from generic indeterminacy toward a specific perfection, that is organic, psychic and intellectual development as this is mediated by potency-*form*-act conjugates. GEM uses genetic method to link our sensate and intellectual knowings and to order the functional aspects of a concrete person's AIRR ope*ra*tions on the mo-del of how mathematicians handle infinite possibilities. There is initial indeterminacy. Organic functioning reveals similarity in its early stages. Psychic development concerns character, temperament and skills.[83] A study of human development includes heuristic, 4-3-5 foundational categories. We live one day at a time. Each day people suffer, kill and die. GEM, addresses life's absurdities, but its allelic in-betweens help us mediate between the sublime and the absurd. If like Hawking, some remain skeptics, GEM invites us to conversion. "5" in my 4-3-5 analogy is the key trans*form*ative pivot that allows me to compare physical and spiritual genomes. The series of 1-2-3, 1-2-3-4 or 1-2-3-4-5 feedback ope*ra*tions implicit in figures 1-4 are "series" comprising a quasi-infinite numbers of ope*ra*tors that are to be spiritually *and* ethically grounded. Unlike the absolute in Hegel, I advert to apocalyptic literature's ethics in addressing the "black hole" of strife or Hawking's skepticism. I let Bellah or Covey's habits[84] be guideposts to a proactive way of putting first things (4-3-5) first.

4c A 4-3-5 Spiritual Topology and "4-2 Progress" in the Light of Eternity

Progress in science is attained through discoveries that eliminate reigning theories such as occurred when Lavoisier helped displace "phlogiston," Michelson and Morley disproved "ether" and Einstein supplanted Newton's absolute space. Such feats reflect the trans*form*ative abilities of the human spirit. GEM's AIRR cognitional structure helps us trans*form* our limited insights into broader, more encompassing (4-3-5) ones. As the frontiers of knowledge expand through verified experiments, so reason-faith's allelic in-betweens can help us ethically trans*form* our world by enabling it to integrate its various traditions, if and when humans do appropriate their cognitional structure. Einstein's use of the rigorous geometric concept of complex numbers as ordered pairs of real numbers finds an analogy in AIRR allelic loci able to improve political realities; based on the immanence of one's self to self, on a *loving*, empathic sharing in the immanence of others. Such loci enable us to use our AIRR *opera*tions in 4-3-5 *ideal* cooperative ways with God and others.[85]

A brief survey of the progress of Western music from the rise of the symphony in the mid-eighteenth century to today's cacophonies may illustrate my point. From 1760 to 1810, Haydn, Mozart and Beethoven perfected the symphony at the very time that the foundations of the old religio-political order were crumbling. On another level, every sensitive, alert person, even today, hears background symphonies despite the cacophonies that may surround him or her. An allelic spiritual genome (based on 4-3-5 analogies, not on 4-2 correspondence) puts this in perspective. Rather than trusting in idealist philosophies, it appeals to the ideals of transcendent love and of a creativity practiced by Mozart, Beethoven, Brahms. These composers' symphonies were, within 100 years, followed by atonality and cacophony. While Christianity sees itself attacked by a would-be all knowing laicism, it will miss the boat if it does not grasp that an "atonal" Buddhism is complementary to it. The three deaf, mute, blind monkeys of Nikko provide 4-3-5 metaxic hints of Jesus' words. Each one of us is called to act as these wise monkeys in non-judgmental but virtuous actions. We oppose evil by fashioning wise, virtuous trans*form*ative 4-3-5 allelic spindles.

Lives are broken - persons suffer immeasurably –
yet GEM helps us transpose 4-2, 4-3-4 insights

Since our social order is threatened, ethical calls are being made for federating our world. Swedenborg's notion of "correspondence" to localize mental processes" anticipates" the idea of a genomic analogy. Scientists can split electrons into a negative or positive spin and shoot them off in opposite directions so that they causally lose any possible link with one another. Changing the spin of one part allows the other 1/2 switches to retain the balance; this "could theoretically" occur across the entire expanse of the universe, but is probably impossible. Still, the two electrons remain in correspondence with one another. As a term, "correspondence" describes observations while acknowledging the inexplicable nature of the event; it is a reality that describes inexplicable links between phenomena. While some cognitivists use the same term to describe brain-mind, the question that Heelan and I address is "How can correct linguistic *form*ulations be descriptive and explanatory in analogical (allelic) ways?" Meta-SAS frameworks, typified in Feynman's diagrams (the qualia of our minds expressing the quanta of physics), in Heelan's transpositions or in Bion's axes are ways to enable "splendidly isolated SAS's" to transcend self and communicate with the trans*form*ative AIRR loci-languages of other cultures or religions. GEM empowers all persons by enabling us to relate the in-betweens of spirituality (inside) with ethics (the outside). Unlike cynics who disparage virtue, GEM artists have a healthy skeptical attitude open to and able to grasp the wisdom at the core of Buddhist teachings. My blending of the insights of such disparate men as Bion, Feynman, Heelan and others is meant to recognize and integrate the different phases that most thinkers undergo. Kant, Heidegger Lonergan and others had later insights that altered many of their previous ones. Music and art, in general, and individual thinkers all evolve. I argue that 4-3-5 metaxic ethics can help us integrate and sublate the AIRR insights that guide many thinkers.

Humanity relentlessly transposes one cultural frame into another. There are many theories on Shakespearean authorship, on religious views. GEM helps us transpose the phases of personal and cultural trans*form*ations such as those of Elizabethan-Stuart or Catholic-Protestant political factions. It transposes 4-2 factional interests into an agenda that might lead to a federated world. Particular religions or cultures must transpose artists' AIRR frames or technicians 4-3-5 ideal visions.

This chapter has explored the mathematical notions of loci, points and tensors. Einstein used the generalizing, trans*form*ative properties of tensors to arrive at his GTR. We seem to live in a three-dimensional world; after Einstein, we know that we are actors within a 4-D universe. As Gamow helped geneticists locate the template within which DNA *opera*tes, so AIRR ideals can help philosophers deploy their allelic insights into being and nothingness. Part Two will explain how our AIRR acts provide 4-3-5 foundations for science and philosophy by relating such acts to all reality.

Third "Let's Get Real" Concurrent Dialectic

Realist: John, get real will you. Okay, big brains like Einstein may have got their stuff together but look at me, just an everyday struggling guy. What gives here? How does that affect me? All those big ideas about a GEM intellectualist method? Who has time for such 4-3-5 stuff?

John: To *tick* means to reach a modicum of authenticity or even full personal authenticity within a circle of friends open to the good. GEM points us in new directions in philosophy and theology by reconciling scientific, religious and ethical AIRR alleles.

Part Two will argue that GEM integrates our daily life's common sense with an ability to achieve a co*oper*ative world ethics and to effect mutual trans*forma*tions between East and West, North and South. It invites us to take the time out to examine the roots of our personal identity so we can communicate with others.

CONCLUSION TO PART ONE

Part One has examined some aspects of an ATGC-AIRR analogy. The analogy holds from a structural viewpoint; it is also illustrated in the way Crick and Watson co*opera*ted in discovering DNA. They realized that scientists *opera*te at their best by co*opera*ting. Physical genomes, too, demand the "co*opera*tion" of chromosomes on a spindle. An AIRR-structured, metaxic "ethical 4-3-5 feedback spindle" enables trans*form*ations based on human co*opera*tion. If it is more difficult to get to know the inside of one's self than it is to know the outside, I have illustrated in-betweens of what is inside us, how we (ethically) share that inside with others or how we hinder such sharing. Human excess manifests itself, [86] from totalitarianisms to adware that hijacks one's computer. Because mystic experience may be a necessary integrator of our outside and inside world, I rely on GEM to 4-3-5 integrate (social) ethics' various levels with mysticism.

Part Two

INTEGRATING IDEAL TRANS*FORM*ATIVE ACTIONS IN FEEDBACK WAYS

Introduction to Part II

This book links GEM's insights into cognition to a hope that experts will apply GEM to life's secular and religious dimensions. Can we integrate the allelic in-betweens of our analogically structured physical and spiritual genomes in a world now able to shape life in a lab? Part One mapped allelic loci in genetics and mathematics. Noting the trans*form*ative facets of DNA-RNA and AIRR loci, it touched on life's imponderables. Relying on religion's fuzzy logic ability, Part Two explores AIRR allelic feedback so as to relate secularism with ethics. Because of the developmental phases in such philosophers as Kant, Heidegger and Wittgenstein whose later views diverged from their earlier ones, it grounds our AIRR poly*morph*ic consciousness' in-betweens through difference within 4-3-5 unity. To go beyond representational theories of mind that focus on mental states as internal to the mind but separate a self from the environment, it contextualizes a view that the absolute has no unmediated existence apart from the relative. If a genome's haploid sets of chromosomes use a spindle, GEM's heals the split between matter and our psyche inasmuch as one's psyche is not a multiple personality but merely multi-sided. While recombination frequency is proportional to the distance between genes' point-loci on a chromosome and while such loci can be ordered relative to each other by recombination analysis, GEM o*pera*tes on cognitive data. Its AIRR loci confront the 4-2 hubris of "progress" by helping us ethically integrate reason-faith alleles which struggle, a la Buddha, Job, Socrates and Jesus, with the in-betweens of good and evil. We cannot play God since we are not God, but we must 4-3-5 judge as to the wisdom of 4-2 science.

A good place to start integrating our lives is for East and West to encounter one another through their 4-3-5 ethico-mystical perspectives on being and nothingness. GEM is like a painter's vanishing point. Enlisting the imponderables of virtue or character, it helps us integrate the *virtual* of nothingness that both contains and trans*forms* contradictions. The sheer speed of ceaseless technological innovations tends to unsettle many, but invariant yet trans*form*ative AIRR loci order the chaos of relentless change.

In *Method in Theology*, Lonergan shows our AIRR o*pera*tional feedback ability to "4-3-5 correlate" transcendence and immanence. Gradually, we become aware of our fuller self; we seek not just data "but the idea or form, the intelligible unity or relatedness, that organizes the data into intelligible wholes."[1] Seeking to resolve our conflicts by having us appropriate our own immanent AIRR loci's openness to grace or to a transcendent spirituality, GEM relates human commitment to an eye of love that seals our interdependence. I turn to peer into East-West divides so as to span them with a metaxy-bridge; the bridge begins in GEM's pure, disinterested desire to know; it moves us from theoretical detachment to public responsibility by having us appropriate our AIRR o*pera*tions in such a way that we advert to the in-betweens of the o*pera*tions themselves. AIRR loci function analogously to biological and mathematical loci. Loci in mathematics are paths traced by points as they move according to a definite rule; an arbitrarily small change involving an infinite number of *opera*tions in a dynamic system can produce chaotic behavior. GEM trans*form*s our AIRR loci with 4-3-5 conversions that can convincingly resolve our ambiguities in ways that map not a dynamic system (as a set into itself) but love's potential.

CHAPTER 4

EAST-WEST PHILOSOPHIES' TRANS*FORM*ATIVE FEEDBACK ALLELIC *OPERA*TIONS

This chapter examines some of the ways in which East and West differ in some of their philosophical stances and how GEM's trans*form*ative feedback and allelic *opera*tions reconcile basic differences by rooting those differences in our 4-3-5 structured ways of knowing and doing. Chapter 5 shall then contextualize and implement some of GEM feedback's ethical in-betweens.

Ethics helps us construct a just, peaceful world but it, too, can benefit from a sound mystic spirituality; to reach the boundaries between the outside and our spiritual side, we must appreciate the power of emotions and feelings and the insights of Eastern and Western mystics. AIRR allelic in-betweens are able to "glide" between the uncertainties of chaos or of complexity (broached in automata systems and in*form*ation theory). Such AIRR in-betweens are interrelated with categories verified in judgments of fact and of value lived out in co*opera*tive, trans*form*ative ways. GEM's heuristic structure moves us beyond a 4-2 cognitive science by integrating 4-3-5 in-betweens of mysticism and of ethics within scientific and philosophic methods (fig. 3's trans*form*ative triads).

Beyond the Limitations of 4-2 Cognitive Science

Cognitivism adheres to the representational theory of mind; its focus on mental states as internal to the mind, is quite susceptible to the dualistic separation of self from the environment. Tending to separate the self from its embodiment, it is unable to explain how the two seemingly unrelated spheres of molecular biology and of our psyche-spirits interface. To avoid the danger of 4-2 cognitivism, it is well to remember that perception not only provides in*form*ation for the distinction between self and environment, but also gives us a means of keeping in contact with the world through memory which bridges earlier and later elements of one's experience. Perceiving and remembering touch on the self in different ways. Perceiving is a spatio-temporal process that "provides a continuous flow of information about the embodied self" in its encounters with the physical and social world. Autobiographical memory involves a duplication of the self so that the "me-experiencing-now" can be related with a prior "me-experiencing-a-prior-environment."[2] How can a perceived self give rise to a remembered self and how can the two be trans*form*atively related? I answer such a question indirectly in two ways. First, I instance the mind's creative abilities whether illustrated in art or in mathematics. Second I go beyond the creative abilities of individual persons who perceive and remember to interrelate such abilities with those of others.

First, just as the abstract painter Paul Klee created a new trans*form*ative language of color, *form* and space with his deeply communicative symbolism, so Riemann and Einstein embody the cognitive sources of complex numbers. Riemann used the notions of con*form*al (a map projection in which small areas are rendered with true shape) and of conjugate (inversely related properties that differ only in the sign of the imaginary term). Einstein generalized Gauss' quadrature method. Just as these brilliant thinkers had a self able to trans*form*atively project thought onto reality, so I project a perceived, remembered, interacting self unto the wider aspects of reality by using GEM's feedback ability (based on personal and mutual per*form*ance). Our cognitional-doing per*form*ance, as Gauss and GEM insist, must delve into the cognitive realm—but also reach beyond that realm.

Second, I go beyond yet interrelate individual creators' abilities. An organization called "AoA" is guided by two basic philosophies: "the first is the Triad of inner strength from which we gain our strong sense of unity and trust for each other. The second is Balance from which we gain an outer strength. Together they form our core guild beliefs and guide us on our great adventure." These simple principles parallel this book's aim, the first Part of which sought to strengthen our inner self. Part Two seeks to use the imponderable allelic in-betweens of inner strength and the art of ethical love to promote a balanced, co-*opera*tive outer strength by deploying the AIRR allelic in-betweens of East-West thought. Just as DNA-RNA works through a 4-3-5 structured chain of bases, so GEM includes but reaches beyond the cognitive realm by integrating levels of our AIRR structured *opera*tions. Its potency-*form*-act and body-mind-spirit triadic functions *opera*te in and interrelate our realms of theory, common sense and interiority so as to lead to 4-3-5 authenticity.

Yves Raguin has compared Chinese spiritualities with Western mysticism. Immersed in Teilhard de Chardin's *Divine Milieu*, Raguin peered into the depths of his own being as a simple way of structuring contemplation. Psychologically, we first become aware of what is outside of ourselves (compare Cezanne or Van Gogh who imagined themselves as *being* the landscapes they painted). "Although we know that there is within us an inside, we do not become aware of it immediately as it is more difficult to penetrate the inside of ourselves than to grasp the external world."[3] In this process, we gradually become aware of ourselves, of others and of the limits of our own world. In negotiating the boundaries between our outside from our inside, what matters is not discovering another world, independent of mine, but being aware of other personalities different from mine. This structure of the world of spiritual experience is intimately connected with a symbolism built into our own deep psychology. Symbols are indispensable to spirituality.

What we experience is not perceived outside of psychological and mental structures. To become aware of my inner life, I first get absorbed in my own thoughts and feelings. Eventually, I begin to discover my own interiority as center of activity and thinking, fully aware of who I am. By turning toward my inner being, I realize the difference between my outside and my inside. Our feelings or emotions are a rich field of negative and desirable impetuses that guide or impede one's ability to appropriate one's "inside." Turning to my inside means that I seek not an object outside of myself, but myself. One's inner self is an integrating *Gestalt*—a unified physical, psychological or symbolic configuration that cannot be derived from its parts. Raguin integrates what seem to be disparate scientific and spiritual insights. In his steps, I develop an integrative structural analogy based on the roles of chromosomal spindle's trans*form*ations through amino acid triplets and on an ethical, self-corrective feedback AIRR spindle of interrelated love. GEM's trans*form*ative potency- *form*- act conjugates are in-betweens for helping us mediate Buddhist-Christian ideals—even if the ideals are expressed in different allelic categories. ATGC and AIRR are analogous; both promote creative trans*form*ations. If a chromosome's spindle includes amino acid triplets' trans*form*ational properties, an AIRR *coopera*tive feedback-spindle centers on a potency-*form*-act triad that can be energized by prayer (a partial immersion in God who empowers us with trans*form*ing symbols).

Few persons appropriate their consciousness so as to reach a mystical state. Seeking to integrate our inner-outer self in East-West co*opera*tive ways that do not neglect but integrate metaxic love, I retrieve the loci of our inner self as interrelated with all of reality. Westerners' failure to discover zero (0) may be due to their mental orientation, but they have learned from Zen that "emptiness" can also mean holistic fullness, a whole greater than its parts. Zen and mysticism are possible 4-3-5 paths to God; both take us beyond "things" and may lead to one being grasped by Ultimate Mind. To grasp something complex, one turns to its simple *form*s. 4-3-5 mystical experiences may be just such a simple *form* of human consciousness. A mystical state is a simplified mental activity that slows down the thinking process but intensifies consciousness. One begins to pay less attention to bodily sensations or daydreams so as to become fully silent inside. Such a silence is a pure consciousness event (PCE) experienced by mystics of many religions. As heightened cognizance, PCE's are "a perceived unity of one's own awareness *per se* with the objects around one, an immediate sense of a quasi-physical unity between self, objects and other people, ... (a state one) may call the unitive mystical state."[4] They may well be the E. coli of consciousness studies, the least complex encounter with awareness *per se* sought by students of consciousness. There is an imagistically filling (*kataphatic*) mysticism and an emptying (*apophatic*) one; the latter is devoid of the sensory language used in the former. PCE's prod a "subject as subject" to nurture 4-3-5 love. Regular, long-term meditation leads to the advanced experience Buddhists call *enlightenment*. It results in a deep shift in one's knowing structure; experienced relationships between the self and one's perceptual objects change deeply. In some people, this new 4-3-5 structure becomes a permanent, inner stillness to integrate the outside and inside into which we divide the world. Such a stillness perdures, even while engaged in thought or activity. It enables one to de-intensify emotional attachments and to progressively sense one's quiet interior.

To evaluate the 4-3-5 authenticity of mystics' first-person reports, one uses criteria based on common sense and on correctly judging whether reports are delusional or wise. Assuming reasonable cultural-linguistic differences, one can find family resemblances in mystical data. St. Teresa of Avila describes PCE as an "orison of union" during which she is deprived of every feeling, being unable to think of any single thing. Still, she remains awake and returns to her practical way of life as a leader. For Eckhart, there is an absence of sensory content and of mental objects, an experience the Upanishads had described long ago: "If a knower restrains his mind from the external, and the breathing spirit (*prana*) he can put to rest objects of sense." Let him then continue "void of conceptions."[5] Being influenced by what is not breathing (*purusha*) one be-comes aware of consciousness itself. One is, as it were, nothing but consciousness itself. By clarifying how our inside "trans*forms*" outside reality, mystics reinforce GEM's conscious-raising awareness of self as being linked with all reality. I turn to Buddhist thought so as to lay a basis for a feedback way of outlining a trans*forma*tive AIRR matrix that can guide our lives in truth.

Empowering an East-West, Buddhist-Christian Dialogue with Buddhist-GEM Truths

I now turn to evaluating 4-3-5 Buddhist-Christian truths. Faced with the fatalist teachings of *karma*, Buddha sought to free us from ignorance and illusion by teaching such ideal constructs as non-self "*anatman*,[6] a causal Chain (*pratitya-samutpada*) and his four Noble Truths. His "Chain" applies to humans in empirical, *non-scienti*fic ways the principles of causally conditioned phenomena; it teaches that all things exist within a *flux* of phenomenal events related in a twelve- linked Chain: our lives depend on 1) *avidya* (ignorance) and 2) revived residues from the past; 3) our conscious recognition (not mere awareness)[7] *of* objects 4) uses names and *forms* (*nama-rupa*); 5) our minds coordinate senses' perceived objects, 6) contact with which yields 7) sensation and 8) such desires as 9) sexuality that set in motion such processes as 10) becoming, 11) birth, 12) aging and death. The Noble Truths (1: all in life is suffering; 2: the cause of which is desire; 3: suffering ceases by detachment from desire; 4: the eightfold path leads to detachment) are in tension with one another *and* with the causal Chain. The ethical path's "*subjective* ethics," outlined in Truths three and four, is weakened if one prioritizes the first two cosmic Truths' "karma" and the Chain's "*objective cosmology*." Buddha's view on a conditioning of a self within five aggregates (*skandha*, a changing conglomerate of *form*, sensation, perception, character, and mental activities making up the human personality) is another important facet of his teachings.[8]

Early Buddhism stressed a simple rule of life; this gave way to philosophical schools that, confusing the key notions of impermanence and momentarness, viewed "substance" as underlying a non-determined type of psychic-moral causality (as did Locke). Nagarjuna was called "a nihilist" for rejecting such views. Opposing theories of "inherent nature" or the world as a cosmic flux of momentary events, his *identity-of-Emptiness* dialectic held that neither the flux itself nor our consciousness of it is real. All things *originate dependently*; their causal factors ever change. Like Socrates or Descartes, Nagarjuna doubted conventional explanations. His doubt was an "epoche" that suspends judgment about a state of affairs or an assertion's correctness. Like Pyrrho, he doubted all claims including his own claim to doubt all claims. His Madhyamika's "Middle Path" attempted to mediate between "all is real" and idealist positions. His insights into constant change led him to conclude that, since all things, concepts and persons evolve, they lack a fixed essence. Change is only possible if all entities and our conceptualizations are void of an eternal, immutable essence.[9] The ineffable void of enlightenment is the one truth, the state of being "thus" (*tathata*).

Around the 4th century CE, Yogacara (practice of Yoga or "path of consciousness")[10] challenged Nagarjuna's view of the ever changing nature of all phenomena. For it, existence is composed of discrete, mutually interdependent, ultimately unanalyzable elements. Denying reality to external objects, it speaks of mind as the sole reality; it admits eight consciousnesses. The first five of these are our senses which the sixth, thought, unifies. Judging leads to its eighth consciousness which receives the impressions of the first seven but is also the object of a false clinging against which it stores "seeds" of all *dharmas*. This eighth "seed-storing (*alaya*) consciousness" seeks to get us beyond delusory concepts since words (*vikalpa*) are unable to reach a first-order reality. It retrieves the seeds of one's memories which, in turn, involve an interplay between the subjective aspect of consciousness (*citta*), and its objective aspect (*caitta*). In this interplay, as in GEM, one reaches *nirvikalpa*, an apophatic state of peace. If one insists on labeling Yogacara as "idealism," it is one that accepts that matter exists but denies that it can be known in itself directly without mediating mental representations. Its mystic stance reaches an absolute in a state of rapture that transcends subject-object dualism; its seemingly monistic assertions are mystic ones opposing views that fail to distinguish between imagined phenomena and ineffable reality. "Within one's mind to which one returns is stored the source of the mind of all living things, that is to say, the place of *prajna*-Emptiness which is oneness with things as they really are."[11] If Husserl and GEM correct Kant by showing that the self can be an object, not just the condition of consciousness, Yogacara lets mind (*manas*) coordinate the senses; its eighth consciousness is the source of, what gives rise to the nature or character of all *dharmas* (things). It maintains that things lack a reality of their own by letting mind construct things' "reality." It can be reconciled with GEM by way of an interrelatedness that integrates words in undiscriminated consciousness and reaches an absolute.

Constructivism correctly asserts that we learn by reflecting on our experience and that we must assess what we learn. Like GEM, it strives for noncircularity amid theory-ladenness based on *opera*tions; yet, its Kantian model of reality is not up to bridging the world of matter with that of spirit. Constructivist theories reject rationalist and empiricist epistemologies—as do GEM and Yogacara. But the latter two stress the roles of judgment and of mystic experience. This sets them apart from Kant's categorical imperative. A "4-3-5 constructivist" encounter between Buddhism and GEM uses the threads[12] of our own lives to empower us; it transcends boundaries to relate an individualist subject as subject to all of reality and to help East-West dialogues so as to effect mutually empowering, "realist" encounters. Nagarjuna's dialectic (that anticipated postmodern claims that transcendence is illusory) is compatible with GEM (if hermeneutically contextualized).

Nagarjuna's nondual, apophatic Absolute frees us of thought *form*s but opens to wisdom. Magliola's deconstructionist Buddhist logic focuses on *and/ or* between the and/or implicit in Nagarjuna's void.[13] Buddhist schools known in the West *are* logocentric in Derrida's sense: we think of *identity* or causality and label them "ideas." The void's unheard-of thought is not a logocentric variation of *logos*. "With one and the same stroke," it allows us to have it both ways in nonparadoxical, ever altering ways that reinstate a logocentric. One must guard against a misplaced absolute that mistakes relative truths as final. For Buddhists, the lotus symbolizes dependent origination. Its flower is not produced by the seed. For Magliola, the lotus exemplifies Derridean *differance*: an effect (signified) is not produced by a "cause" (signifier). Buddhism's two truths (religion's *paramartha* absolute truth, science's *samvrti* relative truth) anticipated the multiple universes now proposed in physicists' anthropic principle. Such truths can reconstruct in deconstructive ways a 4-3-5 ethics. Lest Buddhism fall prey to a cosmic reductionism not unlike Freud's, GEM sublates *karma* and Buddhist dogmatic cosmologies within ethics. It lets void and being "empty-fill" one another on the analogy of how quantum mechanics (as interpreted by Dirac or Feynman) rescues GTR's inability to deal with a universe that is "zero size." As spacetime is always smeared out and "occupies some minimum region,"[14] so GEM links the Noble Truths and the cosmic Chain's tensions through a personalist ethics. It restores ethical primacy to Buddhism by reconciling its two cosmic

Noble Truths (on the necessity of suffering) with its Noble Truths that prioritize an ethical liberation. It lets a cosmos in process be en*form*ed by a 4-3-5 ethics in which a spirituality, specified by our lived socio-ethical judgments, plays a key role. In this sense, GEM and Nagarjuna's *"differances"* are dialectical tools seeking an AIRR foundational matrix.

GEM's critical realism sublates Berkeley's perceptionism. Unlike Locke,[15] GEM and Yogacara accept the primary and secondary qualities of consciousness that, though inconceivable and incommunicable, return to objects of sensation. Distinguishing ideas from reflectivity, such qualities preserve notions of unity between concepts and individual data and *open* us to reality rather than *verbally* separating us from it. A trans*form*ational metaxy finds a basis in Yogacara's notion of *asraya-paravrti* (*asraya*: ground, basis; *paravrti*: trans*form*ation).[16] The expression means the basis on which one relies, only to turn into a different basis (or non-basis) upon further illumination. Like Spinoza, Kant is a monist about phenomena, but, unlike Spinoza, he is a pluralist about noumena. Freud viewed mystic consciousness' trans*form*ations from an angle of neurosis. Yogacara and GEM view them as possibly leading to mystical states that can facilitate conversion in a mentally alert person.[17] In both, the senses apprehend; intellect *constructs* and judges. A 4-3-5 metaxy intellectually and ethically integrates sense consciousness. An antecedent willingness of faith, hope and love (*Insight*, 726) and an ability to meet human needs, by going beyond them, trans*form*s problematic *axio*logies as 4-3-5 points of insertion in pursuit of truth.

The Fourth
"Let's Get Real" Concurrent Dialectic

Realist: Okay, John, with GEM, you speak of a dialectic that helps us get to the root of what divides people so as to overcome their differences. How does that get us off to a new start?

John (finally able to ground his ideals). Thanks for your patience. We are now ready to talk about why the art of love (an ideal ability to transcend oneself) is also an ethical foundation. Let us try to link trans*form*ative ethical loci in Buddhism and Christianity which, as spiritualities of universal interrelatedness, must themselves be interrelated through a spiritual genomic metaxy.

Chapter 5

Contextualizing and Implementing GEM Diphase Feedback's In-Betweens

Preliminaries to Instituting a Buddhist-Christian
Ethical Encounter's Two Dialectics

This book seeks to empower philosophy, artists and science with trans*form*-ative insights linking GEM with Buddhist-Taoist-Christian mysticisms. It has touched on many issues, arguing that we must advert to the ideal in-betweens of our AIRR oper*a*tions (feelings-virtues and reason-faith alleles) lest we exploit them in self-contradictory ways. Appealing to those able to *temper* their sensibilities and to translate dreams into realizable (political) goals, it seeks to go beyond isolated subjects as subjects. GEM is an ethical anti-structure that opposes 4-2 oppressive control systems. Believing in love's viability, it targets our hearts. This final chapter implements GEM's "artistic feedback" so as to activate our integral heuristic structure. Lest we reduce consciousness and free will to the status of delusions or leave subjects isolated within self and/or self-serving communities unaware of their dependence on all of reality, I focus on interrelated selves. As there are many levels of complexity that separate ATGC-U nucleotides from how AIRR ideals per*form*, many reason-faith in-betweens are needed to erect two diphase complementarity-co*opera*tion dialectics between GEM's AIRR ideal levels and its eight functional specialties. Our study of 4-3-5 structures has prepared us to interrelate our AIRR levels and GEM's eight functional specialties.

In mechanics," phase" is the fraction of time required for a point to complete a full cycle after last passing through the reference or zero position. I view diphase GEM as enabling us to extract, as it were, the phase shifts relative to the driving forces of our physical, psychic and ethical states of being. This chapter relates, in two phases, input from those engaged in various *form*s of functional specialization; with GEM, it distinguishes and separates the input as it moves from data to results. Fig.1-4 illustrates a "4-3-5 diphase stance" by using notions of feedback spindles and a trans*form*ative matrix. If a *Gestalt* refers to complex data that require more than sense experience in being perceived, the values one places on various objects can become bases for a personal, social or world ethics. Lonergan distinguishes his method from that of field specialization, which divides and subdivides the field of data, and that of subject specialization, which classifies results of investigation. For him, method is a set of related and recurrent AIRR *oper*ations cumulatively advancing towards an ideal goal. His method of functional specialization involves two phases. There are two reasons for his diphase approach.

First, we read about and assimilate traditions so as to encounter the past. But we do so only to move on to the future. The second reason for two phases stems from the fact that our conscious and intentional *oper*ations occur on four distinct levels and that each level has its own proper achievement and end. The two phases, based on a reduplicative use of our AIRR levels, cover all human activities. In the first phase, GEM explains how humans do research, interpret texts and history or sort out linked but opposed principles. In the second phase, it explores the relational foundations that lead to sound planning and holistic ways of communicating. While Claude Shannon laid the foundations of in*form*ation theory by reproducing at one point either exactly or approximately "a message selected at another point,"[1] GEM lays the foundations of a self-transcendent ethics. If cybernetics foreshadowed complexity theory, 4-3-5 meaning needs a brain-spirit dimension that explores the AIRR in-between boundary regions of 4-2 science and a possible "4-3-5 faith-cybernetics." Gregory Bateson speaks of the "unconscious" algorithms of the heart that transcend the algorithms of language." Since a great deal of conscious thought is structured in terms of the logics of language, the algorithms of the unconscious is doubly inaccessible...The operations of the unconscious are structured in terms of *primary process*" characterized as "lacking negatives, lacking tense,"[2] lacking in any linguistic mood. The discourse of primary process is metaphoric. Bateson's insights coincide with GEM. I transpose his cybernetics into an AIRR-4-3-5 epistemology of a modern wise man who realized that AIRR-consciousness' algorithms are more mysterious *and* relevant than Freud's "4-2 unconscious."

Since the days of Socrates and Jesus, we know that teaching philosophical or religious wisdom is difficult—it can even be a fatal enterprise! In fig. 4, on an analogy of a spiritual genome, first AIRR phase *loci* (AIRR experience-research, interpreting-concepts, judging-history, deciding-dialectic) can be considered as alleles interfacing with other alleles; second RRIA phase *loci* (4-3-5 foundations, policy, systems, communications) "*redefine*" allelic terms and act as "anti-structures" whose job it is to re*form* and trans*form* inadequate structures. Fig. 4 summarizes GEM's 4-3-5 trans*form*ative loci that structurally affect AIRR *opera*tions through metaxies of love implicit in the *opera*tions but made *explicit* in the functional specialties. It maps "equivalence trans*form*ations" between science and such metaxies that seek *sophia*-wisdom—not a *sophi*sm impervious to moral or religious conversion. A spirit philosophy is an art of love that helps us trans*form* one's loving potencies into loving actions. If 4-3-4 mathematics analyzes, GEM posits the trans*form*ative abilities of a diphase 4-3-5 social ethics. Analyzing 4-3-5 phase-bound realities in cells and in our actions, fig. 1-4 rely on the synthetic *opera*tions of group theory; but they ground such a theory in AIRR ideals. If, for Freud, repression was a rational way of "explaining" the unconscious revealed in dreams, GEM's functional specialties (pivoting on notions of AIRR converted consciousness) can help us communicate with all people. Insisting that all thinkers be authentic in seeking to rise above tunnel visions, GEM is open to Deleuze and Guattari's notion of the idiot as well as to the seeker for intellectual truth. Socrates' search for truth is mindful of Job's plight on his dung heap.

GEM considers subjects as dynamic, developing persons faced with the tensions between limitation and transcendence and an unwelcome invasion of consciousness, which, to be genuine, they should acknowledge (*Insight*, 477). In various fields of study, there is a static unity seeking a logical ideal or a rigorous deduction of possible conclusions. GEM stresses a profounder unity based in the dynamic unity of subjects' AIRR *opera*tions. Development is "from an initial state of undifferentiation and specialization towards a goal in which the differentiated specialties function as an integrated unity. . . . The differentiation of operations and objects necessitates a differentiation in the consciousness"[3] of the *opera*ting subject which is then applied in mediating and mediated phases. Fig. 3 compared the trans*form*ative triadic functions in genetics, philosophy and GEM; fig. 4 alludes to, but skirts the issue of GEM's own development. In *Insight*, Lonergan emphasized the first three levels of intentional consciousness as classically *for*mulated in the potency-*form*-act triad. In *Method in Theology*, he re*form*ed *Insight*'s potency-*form*-act triad with his reduplicative AIRR functional specialties schema where act assumes the double role of judgment and action. In devising his diphase-functional specialization approach, he moved beyond, but did not reject this potency-*form*-act triad. Because this triad subsumes all others, it permits to us to handle the differentiating characteristics of human persons physically rooted in codon-anticodon triplets.[4]

Mathematical loci are 4-3-4 systems of points. Genetic loci use spindles in reproducing cells. AIRR loci work within "a spindle" of feedback phases that help us evaluate our inner-and outer-realities and our traditions. GEM feedback of *interrelated* "subjects as subjects" enables AIRR-co*opera*tion among *converted* persons; its allelic diphase boundaries bridge our thoughts, words and deeds so as to avoid bipolar short-circuitings in life—another way of speaking of the AIRR dynamic iso*morph*ism between our minds and reality. Alleles are different *form*s of physical genes; different philosophical *form*s express AIRR allelic *opera*tions common to all humans. AIRR *opera*tions *opera*te on dynamic levels verifiable not only on experiential levels of perceiving and imagining, but also on the intellectual levels of understanding, *form*ulating concepts, weighing the evidence in judging and acting. Each level has its own proper end. Fig. 4 outlines GEM feedback and links AIRR operations to our spiritual genome's higher spiritual faculties.

Deploying AIRR loci functioning as diphase feedback spindle, fig. 4 suggests how we are able to integrate our reflective judgments with right

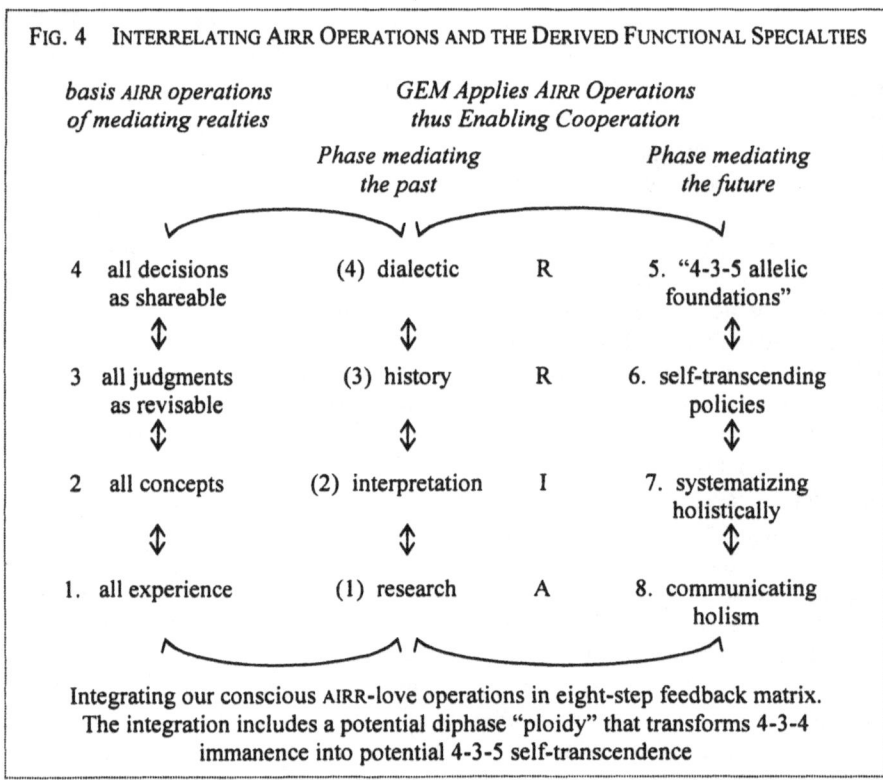

action. It is both a functional and a foundational schema. We appropriate and objectify AIRR *opera*tions in interpersonal and personal feedback. In everyday per-*form*ance, all four AIRR levels are employed continuously without any explicit distinction between them." In that case, no functional specialization arises, for what is sought is not the end of any particular level but the cumulative, composite resultant of the ends of all four levels. But in a scientific investigation the ends proper to particular levels"[5] may become the objective sought by *opera*tions on all four levels. Rather than inquiring into our neural or organic states, GEM grounds AIRR ideals within living contexts. The fourth AIRR level, locus of conversion, has a foundational, bridge-to-infinity role in religious praxis that mediates being-void alleles and fosters ethics. In fig. 4, AIRR stands for series of complex *opera*tions, for *opera*tionally functional specialties verifiable in a 4-3-5 trans*form*ative feedback scheme of ethical judgments and acts. As Zen insists that the habit of action, perception or thought sinks to deeper and deeper levels of the mind, so with Bateson, I consider neatness, boldness of control "as metaphoric and therefore as linked to those levels of the mind where primary process holds sway" (134-35). I am *not* referring to Freudian primary process (repression) but to AIRR algorithms of the heart that our poly*morph*ic minds integrate "allelically." Fig. 4 suggests how the functional specialties integrate decisions and ground a 4-3-5 metaxic feedback that ethically redresses human chaos in ways that respect each person's uniqueness. Its AIRR matrix per*form*s roles analogous to DNA-RNA's amino acid triplets and chromosomes' trans*form*ative abilities. It suggests how diphase GEM has us first convert our inner self before addressing others in viable ethical East-West encounters. Stressing GEM's opposition between self-transcendence and the self as "4-3-5 *transcended*," it maps an AIRR eight-step feedback matrix to "cross-fertilize" cultures. Its "vector arrows" suggest how a subject in *any field* cumulatively assembles and systematically patterns sets of judgments that are revisable through a feedback whose AIRR *ideals can* trans*form* us in mediating and "4-3-5 mediated" phases.

Politics and religion, capitalism and socialism make strange bedfellows; their proponents often clash, but must at times compromise. In dialoguing with the West or with Christianity, the East tends to situate humans within the harmonies of nature. Still, all sides must be ready to tackle new ways of think-ing and acting so as to build a peaceful world. This chapter's two trans*form*ing complementarity-co*opera*tion dialectics apply GEM feedback ability while incorporating holistic Buddhist teachings (fig. 4). Rather than focusing on concepts and words—the *results* of insight—I focus on trans*form*ative insights which give rise to concepts and words. By implicitly accepting the traditional body-mind-spirit triad, GEM views each person as a 4-3-5 socially interacting self caught in a gray, in-between mixture of right and wrong. My survey of the eight specialties limits itself to ethically relating the personal and social self. It suggests that Lonergan's emphasis on potency-*form* act triads in *Insight* and his later functional specialties are analogical to the 4-3-5 structure of our physical genome but affect the 4-3-4 structure of spacetime in which we function.

SECTION ONE

A First Dialectic
Avoiding a 4-2 Brain-Mind Reductionism

I proceed to deploy two dialectics that nuance meta-SAS views from mere

SAS ones; like Stoicism, GEM's trans*form*ative feedback lets us transcend boundaries of race, status or sex by internalizing 4-3-5 virtues. Such virtues motivate our will, which, as Epictetus and Schopenhauer argue, guides our lives. GEM helps convert us into trans*form*ed self-transcendent trans*form*ers.

We are linked to one another in a "total" but not absolute relatedness. Our feedback structure (illustrated in a spirit philosophy and a spiritual topology) allows us to interrelate the invariant manifolds of our AIRR allelic *opera*tional loci within love-nothingness metaxies. Nishida discovered parallel trans*form*ative loci when reflecting on East-West ways of thinking. He and his disciples focus on a holistic approach to reality as expounded in Taoism and Buddhism. I shall relate such an approach to our AIRR ideals so as to integrate the in-betweens of Western logics that accept the principle of non-contradiction with the demands of the psyche that in fact, ignore that principle.

The absolute has no relation to anything, yet the idea of salvation implies "some kind of contact or fusion between the Conditioned and the Unconditioned. This idea is logically untenable,"[6] but *is* embraced by Buddhists for whom difference is the non-difference between yes and no. The truth escapes us when we say "it is" or "it is not"; it lies in a "metaxic in-between" asserting and non-asserting. It reflects an allelic language of men and women who think clearly and act virtuously. DNA-RNA trans*form*ations are due to ATGC-U bases and mitotic-meiotic phases. GEM effects analogical trans*form*ations using two feedback phases in the first of which one encounters the past (Section One). In a second phase (Section Two) persons, enlightened by the past and fortified by love, confront present problems. This chapter's two sections relate our AIRR *opera*tions in a 4-3-5 loci-spindle or a trans*form*ative feedback topology grounded in love-nothingness metaxies.

Postmodernists focus on words. GEM touches on our hearts' ability to face reality. If RNA's catalyzing role is due to its uracil base that replaces DNA's thymine base, GEM helps us solve the riddles of self-absorbed people, of thinkers stuck in 4-2 or 4-3-4 linguistic theories. It differentiates science's functional loci from the AIRR foundational loci that interrelate functional loci by grounding them in-between metaxies reaching for relational love. Cells assemble a *thread-*like spindle as chromatids separate at anaphase and move toward opposite poles in a cell. GEM's feedback spindle allows us to analyze, relate the developmental phases of thinkers and of irrational movements. It enables us to account for and ground personal or societal[7] interchanges by AIRR localizing mental processes within a metaxy. I transpose mathematical and ATGC loci by focusing on in-between AIRR-4-3-5 alleles. As mathematicians define real numbers to include rational and irrational numbers, so we (and the physical, social and moral sciences we devise) contain rational and irrational elements that need mediation. If Gauss refined complex numbers, GEM locates AIRR trans*form*ative loci in metaxies of love or of nothingness that are to be reconciled in an 8-step AIRR-4-3-5 feedback process. I turn to map this eightfold process that like Boulez' music explores the deep resonances of matter not to foster a secular materialism but (on an analogy with Fourier trans*form*s) to test how AIRR invariant ideals may engender a 4-3-5 ethics. I plunge into Deleuze and Guattari's chaotic immanence so as to map a 4-3-5 transcendent alternative that does justice to in-between cultural, psychological, trans*form*ative influences.

Both of this chapter's eight loci begin with an "a)" section that suggests limits to "mere SAS" interpretations; this unsatisfactory stance is followed by a "b)" meta-SAS section based on a 4-3-5 Buddhist-Christian ethics. This procedure will help show that a GEM feedback ethics is open to a transcultural social ethics, to "4-3-5 emptiness." I map a creative love open to a healing-creating scissors' action that moves from data to a universal, meta-sceptical 4-3-5 ethics in touch with material systems. In each of the ensuing summaries of the functional specialties, I first speak of the subject as subject as a person and then of that person as 4-3-5 ethically committed to a Christian (Buddhist) social ethic. Key to the procedure is an "AIRR localizing" of mental processes in the ways explained in this entire book.

1a) *Our Experiences and the Data of Research on the Personal Self*

Psychologists base their theories on observation, but interpret their data differently. Based on his studies of comparative education and anthropology, Erikson used the notion of identity to show that human development involves conscious and unconscious integrations of earlier psychosocial and psycho-spiritual identifications. Postulating eight different developmental stages that humans go through, he studied the crises one may undergo in each of these stages. In the last integrative stage of adulthood, one accepts the fact that one is responsible for one's identity. But, unless one has integrity, one can be led to disgust or despair. Piaget and Kohlberg did analogous studies on the stages of moral development that result from interpersonal interactions and the moral reasoning that lead children to arrive at "fair" solutions.

This agrees with the versatility of our AIRR *opera*tional ideals that can lead to self-seeking, to self-transcendence or to varying mixtures of the two.[8] GEM uses Piaget's insights into how children resolve moral dilemmas. It realizes that humans must assess and reassess inherited standards of development, including moral development. How is it that humans behave in such varied ways? Recall that psychons can be interpreted as entities approximating holist AIRR *opera*tions and lead to a 4-3-5 ethics or fail to do so. Each mental experience is reciprocally linked in a unitary manner to dendrons by way of unit psychons. Psychons are not perceptual paths to experience but holistic potentialities. While our ATGC-U allelic loci are genetic phenomena, AIRR ideals can be shared with others due to the reduplicative feedback nature of the allelic AIRR *opera*tions in self and in others. Heart-to-heart dialogues must be integrated with the in-betweens that may separate us from self or other selves.

1b) *Data on a Meta-SAS Self as Engaged in Society*

As Frechet founded a theory of abstract spaces generalizing traditional definitions of space as a locus for comparing figures, so I argue that the 4-3-4 configuration of spacetime in which we are born and live are a matrix wherein we can reach 4-3-5 ethical certitude in the face of our uncertainties. Pythagoras, Gauss, Riemann, Cantor, Frechet and Einstein have taught us some of spacetime's 4-3-4 properties. Such philosophers as Aristotle, Aquinas, Hegel, Peirce and Deleuze each devised their own *form*s of triadic functions. DNA is trans-*form*ed by 20 amino acid triplets. GEM links its own triads to AIRR ideals, empowering us by having us appropriate our own 4-3-5 structure. In its eightfold functional specialties, it interrelates our 4-3-5 structure in feedback ways to include economics.[9] Overlooking the creative distance presupposed in scientific inquiries, the reductionist "laws" of Comte, Spencer and Summer that would determine our nature are mere 4-2 constructs. In fact, humans can transcend their situation. As Lewis Mumford[10] puts a humane perspective on urban planning, so GEM helps us understand how a self or several selves (even with various culturo-linguistic backgrounds) develop meaning through free interactions. A self or various types of communities interpret data or meanings through ongoing, ethical 4-3-5 feedback.

2a) *Interpreting Meaning and the Limits of Isolated "Subjects as Subjects"*

Lonergan notes how introducing tensor fields and eigen-functions into physics raised barriers between the theoretical physicists, who grasped the mathematics but could not handle laboratory equipment, and the experts in experimental work for whom recondite mathematics is "sheer" mystery. If mathematics provides physicists with a well-defined field of sequences and relations enabling them to anticipate physical theories' general tenure, GEM provides a sketch for a method that hermeneutists can use in "AIRR-interpreting" texts (*Insight*, 579) non-reductively.[11]

Mathematicians are trained to discriminate between logical inferences that are universally true and those that are not. Because our perceptions of the physical world are ultimately private, scientific method subjects our personal experiences to intersubjective agreement. It trains us to abstract from our personal experiences the universal aspects that are independent of the observer. GEM helps us distinguish between the personal elements of spiritual experience and its universal elements by subjecting these experiences to independent verification. Transmitting mathematical or spiritual knowledge depends on a receiver's abilities. Mystics' testimonies seem contradictory; but mathematical-scientific theories can also clash. Dedekind and Cantor revised concepts of continuity with more basic set-theory notions that clarified the principles of mathematical analysis. If Frechet's allowable trans*form*ations built on Riemann and Lebesgue's insights into integrable functions, GEM incorporates the in-between allelic AIRR loci all thinkers use. Today's globalizing crises require new 4-3-5 feedback ways of trans*form*ative AIRR verbs that can mediate our crises.

2b) *The Social "Meta-SAS Self" as Related to Other Persons and to all of Reality*

Some label Lonergan's method a "transcendental Thomism," but Lonergan insisted that GEM (as verb, not as noun) dynamically transcends Thomism; it counters Kant's de-facto dualism by heightening a self's awareness as conscious of thoughts and objects—a cognizance that involves a perceived unity of one's own awareness with surrounding objects in what one might call an immediate sense of a quasi-physical unity between self, objects and other people. It stresses that an "interiorized self, able to de-intensify emotional attachments," is subject to the epistemological conditions involved in all facets of human life. Meaning mediates the mediator to self and there arises a nuanced meaning of feedback self-mediation as well as interpersonal mediation. Meaning regards a universal; yet, most human speech or action is concerned with the particular and the concrete. While there are structural and material invariants to meaning, there "also are changes that affect the manner in which the carriers of meaning are employed, the elements of meaning are combined, the functions of meaning are distinguished and developed, the realms of meaning are extended."[12] In a fully differentiated consciousness there are four realms of meaning, the first of which is the realm of common sense with its meanings expressed in everyday language. In a second realm, that of theory, language is technical, objective in reference; it refers to the subject and his/her *opera*tions only as objects. In a third realm, that of interiority, language also speaks of the subject and his *opera*tions as objects, but this time, language rests upon a self-appropriation that has *verified* in personal experience the *opera*tor, the *opera*tions and the processes referred to in the basic terms and relation of the language employed. In a fourth realm of transcendence," the subject is related to divinity in the language of prayer and of prayerful silence" (*Method*, 257).

GEM's four genetic horizons and realms of meaning overcome the problem of something arbitrarily signifying what a given individual may choose it to "mean." The cognitive function of culture moves into the third stage of meaning in which consciousness grounds both common sense and theory in the realm of interiority that is in "a transforming immanence of the transcendent."[13] Nevertheless, stages of meaning are often resisted; this leads to ideological warfare or to collapse.

Getting to the roots of our 4-3-5 structured spiritual genome helps us bridge East-West differences. Various triads proposed by philosophers or social scientists reveal how poly*morph*ic our consciousness is. As physical genomes depend on the mediation of triadic genetic codes, so GEM artists use their AIRR *opera*tions in ways that reflect but transcend the private nature of our personal perceptions. GEM integrates spirituality rather than reducing knowledge to a brain-mind interaction. In both spirituality and science, a personal component does play an interpretative role whereby one integrates common sense and perceptions within a larger framework of a received tradition as mediated by peers. A 4-3-5 spiritual topology uses AIRR knowing-doing *opera*tions common to all humans. Mathematicians use symbols and words to communicate their insights to others, but underlying the insights is our 4-3-5 structure. Lest it be mistaken for individualism, I argue that the SAS *of itself* is not a sufficient ground for erecting a social ethics, for engaging in interdisciplinary studies or for carrying on interfaith dialogue. Culturo-spatial separations have led East and West to develop variant, allelic versions of philosophy and religion. Traditionally, Asians and Africans have opposed individualism, preferring to sub-ordinate self to the greater community. Focusing too much on a self-centered, self-sufficient person has led to many contemporary identity crises. A trans*form*ative Buddhist-Christian ethics' metaxy links East and West with 4-3-5 ideals. While some GEM experts focus on its "explanatory abilities" or the subject as subject (SAS) as a sufficient ground for interpreting GEM's originality, I argue that philosophy and science can be best empowered by GEM artists who build mystical and ethical bridges. How can historians (3a) help social ethicists and GEM purists adjudicate meanings in reflective meta-SAS feedback ways? (3b)

3a) *East-West Historical Contexts on the Self and Reflective Judgments*

If chemists were long unable to analyze DNA molecules' immense size and complexity, or if mathematicians had to wait for Newton's analytical dynamics to understand the roles of *form*s and *opera*tors as ordered sets, GEM studies analysis before moving into the judgments that posit synthesis. It ethically evaluates system analyses of the type pursued in *opera*tions research, which builds a two-part model for each system under study. Such a model consists of an equation in which the appropriate measure of system per*form*ance is a function of the system's uncontrolled and controlled variables and of a *form*ulation of the constraints within which controlled variables can be manipulated. Different systems can serve as analogues for other systems. Diphase GEM is not a two-part model for physically controlling systems; rather, it integrates deductive reasoning by positing syntheses based on trans*form*ative feedback in ways that are analogous to Bion's grids.

For GEM, the premises for a concrete deduction must be both synthetic and a priori. They must be synthetic for, of themselves, mathematics' analytic propositions lack relevance since they regard all possible worlds. They involve the a priori of insight since every insight is an a priori that follows upon another insight to correct and complement its predecessor. Only the synthetic a priori premises of a mind that does not look upon nature as if in a mirror can per*form* concrete AIRR deductions; the mind processes materials supplied by outer and inner sense into appropriate syntheses. GEM is a series of concrete deductions, none of which is certain but reflects the best currently available scientific opinion. The mind is not a factory with a set of fixed processes; it is a "universal machine tool that erects all kinds of factories, keeps adjusting and improving them, and eventually scraps them" (*Insight*, 405-06) in favour of a better design. The basic concepts about the structures of reality reside in a subject. Concepts issue from insights; insights stem from questions.

GEM approaches "history"[14] and the judgments that historians make by noting what is peculiar to human relationships. Oriented toward concrete situations, we use our invariant, yet trans*form*ative AIRR structure to get us through the day. Historians are concerned about knowing what many people did to create "history." The word "history" is used in two senses, the history that is written about and the history that is written. The latter seeks to express knowledge of the former. The difficulty of writing history lies in the fact that few people possess a "satisfactory cognitional theory."[15] Writing history and accounting for the incarnations of knowledge thus coincide in that writing history also involves knowing what knowledge is and how one comes to understand and know. For GEM, human knowing is not just experiencing but involves the triad of experiencing, understanding, and judging. Our immanent structure of recurring *opera*tions is also the heuristic source of how historians proceed to understand history. Their insights do not differ from the insights of those engaged in the physical sciences for both arrive at acts of understanding that are antecedent to the propositions, words and concepts they use to express the content of events. But historians and scientists express their respective sets of discoveries differently. In history, verification is "parallel to the procedures by which an interpretation is judged correct."[16]

Historians' discoveries are expressed in narratives that regard particular persons, places, and times; they make no claim to universality. They can help us trans*form* the future if we can link historic East-West insights. Scientists study universal systems that can be refuted by contrary evidence; they remain on the level of invariant expressions that abstract from concrete extensions and durations which each person views differently. I turn from an SAS who correctly understands history to the standpoint of a Buddhist-Christian ethics and of meta-SAS communities willing to advance AIRR ways to peace in the face of conflicting values in 4-3-5 faith and 4-2 globalization.[17]

3b) *Interacting "Meta-SAS" Selves in an East-West Dialogue*

Questions have birthdates, parented by answers to previous generations of questions. The "so-called *raw* data are already shaped by the questions that occur to an inquirer. These questions, in turn, contain clues to their answers insofar as the insight we expect is related"[18] to the kind of expected judgment. It could be a logical conclusion, a judgment of fact or of value, or a judgment that an explanation is correct. The roots of such judgments are based on individual inquirers' insights; yet, all inquirers depend on a *community* of inquirers. Science is an ongoing process that moves from subjective judgments to community verification. The verification process was born with the type of wonder exemplified by Thales' falling into a well when gazing at the stars. GEM asks why we wonder; it evaluates the results. It explicates this wondering process' potency-*form*-act triads that move from experience to understanding to judgment and results in a knowledge iso*morph*ic to how we know. The community of inquirers' methodology rewards those who ask the right questions and who can verify their hypotheses. Asking the right questions and making right judgments is a latent ability that the community of inquirers authenticates. The larger society then AIRR decides whether a particular discovery has merits for the greater good of humanity.

Psychologists focus on the self; social scientists study the social self. Empowering science and philosophy means integrating sociocultural views on persons, societies and development. An intentional self is situated in socio-cultural worlds through its orientations as a perspective on these worlds but this self and its perspectives cannot be reduced to 4-2 structures. On the level of theory, I study how the data on interacting selves can lead to understanding our global village's problems so as to erect a viable social ethics. GEM's radical notion of the subjective meaning of the social world helps us get beyond 4-2 reactive meaning. If a physical genome's triadic amino acids' interplay is constrained by chemical laws, on the intellectual level we are free to develop various theories on how a spiritual genome might work. Such a genome is based on a reflective self-transcending social self as related to other persons and all of reality; a danger is that a subject or self remains isolated within the constructs of one's self image. We interrelate intercultural and interfaith values by relating persons of one culture or given milieu with their counterparts in other cultures or milieux. In so doing, we address reductionist ideologies with GEM's 4-3-5 structured feedback that allows us to build a broadly conceived spiritual world ethics. Spiritual blindness is worse than physical blindness.[19] Structurally, we function with the allelic in-betweens of faith and reason, good and evil, our ideals and life's "realities." Functionally, we *ope*ra*te* with a potential 4-3-5 ability that works analogously to how mathematicians order our 4-3-4 spacetime limitations within potential infinity. This involves mind's "subjective nature." In GEM, intelligibility and *form* correspond to what scientists call the "nature of" which includes the subjective side of our minds and its metaphysical and epistemological implications which 4-2 reductionists overlook or distort.

The trans*form*ative power of our minds is mediated through other persons. Mind and body function best within a healthy spirit. GEM locates trans*form*ative ideals in the 4-3-5 structured verbs that function as dynamic in-betweens linking our minds' synthetic and analytic abilities with the concrete reality of our daily lives. As spiritual templates, such "ideal AIRR verbs," help us grasp how mathematicians go beyond analysis to "reach out for the infinite." Mathematicians excel in analysis, but it takes physicists to synthesize their analyses and *apply* them. I contextualize GEM artistry lest we mechanize spirit along the line of how science seeks to mechanize the universe. GEM ethical artists such as Pasteur and Einstein pioneered ways of understanding the complexity of life and of the universe without trying to mechanize either; their scientific work was not divorced from the ideals of a trans*form*ative ethic. Since our physical and spiritual genomes have 4-3-5 structures, I argue that "your 4-3-4 spacetime relatedness" to the universe encounters "my 4-3-4 spacetime relatedness." Such encounters should not neglect our ideal AIRR-4-3-5 feedback structures that *can* be used in co*opera*tive ways—or be reduced to mechanizing 4-2 structures.

GEM's ethics is built upon its basic metaphysical elements. The *goodness* of the universe and its potency for higher systems lies partly in its AIRR potential for more intelligible organization. Physicists follow the simple rule that an X either exists or does not exist. Ethicians study how humans, endowed with the universal potency for higher (trans*form*ative) *form*s, can make value judgments that go beyond such a simple rule and ask whether a thing should or should not exist. To recognize that the universe produces normative acts of consciousness is to recognize that it is more than a massive factual conglomeration: it is a self-organizing, dynamic and *improving entity* whose moral character emerges most clearly when we raise moral objections, when we 4-3-5 anticipate that any existing thing may potentially be part of something better, or sadly, when we act "against our better judgment."[20] GEM's notion of human development has us strive for the ideal of genuineness without being "idealist." GEM helps us integrate the various levels of ethics with spirituality—which is another way of restating how our metaxic feedback structure works. Its notion of integration within human development and of the integrator that effects the integration is the key that enables us to go beyond the analytic procedures of *opera*tor theory and *opera*tions research and to *posit* synthesis. I have used a poetry of verbs and a 4-3-5 topology to approach judgments that *posit* synthesis. Within such a topology, the integrators and *opera*tors at work within genetic method (the laws of human development) deal with emergent trends. Emergent probability is an *opera*tor. God's love is a quasi-*opera*tor that alters laws to which we are subject. GEM, aware of *opera*tors' incompleteness helps us integrate God's love with 4-3-5 ideals, that is it helps us struggle against prejudiced biases and act responsibly in alleviating the needs of others.

Scott Peck's *The Road Less Travelled* is an encomium on love, an ideal which he admitted he did not always live up to. GEM helps us seek God's love so that we may offset human fallibility. It seeks the dynamic in-betweens in*form*ing theory and practice so as to mediate life's difficulties.

A narcissistic focus on self or one's limited group creates more problems than it solves. To place the self within larger contexts, Gibson Winter opposed a privatizing ethics. Synthesizing the views of G. H. Mead and Alfred Schutz, his social ethics is based on the origin of meaning. Mead had *form*ulated the problem of the emergence of mind in society by delving into what constitutes a *triadic* bridge between the self as "I" and "me." Schutz had analyzed Max Weber's views on the methodological foundation of the social sciences and concluded that Weber failed to distinguish between an action in progress "and the completed act, between the meaning of the producer of a cultural object and my own action, and the meaning of another's action." Nor had Weber tried to identify the unique, fundamental relation existing between a self and other selves. The clarification of that relation is essential to a precise understanding of what it is to know another person within "lived relations." Schutz insists that we must ask how an actor's meaning is constituted and what modifications such a meaning undergoes both for his partners in the social world and for a non-participating observer. He found Weber's basic concept of *Sinn* to be ambivalent because it was not distinctive enough of human action, as opposed to a mere reactive understanding (*Verstehen*).

Acts of reflection are important for they let us properly distance ourselves. Only through acts of reflective turning-toward (*Zuwendung*) do our experiences attain meaning (*Sinn*); such acts allow an experience to be "lifted out"[21] of the stream of duration so as to become a clear and distinct entity. Schutz turned to Husserl for a consistent theory of meaning, to Heidegger's notion of project of the action and to Bergson's stream of consciousness. This enabled him to explain why Weber did not have a radical enough notion of our intentional consciousness as creative reality.

Like Lonergan, who enlarged his earlier version of potency-*form*-act, Winter implicitly uses a 4-3-5 structure to adapt the four styles of social science to reorder Mead's triadic scheme.[22] He interprets selves in contexts of caring selves. Being aware of the not-self, is an awareness of the other. Winter also helps us free the human sciences from behaviourist, functionalist and voluntarist styles. He safeguards the ethical bases of society by critiquing the four styles in the light of his revised triadic scheme to yield another instance of a 4-3-5 approach to a social self. A properly radical notion of the subjective meaning of the social world sets limits to a science of that world; it transcends a privatized "SAS ethics" by elevating it to the social level. In Winter's steps, I seek to empower ethics with a Buddhist-Christian feedback model. For Winter, the intentional self is situated in social and "cultural worlds through its orientations as a perspective on these worlds." Such a perspective cannot be subsumed under such worlds' structures even though the conditions and possibilities "open to that perspective can be detailed through these structures."[23] Role structures define the *situation* of the "I", not the "I" itself. The data of interacting selves are not ends in themselves but supply meaning for ethical actions; such data are a first level for reflection.

To judge correctly or to write history properly, one has to clarify how acts of turning-toward (*Zuwendung*) allow one to know (or empower) a person. As in the sociology of knowledge, one moves from a static social dependency of truth to a dynamic, relational (non-4-2-relativist) one.

GEM's ascent through a cognitional theory and an epistemology to objectivity opens up vistas for co*opera*tive endeavours through its reduplicative AIRR feedback method. There are many ways to interrelate the various social orders that our poly*morph*ic consciousness allows us to erect. A spiritual genome's in-between allelic loci allow us to interrelate psychologies and their cultural expressions and to critique political establishments. While some maintain that even physical reality, like social reality, is a linguistic construct, GEM locates the constructs of an ever-revisable language in our trans*form*ative *opera*tions. Our minds are confronted with endless varieties of in-betweens. GEM's iso*morph*ism of knowing and known implies 4-3-5 trans*form*ative feedback that lets Mead, Winter and Levinas' views of self and alterity be guided by an *il y a* realist ethics.

GEM helps us reconcile our subjectivity within an objective, ongoing feedback that bridges the gaps of history. It invokes the *opera*tions underlying the virtually unconditioned behaviourists use. Eugene Ehrlich recognized two complementary sources in law, that of legal history that studies useful precedents and that of "living law" embodied in current social custom.[24] If his sociology of law studied social contexts, diphase GEM's foundational ethics transposes traditional values without changing the basic thrust of ancient wisdom. It trans-poses the illusions of self-sufficiency by situating us in the "real" world. In con-fronting the longer cycle of decline or the shorter cycle of group bias (*Insight*, 222-25), we must 4-3-5 assess which traditions lead to progress or decline.

The economically or politically powerful elites have their ways of enforcing their views. In the light of this, activist groups, NGO's and other far-seeing advocates seek to make a difference. They seek to find the ways that can move us from the *status quo* to trans*form*ative judgments that interrelate all persons for the common good and the survival of the planet. The in-betweens of a 4-3-5 spiritual topology seek to relate such trans*form*ative judgments in feedback ways to all four AIRR *opera*tions and the functional specialties they generate. Part One proposed feedback spindles, trans*form*ative matrices and a spiritual topology that help us parley heart-to-heart intimacy into sensibilities able and willing to reach out to society's larger needs. Part Two is a spindle feedback attempt to interrelate our 4-3-5 ethical concerns with our minds' data. It seeks to interweave the in-betweens of philosophy, mathematics and AIRR ideals that I identified in Part One. This chapter interrelates "GEM-converted subjects" with "non-converted ones" within the larger dimensions of intercultural realities. In doing so, there arise such problems as private gain versus the common good. Just as virtuoso's abilities often depends on adapting his/her virtuosity to fellow musicians, so GEM depends on our converting our AIRR *opera*tions and blending them with those of others.

Interrelating AIRR *opera*tions within a given community, culture or religion is complicated. Doing so in intercultural and interfaith contexts complexifies the issue. But only in this way, can we truly relate GEM's subject as subject (SAS) to persons in other cultures or faiths. In *Insight*, Lonergan emphasized the potency-*form*-act triad at the expense of the fourth level of intentional consciousness; the "later Lonergan" makes decisions taken with others and for the good of others pivotal to his 4-3-5 feedback functional specialties. A meta-SAS reaches out to the needy and the dispossessed as well as to those in power. Prioritizing a self-transcendent ethics for society, GEM helps us establish new interdisciplinary, intercultural, interfaith, trans*form*ative self perceptions. Its invariant structure addresses the variants of cultural meanings by keeping the allelic in-betweens of judgments of fact and of value in trans*form*ative equilibrium in conducting its AIRR dialectic.

4a) *A Spiritual Self and a Dialectic of Workable Decisions and Ideals*

Dialectic guides us in acting responsibly despite conflicts." Am I my brother's keeper?" may imply that persons cannot act responsibly unless their groups do so. Addressing tensions between our egocentric-sociocentric drives, this dialectic section lets conscience and our primary knowing-doing structures in*form* our secondary linguistic structures. It *recenters* reductionisms *within* a world nexus. As *utopia*s ("no place") are unattainable, Nietzsche's voluntarist bravado[25] opts for belonging on a *limited* scale. GEM is not an idealist utopia; it is not soft on deceit or lies. It seeks *reform* by trans*form*ing notions of self-serving entities. Are laudable ideals such as a federated world workable? Is GEM's notion of ethically co*operat*ing groups realistic? If codon triplets code 4-3-5 physical processes, GEM frees us with liberating trans*form*ative *loci* that work analogously to how DNA-RNA triads code the processes of life." 4-3-5-enabled AIRR *opera*tions" help us link the phase boundaries of spirituality and ethics with those of science. Conversely, 4-2 brain-mind reductionisms overlook the spirit dimension in*form*ing cognition; AIRR loci sublate the expressions they give rise to by instantiating personal and interpersonal 4-3-5 feedback. One's AIRR *opera*tions *opera*te internally and interface with other persons' AIRR *opera*tions. To "4-3-5 appropriate" one's self-transcendent spiritual genome, one must strive after ethical ideals. Too many people leave the spiritual dimension in abeyance as they *opera*te on 4-2 levels. Without a metaxy of love, we reduce life to 4-2 mind dualisms. This book's DNA-RNA approach seeks to "unfold" the trans*form*ative aspects of our twin genomes that can lead to a 4-3-5 appropriation.

For Deleuze and Guattari, concepts overlap and involve a threshold of indiscernibility with other concepts which reach to infinity and render components inseparable. I trans*form* their view with GEM's experiencing-understanding-judging triad which, being immanently open to the "hidden" transcendent, enables to reach out to others. If a conceptual geophilosophy fails to relate the inner person to the outer; a spirit topology is open to mystical reality. Geographic in*form*ation systems use topology's three basic components of connectivity, containment and contiguity. Using such components in a "topology" guided by AIRR loci's defining boundaries enables our inside to be contingent to outside realities; it 4-3-5 links us to God and others. If there are methods for computing the inverse of a matrix, a spirit topology devises the inverse of a geophilosophy that cuts us off from God; it lets a metaxy of interrelated love connect us to being and to the "void."

What are the dialectical implications of an East-West encounter that can enrich all by re*form*ing narcissist selves? A GEM feedback spindle does not pull persons to a spindle's pole, but leaves them free to per*form* self-transcendent actions—influenced by God's grace.[26] GEM lets a self-transcendent person be partly AIRR-dependent on the self-transcendence of other selves in solidarity with nature as understood in many Eastern philosophies. Respecting our freedom, it has persons interact in self-transcendent ways. It gets us beyond a mere *passive* appropriation of our AIRR oper*at*ions by having us activate the allelic ethics implied in the fifth conscious intentional ideal of "being in love." We move from experience to understanding, from growing understanding to balanced judgment," from balanced judgment to fruitful courses of action, and from fruitful courses of action" to new situations open to an eye of love. Such a loving situation calls forth further understanding, deeper judgment, richer courses of action"[27] and serves as a foundational pivot for GEM's mediated phase. In both of our genomes, the respective ATGC-AIRR analogues are trans*form*ed by their fifth ideal ATGC-U or AIRR-love parallels. As we go through psychic or turf battles so as to live ethically, we need ideals. GEM stresses AIRR ideals of conversion without which one cannot properly understand reality or other religions. I now turn to consider how Eastern ethical and/or "mystic" philosophies situate a subject (SAS) within larger socio-communal frameworks dependent upon nature—a view based on persons' ethically in*form*ed AIRR ideals.

4b) *A Buddhist-Christian "Meta-SAS Ethics": Decisions Made for the Good of All*

Because there are basic conflicts that stem from opposed cognitional theories and/or ethico-religious outlooks, GEM uses dialectic to bring the conflicts to light so as to resolve them.

I appeal to the ideals and ethics of Buddhist-Christian-Taoist-Confucian metaxies. Taoism, Confucianism and Buddhism have influenced one another but their mutual relations are complicated. The three have tended to make Asians less individualistic than Westerners. When introduced in China, Buddhism was confused with Taoism. Confucianism, like Taoism, has a notion of *Tao* as Heaven's Way on which humans should model themselves.[28] Disenchanted with a hereditary nobility's corruption, Confucius advocated the ideal of a virtuous king. Idealizing the Chou dynasty's claim of a "mandate from heaven," he and Mencius stressed a virtuous life based on human perfectibility as embodied in benevolence (*jen*). Adding a touch of elegance to *jen*, decorum (*li*) helped reinvigorate an older tradition, which had become corrupt and *form*alized. Confucianists subject the self to the five hierarchic relationships of ruler-subject, husband-wife, father-son, elder brother-younger brother, friend-friend so as to rear ideal men. A meta-SAS self is a world citizen integrated in his/her community and who respects others and the ways of nature.

In Japan, neo-Confucianists tended to reduce Confucianism to a simple moral code grafted onto a monistic Shinto. Before the Meiji era that led to Japan's modernization, Japanese had partitioned human relations into a triad comprising one's circle of intimates, those to whom one is obligated and those with whom is one unrelated and can therefore be neglected or excluded from one's concerns. If such an attitude helped Japan "make it" in the world, it has also led to *forms* of pathology in the Japanese psyche that finds it hard to accept a realm of the "public." Because Confucianist hierarchic principles tend to clash with new notions of freedom imported from the West and because many Japanese tend to "lack a self," the Imperial system helps the Japanese retain their sense of national unity by serving as a rallying point for notions of a common good. Westerners often say "that when a Japanese says anyone is insincere, he means only that the other person doesn't agree with him. There is a certain truth in this, for calling a man 'sincere' in Japan has no reference to whether he is acting" upon the love, hate or amazement which is uppermost in his heart. It does not always mean avoiding hypocrisy as in the West. Rather, it "is what makes it stick."[29] The "it" refers to any precept of the Japanese code or attitude stipulated in the Japanese Spirit. Japanese put their *whole being* into action. Like the Sufis' quest for *batin* (inner meaning of the *Koran*) or the impressionists' broken colours that force the viewer to look *at* the painting and its surface patterns rather than "through" the canvas, wholeheartedness in our actions is an ideal.

East-West encounters must address such ethico-sociological realities. Eastern religious philosophies have traditionally been more holistic than Western ones. Western secularism, in its academic and political incarnations, keeps religion at arm's length although meditation such as Zen is viewed as "non-sectarian." Within the past century, ecumenical and interfaith relations have moved from confrontation to dialogue; still, religious pluralism can only go so far. A spiritual topology tries to find a way between the universal claims and unique embodiments of a religion by offsetting modern relativism and traditional suspicion of religious competitors with allelic faith-reason. GEM's dialectal-foundational ability integrates spirituality with the rest of our lives. Its 4-3-5 feedback structure opposes a 4-2 brain-mind reductionism that impoverishes humans by diminishing their spirit. I turn to a second GEM dialectic that empowers spirits in the world *if* they base their lives on a coo*pera*tive ethics that (at least implicitly) seeks to implement 4-3-5 ideals.

SECTION TWO

A Second Non-Reductionist Dialectic to Empower Spirits in the World

Our first dialectic was based on the ways our AIRR *opera*tions complement one another in feedback fashion. We can now apply this feedback in non-reductive ways to learn how East and West can complement one another in erecting a coo*pera*tive social ethic for the greater good of all. GEM spiritual artists can "make a difference" in empowering philosophy and science by cross-fertilizing East-West ways of thinking. GEM does not disdain elusive ideals." Elude" means to avoid or escape from by cunning, daring or artifice; "elusive" means *tending* to elude one's perception or mental grasp. GEM does *not elude*; rather, in the "*loci* we call heart, character or spirit, it *finds pivots* that do not seek escape. Such *loci*, rooted in our AIRR-*opera*tions and in love, are *elusive* but retrievable realities that—*analogously* to ATGC-U bases—unify our inner and outer lives. I seek to show how GEM loci's trans*form*ative ability, integrated through the virtual conditioned of judgment, can empower Deleuze and Guattari's "chaos" and their virtual through co*opera*tive feedback not only among East-West philosophers but among all persons opened to the inner promptings of their spirit and to the signs of spiritual life in others. The pluses, minuses of parochial and provincial allelic in-betweens are only partial ("dialectical") embodiments of in-between Kingdom values being realized in the give and take of everyday life. GEM is a supra-catalyst that trans*form*s its practitioners. In reaching the boundaries between the outside and inside, we must also come to terms with the power of emotions and feelings, with the reality of the experiential self as Nishida and Lonergan did. The road to being and "being-as-an-interrelated void" brings us face to face with some central 4-3-5 insights of Eastern and Western philosophies.

5a) *Foundations for a Morally Converted Buddhist-Christian "Trans-self Self"*[30]

I seek to link some central insights of world philosophies and ethics in 4-3-5 foundations. Part Two's feedback spindle interrelates these foundations with transposed cultural matrices that are grounded in our invariant AIRR operations' allelic, creative ability to ceaselessly adapt themselves. Jesus' parables have blinded the minds and hearts of people who refuse the 4-3-5 nature of the parables' piercing challenge. This paradox is alive today and must be faced in the light of a world divided between secularists and various religious orthodoxies unable to find in-between wisdom.

Concretely locating our spiritual genome in the four transcendental imperatives (chapter 2) was the first step in my attempt to combat 4-2 reductionisms that ignore or misunderstand the reality of *spirit*. A 4-3-5 spiritual topology was a second step suggesting that a poetic notion of holding the universe in one's hand is a verb, *not* a noun. Verbs are a way of expressing the body-mind-spirituality triad that distinguishes humans from animals; our (4-3-5) triadic dynamism links us with one another and with all reality. Faith, an irreducibly personal source of authenticity, is to be shared with others. A problem is that faith depends on how the allelic trans*form*ational loci of our AIRR *opera*tions interpret written texts' revelation. Just as the beat-hip generation read into the writings of Sagan or Kerouac, so believers can read into sacred texts. Be it in intrafaith or in interfaith pursuits, God is "involved." Yet, beliefs often set up barriers for they are confessional ways of expressing doctrines and dogmas of a particular religion. GEM integrates beliefs within the larger frame of reference of intrafaith-interfaith realities. Buddhism and Christianity both see humility as needed in confronting evil. We learn to be at peace when we humbly "cross-fer-tilize" the in-betweens of a 4-3-5 "love-void" metaxy, when we begin to realize that happiness depends on being alert to our basic insights, on virtuously sharing and on an ability to forgive. Those with criminal records are ever more exposed to life's vicious circles. On a world governmental level, it is necessary to move toward a world federalism and a 4-3-5 world spirituality to build real peace.

Sensory perceptions do not create our world; they can usher us into a 4-3-5 spirituality. Plato had rejected the pre-Socratic views of such philosophers as Democritus who argued that nature was governed by its own laws independent of any extrinsic power or divine plan. If Augustine held that that God's actions in the created world participated in the eternal realm of God's Ideas (akin to the Neoplatonic doctrine of a World Soul that transmits intelligibility to the earthly plane), a love-nothingness metaxy adapts both Gauss' insights into complex numbers and Nishida's "nothingness-locus." While Augustine and Gauss trans*form*atively revised Plato's cave metaphor to devise foundations for Christianity and mathematics, Nishida and GEM rely on foundational 4-3-5 ideals that do not separate the physical, mental and spiritual areas of our lives. GEM helps us reunite these areas by integrating elements of Platonic, Christian, Buddhist and Nishidan 4-3-5 metaxies. If physical allelic loci determine inheritance, spiritual allelic loci allow for East-West integrations because expressions such as nothingness or "emptying the self" need not be precisely equivalent, or even precise. They are not primarily instruments of reason but ways to convert reason into realization. One step beyond such terms as "nothingness" or "void" is understanding what they really mean. As pedagogical devices for effecting trans*form*ations of knowledge, they stand "between all the contrarieties of the world and a possible release"[31] from 4-2 worlds. A 4-3-5 in-between metaxy responds to nuances of thought, imagination, diplomacy or holiness to address ordinary people's needs. In seeking to live up to 4-3-5 ideals, we come to grips with our interrelatedness. AIRR verbs (dynamic in-between trans*form*ative loci) dialectically link our minds' analytical-synthetic abilities. They invite us to "4-3-5 trans*form*" our poly*morph*ic consciousness into one that iso*morph*ically knows reality, but ethically confronts evil and sin.[32]

Each person views concrete durations and extensions differently. Still, one's AIRR(-4-3-5) *opera*tions can assess the past's concrete deeds so as to trans*form* the future. Ideals call us to act bravely or even heroically, but GEM realism knows that humans are in need of conversion. The difficulties of ethical co*oper*ation are illustrated in the failures of many Christians and Buddhists to resist fascism or communism. GEM transcends our dualisms with such trans*form*ative ideals as guided Einstein's life. Einstein used trans*form*ative tensors when he applied mathematics to the problem of gravitation in his general theory of relativity. Just as Nishida and Einstein located their discoveries in loci (those of Eastern experience or of Gaussian-Riemannian mathematics) so in this section on foundations, I probe further into love-nothingness metaxies' 4-3-5 trans*form*ative loci. Can our brainwaves' quantum dynamic processes be related to such metaxies? As fig. 2 proposed an analogy between the trans*form*ative loci *opera*tive in ATGC-U and in a love metaxy (each of which involves a physical or spiritual spindle) so this section seeks to outline the foundations for the 4-3-5 trans*form*ative loci that can lead to ethical co*opera*tion. Play, recreation, dreams, art (aesthetics) and prayer are all essential to constituting a genuine person. Just as DNA replication and the segregation of chromosomes into two nuclei involve such processes as the building of microtubular centromeres and chromatin, so spiritual allelic loci involve a type of 4-3-5 spiritual spindle that spiritual guides — concerned with mystic prayer[33] and contemplation—call a symbolism built deep into our psychology. Such a symbolism is intrinsic to foundations and is dialectically processed in the workings of linked but opposed principles and in conversion. Thus, ethics, a 4-3-5 spirituality and philosophy all converge in explaining what makes integrated persons "tick."

Choosing our spiritual leaders or religious affiliation requires a personal commitment and faith. Theories of mind are challenged to meet the demands of an ethical faith. Some reject theistic interpretations, but remain ethically committed. GEM probes reason-faith's ethical 4-3-5 allelic foundations which it dialectically interrelates with conscious intentionality's AIRR levels through its detailed guidance for the co*opera*tive effort of those who specialize in one of the eight functional specialties. It helps us trans*form* ourselves in and through the mediation of God and of others. Its foundational feedback works analogously to interacting sets of DNA-RNA ATGC-U nucleotides. Love begets love; conversion invites conversion. The effects of bias, evil, delusion or sin abide; spiritual guides stress our need to be recollected amidst life's distractions. Prayer is a 4-3-5 spiritual way of dealing with our many limitations, leading to conversion. If for Bloy (mentor to such converts as Maritain and Rouault) mystic love is a devouring fire, I hold that a 4-3-5 love guides interrelated Buddhist-Christian trans-self selves able and willing to overcome selfishness.

For Wayne Proudfoot, Schleiermacher's claim that religious experience is independent of concepts and beliefs was "a protective strategy" to preclude conflict between religious beliefs and science.[34] Steven Katz, a linguistic constructivist, claims that no experience is untouched by one's culture and beliefs. A mystic experiences mystic reality in terms of Jesus, the Trinity, or a personal God, not "in terms of the non-personal, non-everything,"[35] (*nirvana*). Others view the core of mystical experience as universal and transcending language, culture or beliefs. GEM helps us relate East-West mysticisms by objectifying mystic experiences. It *form*ulates insights into such experiences' contents in ways that escape constructivist critiques. Far from claiming that religious experience is independent of concepts or beliefs, it *links* these with our experience and judgments.

Mystics of many faiths are helped by the integrating *Gestalt* of medi-tation's simplified mental activity that slows down our thinking process but in-tensifies consciousness. An interior stillness abides as one returns to daily activity. Meditators, little heedful of bodily sensations or of daydreams, focus on inward silence. Brainwave patterns (discernible in meditative or active states) *form* a continuum with one another and other electromagnetic waves. Whether or not alpha, beta, theta and delta brainwave patterns can "locate" love's trans*form*ing loci, patterns of experience are an organizing *Gestalt* in need of an ethics. (To rebut arguments for a human inner-outer dualism, a 4-3-5 spiritual feedback matrix relates brainwave patterns to changes in perceptual objects).

For GEM, our pre-linguistic relationship with God becomes explicitly known in mystical experience. This knowledge is immediate in that we do not make God or ourselves an object of knowing in the ordinary way. Objectifying religious experience (and deepening James' study of this topic) can address claims that mysticism is an essentialist, universal construct[36] GEM helps us identify what is common to mystical experience; it delves into what occurs in the trans*form*ative experiences of *nada* (St. John of the Cross), *via negativa* ("letting go" as in Eckhart's *Gelassenheit*) or the Zen Buddhist *void* in which the mind, emptied of particular objects or images, reaches undifferentiated unity. In foundations, it objectifies religious experience's AIRR loci. Its philosophic language respects the traditions of world religions even as it integrates them in a love-nothingness metaxy.

Zen has remained faithful to the central Buddhist insight that one should not lose valuable time trying to answer unanswerable questions. Unless one attains meditative enlightenment, one is in the existential predicament of being ignorant of the causes of suffering. Japanese exponents of Zen, such as D. T. Suzuki and Abe Masao, have viewed Buddhism differently in addressing Japanese and Western audiences. In the West, Suzuki promoted a personalist, mystical view of enlightenment in which one becomes conscious of the cosmic unconscious and overcomes contradictions through an "unconscious" self-knowledge unable to discriminate or judge. But he failed to reconcile Zen enlightenment with Christians' stress on the reality of evil. To Japanese, he appealed to a native simple faith that still persists despite globalization. Many characters who appear in his Japanese books speak of enlightenment using such phrases as "let things be as they are" or "let others do as they please." This *differs* from enlightened consciousness in Christianity where one self-consciously stands before the Almighty as a responsible person.[37] In Japan, one denies such a spiritual self-consciousness; one accepts the typical Japanese attitude of dealing with other religions as one pleases in a subjective," meta-moral" way. Suzuki "reassures" his Japanese readers that one is unable to judge whether one's intuitions are contrary to ethics or even whether they are reasonable or objective. I argue that such an attitude is similar to the one the Buddha found in the India of his day *and rejected*. Buddhist enlightenment is one type among many. Besides Buddhist-Christian enlightenments, there are also Hindu, Islamic enlightenments and other varieties evident in Confucianism, Greek myths, Shinto or many kinds of folk religiosity.

How can we address the issue of a "culture" that allows the invasive media to deceive us by inducing "needs" or illusory pleasures. Because our culture lets the media suffuse our youth with a plethora of visual images and permissive attitudes, criteria for 4-3-5 ethical judgments are needed. GEM's foundational AIRR-love loci are a metaxy that rectifies the 4-2 reductionisms flaunted in the media. Nature has equipped dogs to smell; humans rely on such sniffing ability, but dogs depend on humans' ability to discern the givens of our poly*morph*ic consciousness. Various traditions express the alleles of common sense and reason, being and nothingness in seemingly contradictory ways. Such alleles at the core of East-West philosophy and religion are a distinctive dividing line as to how Buddhism and Christianity handle a 4-3-5 topology's potency-*form*-act triadic conjugates. The mystical insights of Pythagoras, Kepler, Newton, Cantor or Einstein reveal both the allure and limit of their experiences. For Pythagoras, the essence of harmony was related to numbers' miraculous power. Seeking to represent the motion of the planets in terms of musical notation, Kepler compared Mercury's elliptical orbit in terms of accented arpeggios. As a devotee of the mystic Jakob Boehme, Newton improved Kepler's calculations by mathematically explaining wave motion.[38] Cantor, influenced by his early religious training and by his doctoral dissertation which argued that the art of asking questions is more valuable than that of solving problems, was led to transfinite numbers. In both of these inspirations, Cantor was in tune with a GEM tenet that a 4-3-5 mystic metaxy often underlies and reinforces creative insights. Einstein was in awe at nature's impenetrable mysteries, which we understand only in primitive *form*s. His attitude was not unlike Nagarjuna's who preferred silence to theories of "inherent nature."

Like Nagarjuna and Boehme, GEM opens us to a mystic view of nature but transcends it. On the fourth level of intentionality it uses dialectical foundations to situate subjects as subjects (SAS) within our 4-3-5 feedback structure. Mystic experiences are signs of religious conversion—witness the lives of Sankara, Dogen, Theresa of Avila." SAS mystics hold the universe" in their hands in that they realize their interrelatedness with all. The immanent-transcendent God challenges us through a language of metaphors, of story, symbol and narrative; we appropriate such language with conceptual glasses which is a necessary phase in self-appropriation and in communicating the appropriation. GEM's foundational reality in the subject differs from Kant's. Schleiermacher's notion of *"Gefuhl,"* that attempts to remedy Kantian dualism,[39] can help us in our task. *Gefuhl*, a pre-reflective consciousness, relates faith-reason alleles. It involves two types of consciousness, the first of which, often rendered as *feeling*, is rather an *undivided personal* experience or immediate presence of the whole, that, far from being subjective, leads to self-transcendence. A second type of consciousness, based in knowing-willing alleles, integrates our *unobjectified* consciousness. Schleiermacher leaves unexplained a third type of consciousness that can link the first two types by *objectifying* objects of perception. Lacking the third type,[40] one cannot reach reason-faith foundations. I argue that *Gefuhl* is a *locus* of nondifference, a pivot that transcends affectivity and abolishes oppositions *if* and when it is objectified in self-transcendent feedback. As a *fore*ground that unifies consciousness in the *back*ground of a return to self, *Gefuhl* lets us go *back and forth* among realms of knowing and willing. It is a *pivot* that one experiences when returning to self in the AIRR (+love) moments between knowing and willing. Schleiermacher's notion of *Gefuhl*, as objectified by GEM, is helpful in integrating the ordinary notion of feelings. Feelings, as we saw, integrate percepts by remaining ambivalent about them and by retaining the full texture of their contradictory elements. An objectified *Gefuhl*, based on the analogical functions of physical and spiritual loci, helps us integrate feelings within trans*form*ative, East-West feedback spiritualities.

GEM exponents rightly stress the role of the subject as subject, but let us not forget that this subject is related to other persons—to all of reality—through such foundational categories as faith and ethics. The notion of category has had a complex and inconclusive history. It began with Aristotle's ontological scheme in his *Categories* that he then transmuted into the categories of predication in his *Topics*. This presupposes that language can represent the most basic features of reality. Kant derived his categories from a priori concepts hoping that they could constitute an objective world. For GEM, an insight is an priori that corrects and complements its predecessor.

To correct Aristotelian and Kantian categories, GEM general categories are derived from the AIRR attending, inquiring, reflecting, responsible subject's structured *opera*tions. These AIRR-structured *opera*tions occur as a pattern of dynamic relations that a subject knows from personal experience and that lead from one *opera*tion to the next. An SAS is a person engaged in any practical or intellectual pursuit; the *opera*tions involved are the ones a person has discovered in his/her AIRR *opera*ting. This yields the basic set of terms and relations upon which GEM pivots. A subject's' *opera*tions reveal objects: single operations reveal partial objects; a structured compound of *opera*tions reveals compound objects. As the subject by his/her AIRR *opera*tions is conscious of self *opera*ting, he or she "is also revealed though not as object but as subject."[41] GEM derives its special categories from data based in its intentionality analysis in which love and grace have a role. Grace is God's loving gift to us; it results in a dynamic state manifested in the inner and outer acts of our lives. Because we grow into special and general categories through dialogue and good will, I seek to foster a cross-cultural dialogue that uses GEM's dynamic," loving" feedback as based on enlightened service. GEM's differentiated manifolds of invariant trans*form*ative allelic loci are open to a meta-SAS Buddhist-Christian ethics and to conversion that I now turn to contextualize.

5b) *Religiously and Morally Converted Meta-SAS Selves Who Reach Out*

This section explores the limits and possibilities of immanence-transcendence. It evaluates how Nishida's locus can complement GEM's functional specialties' co*opera*tive feedback matrix. It asks how immanence can be self-validating without banishing transcendence. It integrates GEM and Nishida's immanent loci by rooting us in our self-transcendent AIRR loci and in a 4-3-5 meta-Sartrean Buddhist "void" that virtually draws out all possible *form*s so as to enable us to be more than introverted subjects as subjects. By integrating impersonal, transcendental fields we facilitate interfaith-transcultural dialogues that can link experience and the rational judgments of Lonergan's *Insight* with the trans*form*ative feedback specialties of his *Method in Theology*. In the ideal case, AIRR ope*ra*tions asymptotically converge toward the infinite by overcoming, at various steps, our biases. Plato contrasts cosmic order with the injustice that led Athens to condemn Socrates." *Kosmos*" comes from a word meaning a "well-woven warp and woof." If Plato tried to guide us with his theory of *form*s, I use a 4-3-5 spindle (miniature of a well-woven cosmos) to ethically assess complementary Buddhist-Christian ethics. Molecular biologists speak of DNA *loci*; Nishida spoke of experience-based *loci*. GEM's AIRR feedback *loci* help prioritize the ethical Noble Truths over the cosmic ones *and* move us from Platonic *ideas* to 4-3-5 faith-dependent Kingdom *ideals*.

For GEM, transcendence (attested to in Judaism, Christianity, Buddhism[42] or Islam) has an immanent dimension. Love of God and neighbour mediates between an unrealistic self-sacrifice and self-centeredness. I link Yogacara and GEM foundations by arguing that the former's eighth foundational consciousness that receives the impressions of the first seven and stores memories to guard against false clinging to delusory concepts, is equivalent to our fourth AIRR intentional level. GEM and Yogacara both have a notion of oneness with things as they are. In both, the five senses are integrated in consciousness, and scientific or religious imagination have viable foundations. GEM's central *forms* (concrete, intelligible *unities* known by understanding) replace "substance." Yogacara's trans-self view of reality non-dogmatically corrects an exaggerated 4-3-4 subjectivity.

Humans, reduced to 4-2 mind, cannot reach out to God or to others; this compromises the foundations of science or of a human life worth living. To empower philosophers and scientists, GEM artists (with spirits "imitating" Jesus or Buddha) are needed. One may ask 1) whether the Buddhist notion of interrelatedness squares with beliefs that everything is derived from God and "has being"? 2) does it lead to agnosticism? Long ago Parmenides and Zeno explored infinities in being or fractions. God (the infinite unknown)[43] and nihilism are the two bounds of a continuum *or* a discontinuity that has puzzled humanity as illustrated in world literature including the Bible.

Crossing and crisscrossing such bounds, this book links them with an attempt to overcome the verbal and credal gaps that do divide human beings. It is important to distinguish between "nothingness" (as interrelatedness) and nihilism, on the one hand, and between reason devoid of faith and a reason related to faith, on the other. In interpreting Buddhism, I argue that being's allele, *sunyata* (4-3-5 dynamic "void" or ultimate reality), is not the negation of existence; it is, rather a 4-3-5 metaxic undifferentiation out of which all apparent entities or dualities arise. I set up a multi-step 4-3-5 trans*form*ative matrix that allows GEM to link Buddhist-Christian teachings.

1. *Beyond Ideology* Parallel debates on the limits of fathoming reality have occurred in the West since Plato and Aristotle, and in the East since Gautama. The ideological tones of Christian and Buddhist polemicists in the Victorian era (such as Dharmapala, Olcott and Carus) reflect the period's crises of faith and of colonial hegemony in Asia; the crises were contextual, not normative.[44] Present day meeting points between Buddhists and Christians include Madhyamika dialectics, faith in Pure Land Buddhism, Zen meditation and Yogacara's epistemology on one hand, and a Christian love praxis willing to dialogue, on the other. For Pope John Paul II, persons, knowing they are subjects and objects of experience, realize themselves in their actions.[45] Dogen held a parallel notion couched in the mystic terms of Zen. Such views can help us answer the question posed earlier as to how GEM can bridge Snow's two cultures (based on sensate and intellectual knowledge)." 4-3-5" trans*form*ative matrices trans*form* us through interrelated love; they empower thinkers by conscienticizing them to the art of deploying their own AIRR *opera*tions.

Marxists, Freudians and Nietzscheans insist that consciousness depends upon its material conditions and upon the unconscious. The AIRR in-betweens of committed love nuance such views. Rooted in our physical genome, our spiritual genome nevertheless transcends it. As Buddhist and Christian spiritualities transcend time, so metaxic love occurs within the more comprehensive reality of a pure consciousness reducible to neither of intentionality's subject-object poles. Such a metaxic 4-3-5 love underpins an ethical feedback matrix enabling us to act in self-transcendent ways that oppose evil or illusions. The loving art of trans*form*ative loci suggests that Magliola's view of Derrida's deconstructionism and a 4-3-5 love metaxy *may* coincide. The "3" points to philosophers' various in-between dialectical triads. The "4" (thymine analogue) can be either foundation or its negation (if one ignores the trans*form*ative loving role of the uracil analogue "5"). The "5" is a Yogacara-GEM foundation that unmasks Nietzschean, Heideggerian and postmodernist views. Sadly, bias confronts us at every turn; group and cultural biases divert the *opera*tional efficacy of ethical love to their own perceived ends. As painters use vanishing points, so ethical artists can "handle" a Buddhist metaxic void that virtually draws out all possible *form*s. We must not ignore life's many gray or chaotic areas and in-between ambiguities that nuance how we appropriate 4-3-5 foundations which is our way of reaching for an infinity beyond our grasp. I contextualize ethical foundations by stressing our AIRR *opera*tions' dispositional in-betweens, that is our AIRR *opera*tions' allelic openness to good as well as to their being liable to failure.

A good place to start mending our lives is through East-West encounters that permit us to integrate their perspectives on being and "nothingness." My study of Buddhist philosophies seeks to show that they complement GEM in providing alternatives to postmodern critiques of the subject. While the latter are driven by philosophical, political and therapeutic concerns, for GEM, interpersonal subjects are able to trans*form* external reality. We "AIRR create" the languages we use.

With Buddhists, GEM affirms that all reality is interrelated through a foundational metaxy; but it prioritizes love. It helps us be ethically committed to an interrelated reality. History and today's realities amply disclose aberrations such as deception or tyranny; only ethically committed persons willingly oppose such aberrations. In developing GEM's 4-3-5 trans*form*ative aspects, I appeal to the pure consciousness that grounds Buddhist emptiness as expounded by Nishida and Nishitani both of whose ethics provide a philosophical basis for meeting Kantian and postmodernist views.

2. *Nishida*   His thought went through several stages. Having probed, early in his career, the thought of Kant, W. James and Bergson, he concluded that these men could not help him in his attempts to bridge East-West thought. Moving away from his transcendental idealism, he went back to Plato and Aristotle's philosophies which he found less given to a subject-object cleavage. He began developing a metaxy that integrated but trans*form*ed his previous standpoints from a Buddhist perspective. His thought does show continuities as he moved from stressing experience to his bedrock general scheme for explaining experience. His first work, *The Study of the Good*, tried to trans*form* James' notion of religious experience into one of pure experience that cast away all reflection so as to arrive at a conscious, direct experience where there is neither subject nor object. In his turn to Bergson and the Neo-Kantians, this basic notion perdured, but he tried to express pure experience in ways that did away with his previous reliance on psychology.[46] He nevertheless, found himself standing at the end of a blind alley that could not accommodate a logic of locus (*topos*, place) that he was trying to develop.

Abandoning his metaphysical absolutes (pure experience, will, nothingness) and ideal *form*s of consciousness (self-awareness or active intuition) he developed a logic of nothingness in which there is "self-identity in absolute contradiction." To do this, he developed Plato's "*topos*" in the *Timaeus* into a *topos* or locus in which nothingness is the uniqueness of that locus. Like Plato's metaxy, Nishida's Buddhist metaxy is a mystic one in which the self, as unity of thought and intuition, finds self in an abyss of darkness enveloping the light of self-consciousness. For Nishida, it is not an individual that has a given experience; rather the experience is the one that "has" the individual. Events occur within a comprehensive reality not reducible to intentionality's subject or object poles. His logic of locus is an in-between metaxy that "does not point to a particular ideal or principle or activity, but rather to a general scheme for 'locating' all of these things." It would have us *dislocate* the self from its apparently fixed abode on a landscape of subjects and objects and to *relocate* it in its true landscape, a metaxy of mystic nothingness. Based on mystical experience, Nishida's logic does not refer to timespace but only to the abstract "point" at which activity takes place. Refusing to think along the lines of something based on the intuition of a subject-object unity, he sees all things that exist as shadows reflecting the self within a self that has nullified itself, a kind of seeing without a seer into the bottom of all things.

He turns the image of Plato's cave on its head. Rather than seeing "freedom from illusion as leaving the half-light of self-opinionated, self-enclosed ignorance, where the world can only appear as shadows dancing on the wall, for the bright sunlight of reality where things can be known as they are," Nishida seeks a standpoint in which the knowing subject, standing foursquare in the sunlight of the real, objective world," can be seen as itself an illusion to be broken through only by negating the self and seeing everything moving around in the world as shadows" of the awakened true self." Replacing the Platonic standpoint of an awakened self with one from which the self can find the truth about itself mirrored in all things just as they are, Nishida puts the I in a somewhat contradictory position." If the I is indeed nothing other than the self-awareness of an experience, then it must be affirmed. At the same time, since the I of itself does not have any meaning, it must be denied . . . . The I is I because at the same time it is not I. It is, we might say, an 'I-*in*-not-I.'"[47]

More important than modes of expression, is noting that when one speaks of the knowing subject one is abstracting from one point of view part of a wider event that from other viewpoints requires negating the abstracted I. For Nishida, philosophy trans*form*s ordinary consciousness into one's being aware of one's innermost nature—spontaneously *without any* interference. If Gauss arrived at the absolute value of a complex number by adopting Plato's cave metaphor in ways that 4-3-4 trans*form*ed geometry, Nishida 4-3-5 trans*form*s consciousness by turning that metaphor on its head. For its part, GEM grounds 4-3-5 foundational loci in an ever revisable AIRR foundational language of the heart. Nishida's "pure experience" is a to-be-transcended *opera*tional thinking analogous to GEM. On the analogy of the trans*form*ative loci of genetics and mathematics, GEM's AIRR verbs use a spindle of in-between *opera*tionally metaxic reflective feedback loci to mutually link our allelic transcendental dynamism through co-*opera*tive action. If Nishida empties the I so as to fill it with a metaxy of nothingness in which the I or self *reaches beyond* self, GEM allows for an eye of love to effect such reaching. I dialectically relate Nishida's "locus philosophy of nothingness" with a metaxy of love's 4-3-5 trans*form*ative loci. 4-3-5 loci, located in our AIRR *opera*tions, are foundational inasmuch as they enable us to convert the moments of our experience into "understandable" ideals. Rooted in our dynamic pure desire to know, these loci supplant Kant's inability to reconcile the properties of intuition and reflection by recognizing that these are pivots through which a self returns to self, or alternatively, in which self or I, as transcended, can overcome one's worldly illusions on reality. I seek to reconcile East-West thought by relating *our inbuilt*, allelic AIRR loci with Nishida's notion of a mystical experience that "has *us*" before "we have" that experience. Like

Hegel, Nishida and GEM break from Kant by seeing noumena not as unfathomable but as a fact of dynamic reality. Nishida's view of awareness as nonsubjective, timeless, egoless presence is a paradoxical standpoint compatible with GEM's foundational loci.

For Nishida, an event occurs not by distancing self from things but by locating self at the locus of nothingness, by trans-descending to the very pit of immanence.[48] By affirming the world with a *trans-descending* event, he anticipates Heidegger's *Ereignis*. Linking Nishida's *sunya* metaxy with Plato's love metaxy is a way to address the dilemmas of our lives. Even good, intelligent persons sometimes become unreasonable; we are called to deal with the conflicting "in-between" demands of feelings and reason, uncertainty and fears that cloud our reason. To contextualize such realities, I invoke virtue as typified in the paradigmatic examples of Newton, Spinoza, Cantor, Nishida and the mystic qualities that in*form*ed Einstein's lifework. I wed the poetic in-betweens of a life well-lived with the theoretical-cum-practical standpoints of such thinkers. If geneticists show that extensive variations occur in a genome over the span of a single generation, GEM helps us face life's imponderables with a love-interrelatedness foundational metaxy wed to *il y a* realism, that is a view of transcendence compatible with immanence views in Nishida, Heidegger or Deleuze. I *map* multiple entry points for dislodging preconceived ideas, relying not on a unity unable to fix a subject or object (Deleuze) but one that AIRR "locates" (Nishida) our allelic 4-3-5 spiritual aspects.

3. *Nishitani*. Like Nishida, Nishitani borrows from such sources as the Buddhist Kegon philosophy on the "interpenetration" of all things one with the other. He, too, revises Aristotle's "*hypokeimenon*" in his effort to find a concrete reality prior to its being factored into object and subject poles, while allowing subject and object to find their rightful place. He develops Nishida's notion of locus, according to which our everyday idea of *place* no longer refers to a mere *nothing* as nonexistent, nor to an existent *something*—a notion not unlike Jasper's view of "encompassing" (*Umgreifendes*) "that allows things to exist where they are: each on its own, and yet all together in a sort of oneness." He alludes to *Mahayana*'s *prajna* by which one grasps that all reality is interrelated. Comparing *prajna* with Western thought, he seeks to go beyond mere reason so as to reach a *sunyata*-void standpoint that handles the concepts of both substance and subject. For him, this standpoint allows us to pursue in depth such issues as personality and materiality," as well as the problem of the modes of being of things and the self implied in the claim that all things come forth and 'confirm the self.'"[49] One can then return to one's mind and to its interrelatedness. Far from overturning GEM metaphysics, this view confirms it by having us return to our AIRR mind in a 4-3-5 spiritual mode. Nishitani often places *soku* (compenetration of all things and all persons) between two contradictory concepts such as emptiness and *form* to help us realize that the two are "the same." *Soku*, a "non-nihil void-nothingness" virtually draws out all possible *form*s to build society; it draws off

the total reality of two poles into itself as their constitutive, ontological prior unity so as to indicate the only locus (place) at which the opposites are *realized* and display their true reality.

Our fundamental religious option and our historical situation are grounded in a realm beyond space and time, a realm proclaimed in "the mystical experiences of all times and in the basic Buddhist standpoint of emptiness."[50] Like GEM, a "4-3-5 *soku* in-between" integrates our feeling-reason alleles. As Nishitani synergizes a 4-3-5 *soku*, so we can synergize GEM and let it be synergized by 4-3-5 *soku* interrelating us all. Fig. 1 initiated us in a transposition of real and complex human realities analogous to and giving rise to mathematical loci. Scalar fields locate real and complex numbers. Fig. 2 touched on a GEM spindle-feedback allowing for 4-3-4-immanence-4-3-5 self-transcendence. *Soku* integrates impersonal, transcendental fields in transcultural ways so as to link experience with the rational judgments that Nishitani and Lonergan explore. If Eliade and Jung explored Otto's *numinous* that transposed Jakob Fries' view that sensation relates us to *noumena* just as much as does reason (aesthetic feeling being an aspect of sensation) or if Lotze's *axio*logy sought to integrate feelings and evaluations in non-ideal, meta-realist ways, a *soku*-GEM *axio*logy re-evaluates values in spiritual conjugates bridging immanence-transcendence (fig. 1-4). If reality outstrips thought, GEM iso*morph*ic-*soku* alleles help us 4-3-5 link faith, reason and values. Such "alleles" are my way of interpreting our pattern of recurrent and related AIRR *opera*tions. If GEM iso*morph*ically-normatively uses a biological *opera*tor as higher system on the move, as ground of the flexible circle of schemes of recurrence for organic functioning, and if it uses the schemes of organic, psychic, and intellectual recurrence to reach underlying correlations, I use iso*morph*ic *soku* alleles to 4-3-5 link faith, reason and values in ways that the later Lonergan did.

GEM's genetic method studies processes of development; it takes us beyond genetics. If Newton reduced Kepler's planetary scheme of recurrence to his abstract laws of gravitation and motion by using the conjugate *form* of "mass," and if the conjugate *form*s of the organism, the psyche and intelligence are discovered by proceeding from the schemes of organic, psychic and intellectual recurrence to the underlying correlations, GEM's "iso*morph*ic *soku* alleles" take us beyond an SAS view of reality to a world-encompassing meta-SAS view of world communities. My approach to spiritually genomic conjugates is not a natural theology but a social ethics that goes beyond schemes of recurrence to a way of virtuously interrelating immanence-transcendence. A notion of recurrent schemes is one of GEM's breakthroughs; that breakthrough has to be built on, as Lonergan did, in *Method*'s functional specialties that transposed his *Insight*. Poly*morph*ic-*soku* alleles are my way of mapping an art of love analogous to Cezanne's absolute. At each stage of human evolution, artists and mystics "feel," reveal 4-3-5 poetic verb-possibilities that clarify for us a path, a *Tao* to be trod as we reach for personal and interpersonal authenticity. My *Tao* path builds on GEM's triadic conjugates with spiritual, artistic conjugates that take its patterns of experience seriously by transposing them (fig. 1-4) into an AIRR-4-3-5 structure analogous to and building on physical genomes' recurrent patterns. I seek to discover a Cezanne-like 4-3-5 absolute that brings us into the realm of interiority unique to humans and actualized in a meta-SAS ethics.

Nishida's locus and Nishitani's *soku* are 4-3-5 foundational metaxic pivots that root, and are rooted in the allelic trans*form*ative AIRR loci of a spiritual topology; *soku* expresses the "union" with the Ultimate of which mystics and Buddhists speak.[51] If "self" is problematic for Buddhists, meditation's pure consciousness event does not absorb us into God; it frees us for ethics. I would note two differences between GEM and *soku*-loci. First, Nishida and Nishitani seek to get beyond things as objects that appear as realities. For them, a thing is *represented as an object*—as with Kant. Objects, as represented, are an *aporia* inherent in the field of consciousness itself. Nishida remains in the *abstract* realm of self-awareness rooted in an intelligible world if he views pure experience as a to-be-transcended *opera*tional thinking. For Nishitani, the field of consciousness can be "broken through" by allowing "nihility" to open forth at its ground and "nullify" things; he tries to avoid paradoxical representation by letting things escape a subjectivism lurking beyond "external actualities." Subjective existence views nihility as Heideggerian *ekstasis*.[52] GEM's two knowings (that of the senses and the verified) can accept *soku*-locus—but not if cut off from a subject. Second, whereas GEM appeals to a love ideal, Nishitani replaces love with "nothingness," a whole greater than its parts. If one complements this view with GEM's virtually unconditioned, we are more than subjects as subjects (SAS); we are "SAS *soku* (SASS)": subjects realize they are related to all of reality. *Soku* may help individualistic Westerners grasp meta-SAS cultural views.

By reconciling a SAS with its *soku* meta-SAS interpenetration with all reality we move beyond 4-2 chaos. Lest *soku* panentheistically refer to God's Entity rather than God's underlying activity, I liken it to Eckhart's mystic Emptying, a spark that leads to a life in the Spirit. *Form*, linked with potency-act and *soku* is a *form*less *form*alyzable that I use to interpret GEM triads, so as to transculturally "4-3-5 trans*form*" trans*form*ators. Our mind-spirits interface with our bodies. To avoid the clumsy phrasing of "SASS," I refer to our body-mind-spirit as an "*interrelated self*." But let us advert to *soku*'s deeper 4-3-5 metaxic implications. A *soku* metaxy of love confirms a *Tao*-way of living out our 4-3-5 spiritual structure. It is not unlike *todo y nada* in John of the Cross or Socrates and Levinas' primacy of ethics. Not unlike these men, GEM derives its special categories, not from nature but from God's 4-3-5 "loving gift of himself to us."[53]

4. *Prajna*. Emptiness and *soku*-loci of interrelated love build upon our invariant structure of consciousness as discerned in Yogacara, Nishitani and GEM. One returns to the source of one's consciousness but is able to respond to the needs of others. For John Keenan, the languages of Buddhist or Christian doctrines are "empty," provisional constructs, skilful means that point to a larger reality. In the light of GEM, he compares Origen's mysticism of light (knowing

subjects and knowable objects) with the mysticism of darkness of Gregory of Nyssa and of Pseudo-Dionysius (immediacy that precedes the subject-object pattern) and with Yogacara's revision of Nagarjuna's "consistent deconstruction of the previous Abhidarma endeavour." Yogacarins restored some Abhidarma-like "theoretical analysis within their understanding of emptiness."[54] Like RNA, *soku*-loci are both chicken and egg. Presupposing elements of GEM conversion, they place all of us on a path of adverting to our own AIRR *opera*tions and of transcending these through 4-3-5 virtues. They course between what is in-between the conflicting demands of the personal, private self and the public presentation of that self, of faith and a secular neutralism, the chaotic inability of laws to walk the fine line of justice except by letting the judiciary's pet whims interpret or decide issues. GEM, like the scientific method and like Yogacara, present us with a ever revisable foundation that I map as 4-3-5 ethical structure analogous to, interfacing with, transposing physical genomes.

6a) *Privatizing Policies*[55] *Submitted to the Public Good*

GEM revises Aristotle's potency-*form*-act triad that substitutes the facts of experience for Plato's abstract, ideal notion of the good.[56] For Aristotle, virtue helps us regulate our appetites. GEM moves us toward the golden mean in feedback ways by translating imperfect realities with viable (if ideal) policies. Since we share irrational elements with other animals, conceptualist triads need an in-between spiritual anchor. GEM's potency-*form*-act triad has a trans*form*ative feedback in-between ability that "4-3-5 trans*forms*" potency and act so as to link our minds' analytic and synthetic abilities. In both our physical and spiritual genomes, there are analogous life-death pulls and counter-pulls. Spirituality invites us to a higher love. If the tug of history reveals ever new architectural *forms* that fuse previous styles (Romanesque), or if Western education 4-3-4 adapted trans*form*ed Medieval elements, the elusive, abiding 4-3-5 peace of mystics helps us underpin the "realities" of life with a self-authenticating *fifth-ideal* pedagogy of AIRR-love analogous to ATGC and uracil (fig. 1-4). Dialogues between East-West religions and philosophies, should not neglect a mystic love that prays from the heart and corrects verbal *gaps*. In the physical genome, a mRNA uracil function replicates life. An AIRR structured GEM stresses the role of self-transcendent love in reconciling various traditions in a metaxic interrelatedness, in helping teens deal with their dim perceptions of an ever more encroaching 4-2 materialism. Our basic AIRR experiencing-knowing-judging-acting *opera*tions are spiritually allelic loci analogous to ATGC nucleotides of biological life and their genetic loci. These *opera*tions complement one another in their knowing and doing; as AIRR ideals they are to be coordinated with possible AIRR-4-3-5 allelic *opera*tional loci of other persons. AIRR self-transcendence can and should lead to processes of mutual adaptation between persons and various types of secular or religious organizations. In brief, our AIRR imperatives are a *form*ula for what makes persons and organizations "tick" because, rooted in a potency-*form*-act triad and in our body-mind makeup, they underlie and motivate our spiritual and ethical actions.

The "chaos" of our minds as reflected in sleep or alpha-theta waves is a portal to God's mystery of love. GEM's eye of love is linked to faith and hope; it presupposes humility, that is, a self-emptying kenosis prompting us to serve others with policies of mutual self-giving. I will not go into how GEM economics analyzes consumption-production cycles so as to prevent booms and slumps, how it urges consumers and producers to adopt self-transcendent policies; yet, we should be aware of faith-reason in-betweens in working out the functional specialties that link all fields of human studies. Relationships need a certain distantiation so as to ensure privacy. But we should balance this need with an awareness of our biases that discourage co*opera*tion. No one, no group should lose the forest of the public good for trees of self-serving biases. For GEM, our experiencing-understanding-judging involves a willingness to re*form* ourselves by undoing privatizing policies. We responsibly assert our rights by respecting the rights of all. AIRR ideals are mediated according to a potency-*form*-act triad and a 4-3-5 feedback ethics that helps us avoid privatization's 4-2 dangers. Most traditions have 4-3-5 ideals.⁵⁷ An intrafaith-interfaith 4-3-5 ethics contextualizes spirituality's "in-between phase boundaries."

Watson and Crick lifted DNA from its status of a mere acronym; the process of reverse transcriptase uses 4-3-5 RNA as a template to transcribe a single-stranded DNA. GEM 4-3-5 feedback links our AIRR *opera*tions to the functional specialties. Its allelical openness to spirituality enables us to oppose wrong policies. It helps us link the role of virtue to its cognate, the *virtually* unconditioned of judgments. Such a virtually unconditioned helps us devise workable 4-3-5 policies. Many people live in worlds of their own. Born and raised within a locale or culture, they tend to settle down in their own locale.

A globalizing world provokes new developments; it needs ever new adaptative 4-3-5 trans*form*ations. Virtues are guiding 4-3-5 ideals—not just an "operant conditioned" observed in a laboratory. Behaviourists would incorporate neural events into a theory that integrates Pavlovian salience motivation with Skinner's *opera*nt conditioning so as to permit "the operationalization of key inferred processes in psychology such as intrinsic motivation,"⁵⁸ GEM names the routines that secure gains a higher system as integrator. The routines within an emerged system that open the door to a better system are a "higher system as operator." Within a developing moral tradition, value judgments per*form* the integrator functions; value questions per*form* the *opera*tor functions. Value judgments' integrating power is directly proportional to the absence of *opera*tor functions (of further relevant value questions). Provisional value judgments function as limited integrators—limited in that lingering value questions function as *opera*tors, scrutinizing value judgments for bias or factual errors. Feelings function as *opera*tors or integrators. As *opera*tors, they represent "our initial response to possible values, moving us to pose value questions; as integrators, they settle us in our value judgments as our psyches link our affects to an image of the valued object." This linkage of affect and image is a "symbol," an event in consciousness not to be confused with flag etc.)." The concrete, functioning symbols that suffuse our psyches can serve as integrator systems for how we view our social institutions etc. ... making it easy for us to respond smoothly without having to reassess everything at every moment. Symbols also serve as *opera*tors insofar as the affect-image pair may disturb our consciousness, alerting us to danger or confusion, and prompting the questions we pose about values."[59] Freedom integrates intelligence's higher system in psychic representations. Higher-system integrators' conjugate *form*s work on lower physical and biological manifolds. Note that GEM uses "conjugates" in special sublating, trans*form*ative ways.

6b) *Meta-SAS Policies that Transcend Mere "Self-Fulfilment"*

Bernard Mandeville' *Fable of the Bees* (1714) initially appears to credit politicians with originating morality. His strict criterion of virtue scandalized contemporaries by arguing that their flourishing commercial society depended on vices they denounced—such as pride and envy. The dilemma of virtue also arises in the work of Abraham Maslow. Did Maslow err by combining in one theory the two massive defects of the self-fulfilment strategy: the idea of a self as an aggregate of inner needs, and the concept of a hierarchy of being that makes economic security a precondition to satisfying the human spirit?[60] Lonergan accepts Maslow's "peak experiences"; this is nuanced by GEM's stress on mediating the meaning of experience and by how it helps us reshape politics and philosophy. It has us advert to the differentiations in our consciousness based on contextualized subject-object reflections. While one may agree, with Maslow, that our higher needs for self-expression and self-esteem depend on our lower needs of security and food being met, we must inquire as to why neurotic needs arise. GEM, like Mandeville, knows that vice and virtue coexist; still, humans can 4-3-5 rise above their needs by 4-3-5 appropriating their recurring structured AIRR *opera*tions. GEM integrates all studies by turning concepts, judgments and actions into viable policies based on planned execution. Policy involves attitudes and ends, while planning works out the optimal use of existing resources for attaining the ends under given conditions.

Execution generates feedback. Policy making and planning thus become "ongoing processes that are continuously revised in the light of their consequences."[61] While many opt for ever less comprehensive viewpoints and while communication often breaks down, ethical policies are to be based on higher viewpoints. For Gandhi and Martin Luther King, *satyagraha* was a relentless search for truth to be implemented in civil disobedience. For Bion, psychotherapy is a process marked by a split founded on the caesura of birth. To transcend that split, the therapeutist must make choices as to whether a patient's problems are pathological or not." The human personality exists as a whole; we have to split that personality to formulate several possible ideas or interpretations. That I call non-pathological splitting."[62] If a psychotherapist's goal is to help a patient,

4-3-5 GEM's goal is to help us co*opera*te in virtuous ways. I seek to relate Bion's insights on our splits with the biases that exist in the political arena. As Gandhi's concerted actions were based on the power of a 4-3-5 truth hidden within the spirit of all persons, so GEM nudges us toward sustained development by having us appropriate 4-3-5 truth in ways that heal biased splits. On the level of the mind, one reaches transcendence through grasping an unconditioned, but as to the reality of human living, transcendence occurs when an unconditioned is realized," made real."

Man proposes but God disposes. GEM unmasks those who use religion to foster violence. We oppose terror but should not overlook the despair provoking terrorism. If some Palestinians resist encroachment, virtue prompts policymakers to forsake hidden agendas and to devise viable, just policies. All sides must abandon force, terror and lies. Virtues are good habits that enable us to do what is right with ease and consistency; the cardinal virtues of temperance, *justice*, prudence (*phronesis*)[63] and fortitude support the entire structure of moral life. Faith, hope and love "link" us to God. Some may want to escape from this world's problems. Conversely, others may resent the time and money spent in prayer and on places of worship—preferring to work for re*form* in such social evils as poverty and racism. Pope John XXIII harnessed trans*form*ative ideals with a Council that promoted world solidarity. GEM addresses social problems by dialectically nuancing human vagaries. It helps us deal with the intense social conflicts, economic stress and confusion of our age. One must get to the root of the contradictions that thwart justice; moral principles merely express conditioned value judgments. One must look to AIRR ideals so as to foster a co*opera*tion that moves beyond selfish privatization to embrace an ethic of commitment. Only when enough persons pursue policies that avoid the injustices of overprivatization by committing themselves to the ideals of the common good, by acting justly, can a social ethics work. Only then can we find the rules appropriate to our age. GEM artists seek to devise workable policies of ethical change. When comparing the basic biochemical processes with the allelic loci processes of a spiritual genome, I stressed GEM's ability to sublate enzymes' catalysis. As RNA has the catalytic role of mediating between DNA and proteins, so sound GEM policies mediate between good and bad trans*form*ative processes within and among human beings so as to enable them to AIRR co*opera*te.

7a) *Systems and Reconsidering Deleuze and Guattari's Neo-Materialist Geophilosophy*

Philosophy and science achieve their ends differently because the former investigates the virtual of virtue, but the latter is restricted to functives. Eastern philosophy does not divorce itself from religious views; it has a mystical bent, not unlike that of Spinoza and Einstein. Deleuze and Guattari's philosophy of immanence appeals to Eastern philosophies, but it is flawed in that it is based on a third person, abstractive standpoint, rather than on personal appropriation of one's own knowing and doing.[64] For them, philosophical concepts and scientific functions differ due to inseparable variations and independent variables. Events occur on a plane of immanence; states of affairs occur in a system of reference. The concept is a "vagabond, nondiscursive, moving about on a plane of immanence." It is intensional, modular and devoid of reference. Accepting Sartre's view of an impersonal transcendental field, they see us as prone to an "infinite" list of errors, to bad feelings and the "illusion" of transcendence. Reducing the latter to the immanent, they argue that "concepts, sensations, and functions are undecidable" but that philosophy gives "consistency to the virtual through concepts."[65] GEM moves beyond an undecidable chaos because its critical, discursive realism corrects Kantian notions based on intuitions of sense.

With Nishida, it finds a 4-3-5 mystic order within chaos; it links a concept to reference not only in relation to its internal components ("the inside") but also to how we responsibly interact with others and with our environment. It relates the internal and external by postulating four realms of meaning that depend on genetically distinct horizons and on how we appropriate such horizons.[66] Unlike a private Cartesian thinker who thinks for himself, it integrates postmodernist insights into our conflicting emotions. It prizes transcendence and ethics and links them with the realms of interiority and theory. I trans*form* Deleuze and Guattari's abstract ontology with a Buddhist-Christian ethics. If the locus of points at a fixed distance, d, from point P is a circle with the given point P as its centre and d as its radius, GEM invites us to step into the greater circle of grace. Its perimeters incorporate the new within the old. It helps us relocate a revisionist geophilosophy within a 4-3-5 spiritual topology whose feedback ability integrates immanence and transcendence, our "inside" and the outside. These are linked in that our AIRR *opera*tional ideals (the realm of the virtues) help us reach beyond one's self. I relate virtually unconditioned judgments to the 4-3-5 in-betweens of *lived* virtue and with Deleuze and Guattari's noteworthy notion of a *virtual open* to the infinite.

Every *form* may vanish, but, in us, each also invites possibilities of trans*form*ative change *open* to infinity. The in-betweens of virtue can help us systematize the judgments we make in benevolent policies; those in-betweens are concrete. They dialectically oppose the dark side of our personalities, the inner secrets, deceits and guilt that all humans harbour. In this sense, both Buddhism and Christianity are in-betweens mediating personal conversions within culture change.

7b) *Systematizing the In-betweens of a Virtuous Meta-SAS Interrelatedness*

To systematize GEM's integration of the complementary aspects of cosmic and personalist world views, I argue that East-West mysticism and ethics can be reconciled through GEM's trans*form*ative feedback allelic loci located deep within each person. I generalize the notion that GEM 1) goes into experiential data, 2) helps us understand such data, and 3) judge, then 4) act on them. I apply the generalization to the ongoing feedback entailed in functional specialization with a view to "systematize" the in-betweens of a virtuous interrelatedness." Allelic in-betweens" refer to the gray-area ambiguities of life; they oscillate between good and evil, between ideals and the "realities" of life punctuated by our feelings and uncertain fears. To reach feasible solutions, we need wise persons who, knowing the limits of human co*oper*ation, can engage others in the quest for peace and justice. Just as traditional societies insist, not on capitalist notions of maximizing profits, but on the common good, so GEM's 4-3-5 approach gets us beyond Cartesian-Lockean would-be foundational "ideas" by locating ideas in genetic insights. With Dignaga[67] and Berkeley, it knows that perceptions always belong to experiencing subjects; but it subordinates perceptions to an ethical level that maximizes community and co*oper*ation rather than mere personal profit.

GEM takes Deleuze and Guattari's notion of rhizome (a *map* with multiple entry points for dislodging preconceived ideas) a step further than they do by letting virtuous trans*form*ative change be *open* to infinity. As incarnated in ethical persons, it maps 4-3-5 ethical co*oper*ation opposing the pseudo "values" of greed masked as deregulation. From the local to the global, it systematizes the in-betweens of virtuous networks. Rooted in our *intellectualist* potency-*form*-act triads and their underlying AIRR ideals, a spiritual genome offers us a trans*forma*tive ballast that can stabilize scientific or philosophical views. Integrating being-nothingness alleles is akin to the *axio*ms in mathematics and set theory, except that while *axio*ms stress the limits of philosophy or religion as to infinity, GEM opens us to 4-3-5 possibilities of the transcendent infinite in our lives.

Technological breakthroughs in biomedicine, robotics, etc. and the new possibilities they hold for human life have complexified the issues of permissible research and medical practice. Realizing technology's inherent dangers, Hans Jonas moved from theoretical detachment to public responsibility. Concerned more with technology's long-term threat than with present perils, he feared malevolent uses. For those who do deny a trans-human significance for human conduct, ethics depends on a principle that can be discovered in the nature of things; but it should not give in to subjectivism or relativism. Jonas "begins to lose his way when he overlooks the fact that the principle of man's singularity in the universe is also the principle of his universality."[68] His sets of propositions cannot serve as the foundation of ethics; the root of ethics, like that of metaphysics, lies not in sentences nor in propositions nor in judgments but in the dynamic structure of rational self-consciousness. Because that structure is latent and *opera*tive in everyone's choosing, it is universal on the side of the subject; because it can be dodged, it grounds a dialectical criticism of subjects. But since it is recurrent in every act of choice, it is universal on the side of the object. Because its universality consists not in abstraction but in inevitable recurrence, it is also concrete (*Insight*, 604). Our AIRR operations' recurrent feedback ability grounds ethics in that recurrent structure which Buddhism helps us translate into an ethics of universal interrelatedness. The question remains as to how we communicate to the world a holistic Buddhist-Christian ethics. Such a communication involves our tapping GEM's empowering, 4-3-5 trans*form*ative potential.

8a) *Communicating Holism*

Are persons, groups or governments able and willing to act responsibly and discharge their moral duties in the face of contradictions? The world stresses human rights. Too often, we forget that rights depend on fulfilling duties and obligations. God, as Master Builder, leaves us free. GEM counters our suffocating narcissism with an ethics rooted in a 4-3-5 in-between metaxy linking humans to God. It bridges divides by clarifying the issues of how reason-faith alleles can help federate our world so as to rescue victims cut off from their own inner being and from love. Communication mediates a love metaxy so as to save from self-serving. It can succeed only if we accept an unconditioned gift. Can we realistically hope that there are enough persons able to defy postmodernism and unconditionally accept such a gift manifested in the ideals of Jesus' Kingdom?

8b) *Holistic Communication among Meta-SAS Interrelated Selves*

In Christianity, selfless persons share an unconditioned gift. In Buddhism, selfless persons seek to share enlightenment. Buddhism and Christianity have engendered profound philosophies. As religions, they seek to communicate their beliefs. While Christians believe in revelation, they, like Buddhists, preach an ideal of selfless action. Both religions would achieve peace through justice. GEM grounds the ethical roots of peace in our AIRR *loci* that interact with other persons' similarly structured allelic loci. In Russia, Gorbachev's *glasnost* led to capitalist greed, to Putin.

Putin's Russia is a "managed democracy" that threatens/jails dissenters. Limits on one's effective freedom are imposed. GEM artists respect legitimate restraints, but they communicate at deeper levels of practical and 4-3-5 mystic interrelatedness; resolutely diplomatic, they are gentle, yet firm. They know that normal persons must rely on their 4-3-5 structured *opera*tions to empower themselves and to communicate a message of hope. Vatican II had its day; it has been subject to excessive interpretations from both left and right. Patient moderation will empower us.

Concluding
"Let's Get Real" Concurrent Dialectic

Realist: Oh, now I have some idea of how AIRR-love *opera*tions may open us to ideals!

John (thankful for his patience): In-between reason-faith alleles open us to a free space we call virtue. Only an eye of love can *reconcile* chaotic "irreconcilables" with the imponderables of our *seemingly* intractable differences. The best antidote to terror is practicing a peace, nurtured by love. GEM alleles are analogous to the mutuality of physical alleles of which ethologists speak. By grounding our "contradictory" feelings in a metaxy of ethical love, GEM invites us to share in the trans*form*ative conversions that *open* us to one's neighbour—a true receptacle of God's infinity.

ENDNOTES

INTRODUCTION

1. John Raymaker, *Empowering the Lonely Crowd: Pope John Paul II, Lonergan and Japanese Buddhism* (Lanham, MD: University Press of America, 2003). My *A Buddhist-Christian Logic of the Heart: Nishida's School and Lonergan's "Spiritual Genome" as World Bridge* (University Press, 2002); *The Theory-Praxis of Social Ethics: the Complementarity between Lonergan's and Winter's Foundations* (U. Microfilms, Ann Arbor, MI: 1977); "The Theory-Praxis of Social Ethics" in *Creativity and Method* (Marquette U., 1981), 337-52, "The Dilemma Created by the Vatican Letter on Meditation" (*East Asian Pastoral Review*, 27, 1990); various articles in *The Japan Mission Journal* (Tokyo: Oriens, 1983-2003) and other periodicals. Influenced by Bernard Lonergan's *Insight: A Study of Human Understanding* (New York: Philosophical Library 1958); *Method in Theology* (New York: Herder, 1972) I use notions of mathematical and genetic loci in a trans*form*ative feedback dialogue with Deleuze and Guattari, *A Thousand Plateaus*, London, Athlone, 1988 and *What is Philosophy?*, tr. Hugh Tomlinson & G. Burchell (Columbia U.) 1994.
2. Political theorists like Plato, Aristotle, Montesquieu, Strauss address core issues.
3. An Internet quote from A. R. Luria's *The Making of Mind*, tr. Mike Cole (Harvard U., 1979) 43, where he compares his work with that of Vygotsky and Leontiev. The three men sought to devise a psychology that could "discover the way natural pro-cesses such as physical maturation and sensory mechanisms become intertwined with culturally determined processes to produce the psychological functions of adults." As they sought to index the centrality of culturo-linguistic mediations in constituting our psychological processes based on the *relational consciousness*, so I seek to develop a science-spirituality bridge that can transcend usual religious-secular boundaries.
4. If Edward Conze, *Buddhism: Its Essence and Development* (New York: Harper, 1959) touches on Buddhist contradictions, the *Book of Job*, the Psalms, etc. also address human contradictions.

CHAPTER I

1. Marcia Bartusiak, *Einstein's Unfinished Symphony* (Wash, D.C., Henry, 2000) 21.
2. Throughout the text, I use italics in expressing variants of "*opera*tion" and of "*form*" (such as in trans*form*ation) to illustrate and emphasize the important GEM point of how we translate insights into *form*s through our AIRR acts and *opera*tions; this, in turn, enables us to co*opera*te ethically.
3. Robert Thurman, *Anger* (New York Public Library Lecture, 2004) is a Buddhist perspective on the subject that must be complemented by e. g. St. Francis de Sales.
4. DNA molecules consist of multiple copies of single basic nucleotide units, ATGC. RNA uses a uracil nucleotide. If a molecule is composed of a purine or pyrimidine base and a deoxyribose or ribose sugar, it is a nucleoside. Adding a phosphate turns a nucleoside into a ATGC-U nucleotide.
5. Lonergan, *Method in Theology*, 14. The shorthand addresses metalinguistic issues in semantics, syntax and pragmatics; they complement my *Logic*'s AI?R shorthand referring to judgments that shortcircuit meaning. GEM rethinks Kant's categorical imperatives and other idealisms to help us understand historical breakthroughs and co*opera*te

in staving off disaster from a misuse of AIRR.
6. "Eclipse of Reality," *Collected Works of Eric Voegelin*, 28, (Baton Rouge: Louisiana State U., 1990) 157. In "Hesiod as Precursor to the Presocratic Philosophers: A Voegelian View," Richard Moorton, Jr. calls the Pythagoreans an aristocratic political group intent on governing society under the right order of the soul as shaped by consciousness, . . . a differentiation of the regime of *dike* in the just polis as conceived by Hesiod." My in between ideals extend a Hesiod-Voegelin-Lonergan thesis of *dike* as transcendent metaxy that reaches between inner events pulling toward life or producing a counterpull toward death. For Alan Bloom, Rousseau's invention of Romantic love derailed the *Symposium*'s view of eros, and, by implication, the metaxy of love.
7. Like Descartes, Whitehead or GEM, the *Timaeus* uses notions of space and a genesis of events. With Thurber, GEM is aware of the befuddled urbanites coping in a world they fail to understand.
8. Robert Magliola *Derrida on the Mend* (Purdue U., 1984) and an Internet article.
9. GEM uses Rahner's notion: what sublates goes beyond what is sublated; it puts all things on a *new* basis; far from interfering with the sublated or harming it, it includes, preserves "all its proper features . . . and carries them forward to a fuller realization within a richer context." *Method*, 241.
10. Joan Stambaugh, Introduction to Heidegger's *On Time and Being* (New York: Harper, 1972) vii., argues that from the external point view *Time and Being* seems to be the reversal of *Being and Time*. The latter moves from a phenomenological hermeneutic of human being toward a fundamental ontology of Being; the former "uncovers layers of experience, analyzing things of nature (*Vorhandensein*), artifacts and the core of human being in its basic structure of care. These three constitute the original, indissoluble unity of being-in-the-world, a unity that originates in Husserl's notion of conscious intentionality, but that GEM develops without intellectual intuition.
11. Spinoza's *Ethics* opposes Descartes' mind-extension dualism, by letting God contain the notion of existence in Self. Its starting point ("Definitions") is that God is absolute infinite Substance or "that which is in itself and is conceived through itself," consisting of infinite attributes, each one of which expresses eternal and infinite essence." Definitions, 3 to 6 (on modes and attributes) lead to deductivism. Mode is what is not conceived as reality but through and in something else. Attribute is not conceived through itself but has a relation to the conceiving understanding. God's attributes are thought and extension. In Schol. 2, Prop. 8, he concedes that proposition 7 on the necessity of substance to exist is difficult to grasp; one grasps it by keeping in mind the difference between modes and substances. Modes, such as properties of trees, do come and go out of existence, but absolutely infinite Substance has infinite attributes. God, having "infinite attributes, each one of which expresses eternal and infinite essence, necessity exists" (prop. 11). In fact, Spinoza's God is an abstract, non-real pantheist Being. As in ontological argument for God's existence, he uses a *reductio ad absurdum*. His system stands or falls with Proposition 5: "In nature there cannot be two or more substances of the same nature or attribute." Since two substances cannot share the same attribute, and since it pertains to the nature of Substance to exist (prop. 7), he is led to a pantheism. His Appendix to the First Part proposes an *axiom* that man "has a desire, of which he is conscious, to seek that which is profitable to him . . . (though) he is ignorant of the causes" for that desire. For Leibniz, even though Spinoza claims geometric proof that lays out definitions and *axiom*s from which deductions follow, his system lacks mathematical rigor. One must look at the content of his entire system and accept or

reject it on its own merits, rather than from the success of the various deductions. On how Spinoza deductivism inspired Hegel, Lonergan, *Insight*, 445.
12. Frankl, *Man's Search for Meaning: Introduction to Logotherapy* (London, 1964).
13. In mathematics, a "map" means function. Massumi, Foreword, *Plateaus*, xiii, notes that nomad space is 'smooth' (open-ended); it would replace the closed equation of representation

$$x = x = \text{not } y$$

with "... $+ y + z + a + (\ldots + \text{arm}, + \text{brick} + x = \text{window} =)$."
For Deleuze and Guattari's "rhizome" (21), social systems' non-signifying aspects, leave us prone to anarchy. For S. Moultrop, *Rhizome and Resistance: Hypertext and the Dreams of a New Culture* (London: Hopkins, 1994) 301, rhizome is the "concept of social order defined by active transversal or encounter rather than objectification.... Figures for this order include the ocean of the navigator or the desert of the nomad." Lonergan, *Insight*, 440, on representations being erroneously taken as real things. For GEM, objectification and encounter mesh. I remap rhizome from a moving viewpoint.
14. Deleuze and Guattari, 112; they refuse to oppose knowledge through the construction of concepts within possible experience or through intuition because philosophers wonder about being. J. S. Smith, "Deleuze," (Internet) faults Deleuze's "clever hypotheses" on Nietzsche that do "not amount to philosophy" but abetted Nazi claims. Lonergan, *Method*, 33, 273, on Nietzsche's *ressentiment* as that which negatively re-feels a specific clash with someone else's value-qualities.
15. *Insight*, 315; G. B. Sala, "Lonergan on the Virtually Unconditioned as Ground of Judgment"; in generalizations or in provisional analytic propositions judgments yield a virtually unconditioned. Fulfilment is less clear when dealing with evil's absurdity.
16. Lonergan, *Insight*, 432; Deleuze and Guattari, *Philosophy*, 104-05. GEM does not vacillate between impersonalism and personalism as they tend to do. Our trans*form*ative AIRR loci are a sufficient foundation for integrating immanence-concept-personae triad on a personal basis.
17. Soul music, rag or jazz are examples of reinventing music in Afro-American ways.
18. One does not have to accept their characterization of Chinese thought as "an absolutization of immanence" (74), unless located in self-transcendent judgments.
19. Lonergan, *Insight*, 430. Since GEM metaphysics comes *after* self-affirmation, it is not subject to Derridean deconstruction aimed at self-identity as understood in Western metaphysics. Part Two seeks to establish trans*form*ative links between a "universalism in ethics" through AIRR feedback.
20. Lonergan, "Theories of Inquiry," *Second Collection*, ed. B.Tyrrell (London: Darton, Longman, 1974), 34; the *opera*tions & their dynamic relations are experiential givens.
21. Lonergan, "Insight Revisited," Second Collection, 268; Kant"s critique "was not of pure reason but of the human mind as conceived by Scotus," *Verbum: Word and Idea in Aquinas* (U. of Notre Dame) 1967, 25; *Insight*, 314. GEM upholds two kinds of knowings: that of the senses as a kitten knows milk and that of the real as verified through inquiry. The frist, elementary kind is that of experience; in its genesis neither questions for intelligence nor reflection enter. The second, verified kind pivots on questions for intelligence and reflection. Particular sciences are to be left to the scientists engaged therein, but GEM works out the dynamic structure guiding inquiries.

CHAPTER 2

1. Pure conjugates occur in Newton's view of mass, in correlatives implicit "in his law of inverse squares, in the electric and magnetic fields intensities (E and H) defined by Maxwell's equations for the electromagnetic field" (*Insight*, 80). Conjugate potency is potency to conjugate *form* and conjugate act is act of conjugate *form*, where potency *to form* and act *of form* constitute a single unity. GEM's central-conjugate *form*s are part of its strategy of working out the integral heuristic structure of proportionate being as two general cases of realizable potencies-*form*s-acts. The potency-*form*-act triad is that *by which* concrete beings that exist and change *are* constituted; conjugate-central potency-*form*-act triads are heuristic structures in*form*ing our AIRR *operations*. Central *form* (principle of unity) and differentiating conjugate *form*s enable *concrete* predications. Central act is existence, for what exists is the intelligible unity. Conjugate act is occurrence, for what occurs is defined explanatorily "by appealing to conjugate form" (434-37). Lonergan argues, in *Insight*, that the reader of a detective story, given all the clues, is often unable to spot the criminal for failing to organize the clues in an explanatory perspective. Acts of understanding occur in mathematics, but their dynamic *context* is best studied by investigating scientific methods.
2. Watson, *DNA*, 74 on how Nirenberg and Matthaei discovered that UUU (poly-uracil) encodes the amino acid polyphenylalalnine—a first step in deciphering the genetic code. A physical genome codes with triplets; GEM's potency-*form*-act triads variously affect 4-3-5 body-mind-spirit triads.
3. If ATGC bases pair up through *coded* semiotic scripts, a spiritual genome—built a-top our DNA— *transcends* DNA-RNA codes and their nucleotide bases and allows for liberty. In previous books, I spoke of a "TNA *Tata*lytic AIRR feedback" that synergizes us by lessening our alienations from self and others. To *Tata*lysis, based on Japanese *Ta* meaning "Other Power," and *ta*, meaning other alienated ones, I add "-lysis." *Tatalysis* is like catalysis, except that unlike catalysis it trans*form*s persons. I do not use "TNA *Tata*lysis," etc in this book; I have not yet received adequate criticism on the subject. While dancing synergizes Sufi dervishes, some orthodox theologians claim that ascetics are "inebriated" by God. P. Evdokimov, *L'Orthodoxie* (Paris: Desclee de Brouwer, 1980). Perhaps the meaning of orthodoxy and sainthood do evolve.
4. Aristotle, *Nicomathean Ethics*, I, 2. In his *The Nature of Buddhist Ethics* (London: MacMillan, 1992), Damien Keown, takes Aristotle's model as his own. He avoids intellectualizing Buddhism, but one should complement his approach with a more atemporal, spiritual stance such as Dogen's. Padmasiri de Silva, *Environmental Philosophy and Ethics in Buddhism* (Macmillan, 1998) is a helpful contextualization of many themes that I discuss in this book, as implied in the title.
5. Matters of faith are quite personal; no one can fully understand the alleles of someone's faith. I use interfaith reason-faith, being-nothingness alleles as AIRR bridges between persons and cultures. Alain Badiou view and Giorgio Agamben view truth as a trans*form*ative, political process that begins to change the status quo. I root such trans*form*ative process in a 4-3-5 relatedness "void."
6. Kant, *Critique of Pure Reason*, tr. N. Smith (Toronto: MacMillan: 1929) A 7, B 26.
7. Lonergan, *Insight*, 427. His context on the key to philosophy is that of discovering what logicians call a technically accurate meta-language within changing thought.
8. The locus of the equation $2x + 3y = 6$, is a straight line containing points (0,2) and (3,0). The locus of points satisfying a given condition is the set containing all the points satisfying the condition and none that do not; an inequality's locus consists of those points whose coordinates satisfy the inequality. John Austin, *How to Do Things with*

Words (Cambridge: Harvard,1975) on concrete and declarative affirmations referring to truth; constatives do not. Lonergan, *Collected Works of Bernard Lonergan*, 17, *Philosophical and Theological Papers 1965-1980*, 185-86, seems to agree with Austin in that he sees (per*form*ative) meaning as constitutive meaning.

9. W. R. Bion, *Two Papers: The Grid and the Caesura* (London: Karnac Books, 1989). Joris Wiggers, M. D. helped me *form*ulate the relevance of Bion's insights and grid.
10. H. Hunt, *The Multiplicity of Dreams: A Psychological Perspective* (Yale U, 1989) on lucid dreams as non-reducible to only a mental waking up unique to the sleep state. Self-recognition is akin to the development of mystic self-reflective consciousness. Religion, as nurture, fits us into the natural and human environments of our birth; it completes us as human beings. Its *form*al content is the psychological equivalent of the biological genome; it has a similar function. It works in the space of all possible configurations of our minds ("M"); biology works in the space of all possible genomes (G). When we observe the distribution of real genomes in G we can notice a detailed structure attributable to evolution. Religion's evolution has led to similar trans*form*ational structures in the space of mind M (AIRR operational procedures).
12. Michael Guillen, *Bridges to Infinity: The Human Side of Mathematics* (Tarcher, 1983), 33; this legendary account is traced to Egyptian' a respect for harmony.
13. Richard Feynman, *QED, The Strange Theory of Light and Matter* (Princeton U., 1985) 35, 89.
14. William Doheny, ed., *Selected Writings of St. Teresa of Avila* (Milwaukee: Bruce, 1950) 192. "Soul" is derived from the *sawol* from common Germanic *saiwala*, "coming from the eternal sea." I view soul in the Christian sense (influenced by Aristotle) rather than in the Platonic sense. Chapters 4 and 5 will outline how one's unique AIRR *op*era*tions can lead to "feedback coopera*tion."
15. John W. Dixon, "Theology and Form," in *JAAR*, xlv, Supplement, 1977, 644.
16. Donald Watson, MD and Bernard Williams, "Eccles' Model of the Self Controlling Its Brain: the Irrelevance of Dualist-Interactionism," in *Neuroquantology*, 1: 119-28, January, 2003, 119.
17. In "Neocortical Dynamics and EEG" (1994), Paul Nunez describes wave velocity in EEG's as transmitted along corticocortical fibers: cognitive events may be directly related to the continuous "forming and reforming of local and regional circuits which are functionally disconnected from tissue involved in global operation." Events that occur in complex nonlinear systems such as self-organization and stable spatial structure in the presence of temporal chaos do occur in the neocortex and may be closely aligned with cognition. Taoists anticipated the results of EEG's when they spoke of trans*form*ing heavy densities of sensation and energy into higher frequencies of vibration. Internet sites (addressing such issues in terms of relaxation that loosens the energetic knots keeping us bound to our present perceptions) argue for the importance of deep-relaxation alpha waves over theta waves, or link EEG research with mind-control and the Pentagon's Remote Viewing experiments that sought to counter Soviet psychic operations against religion.
18. Eugene Taylor in "Meditation" (Internet) notes that Zen meditators progress from a decrease in alpha wave frequency to the appearance of rhythmical theta chains. Reviewing previous research on meditation and EEG's, Taylor concludes that, on the basis of existing EEG evidence, we can differentiate between meditation and drowsiness. Although more precisely *form*ulated research is needed, Taylor concludes that psychophysiologically, meditation is a finely held hypnagogic state.

19. Karl Popper and John Eccles, *The Self and Its Brain* (New York: Springer), 371, 365-68. Eccles' argument depends on the role of the difficult-to-access thalamus. Descartes' dualist brain-mind interactionism led to Malebranche's occasionalism, Spinoza's monism, Leibniz's divinely pre-established harmony and to mechanistic neuroscience. Vincent Descombes, *The Mind's Provisions: A Critique of Cognitivism* (Princeton U: 2001) on mind's contextual nature.
20. C. George Boeree, "Sleep," (Internet). "Brain, Chaos, Quantum Mechanics" (Internet) argues that at the neurosystems level, experimental evidence points to chaos in the EEG's of some phases of cortical activity, including sleep, resting wakefulness and states such as epilepsy. "The low correlation dimensions of several of these states is consistent with collective chaotic dynamics in neuron populations." A quantum behaves like a particle in terms of its emission and absorption; yet, its wave function extends through spacetime. Models of brain function should consistently describe mind, consciousness and free will, as they link the structural instability of brain dynamics and quantum uncertainty; the quantum-physical brain "may be more than just an interface between sensory input and decision-making. It may be a doorway between complementary aspects of the physical universe, the time-directed nature of real-particle symmetry-breaking and the time-symmetric aspect of the subquantum domain. If so, the role of consciousness and brain-mind duality may be central to cosmology." It has been shown that meditators' brainwaves shifted from asymmetrical patterns (one hemisphere dominant over the other), to a balanced state of whole-brain integration.
21. Lonergan, *Insight*, 313; I transpose this to let a spiritual genomic "being-void" dialectic emerge.
22. Watson and Williams, "Eccles' Model," *ibid*. SELF uses Eccles' ideal of derandomization in his model of synaptic neurotransmitter release based on statistical quantum physics; in TES, SELFs are not limited to humans, but "correspond to the organization inherent in all coherent systems" from photons and beyond; they are prephysical entities whose *opera*tions map elements of matter. Despite Watson and Williams' reservation on "mind," I stress both mind and self. GEM uses the abstract *form*ulation of geometry to go beyond hypothetico-deductive postulation or a descriptive iso*morph*ism of the physical world. An abstract *form*ulation of the intelligibility of spacetime is one of the possible sets of definitions, postulates or inferences that systematically unify relations of extensions and of durations. If geometry studies the invariant properties of given elements under specified groups of trans*form*ations, I extend the principle to AIRR-4-3-5 trans*form*ations.
23. Antonio Damasio, *Descartes' Error* (New York: Avon, 1994). The challenge is to redefine Cartesian dualist-interactionism in ways that avoid the Cartesian body-mind binding problem.
24. Cusa, *De Docta Ignorantia*, I. 3. h 10, on our minds' need to always understand more deeply. "Interval" in *The New Harvard Dictionary of Music* (Harvard: 1986) shows that the harmony problem has only approximate but K*no* exact solutions; this fits in with my "in-betweens."
25. Dean Hamer, *The God Gene: How Faith is Hardwired into Our Genes* (Doubleday, 2004). Geneticists investigate our 3.2 billion chemical bases. RNA is a "given"; a 4-3-5 ethics is an ideal.
26. Tad Dunne, "What Do I Do When I Paint," *Method: Journal of Lonergan Studies*, 16, 2, 121.
27. Matthew Lamb, *History, Method* and *Theology* (Scholars Press, 1978) vi, 170-73.

The notion of the non-intelligibility of random occurrences technically affirms non-identity within the physical sciences. Richard Palmer, *Hermeneutics* (Evanston: Northwestern Univ), 1969, 56-58 on Dilthey.

28. By "diphase GEM," I mean its inbuilt feedback trans*form*ative ability (Part Two).
29. Buddhism enucleated notions of *substance* long before Lonergan did. I relate the enucleations.
30. In genetics, conjugation is the temporary fusion of two single-celled organisms resulting in new allelic loci. In mathematics, conjugates order points within loci. With constructivists, GEM sees scientists as constituting knowledge, but it avoids the problem of being antirealist. Many *forms* of constructivism in mathematics struggle with the relevance of *axioms*. AIRR-4-3-5 loci order GEM triadic conjugates by studying the ways scientists and mathematicians, in fact, attain knowledge.
31. GEM trans*form*ations converge toward the infinite; mathematicians do it speculatively while religious persons to do o in their daily life inasmuch as they strive for virtue and help others.
32. Antonio Damasio, *Looking for Spinoza* (New York: Harcourt, 2003), 30; 195, 198; he accepts Spinoza's use of 'idea' as synonym for image or mental representation. He uses idea to signify an elaboration on images, as a product of the intellect rather than plain imagination" (211). I accept Damasio's view of Spinozan feelings but seek to trans*form* pantheist implications while being open to the transcendent. Spinoza validates the role of our affections, GEM focuses on our pure desire to know that leads to self-knowledge. Important to GEM's ability to replace Damasio's reliance on Spinoza in retrieving feeling as a key element of human identity is its replacement of the notion of substance with that of feedback conjugates or potency-*form*-act per*form*ance triads. GEM sublates Damasio by translating potency and finality in ways that trans*form* our intellectual-moral ambiguities with noetic verbs (an openness to the in-betweens of poetry and mysticism).
33. Damasio, *Spinoza*, 170, 36; *conatus* can underpin GEM's unrestricted, pure desire to know.
34. Lonergan, *Method in Theology*, 31. Here GEM anticipates the nesting principle.
35. Maxwell, Hadamard, Duhem and GEM's view of randomness all anticipated chaos theory. It is impossible to model either a continuous equation or an AIRR-4-3-5 ethics on a computer. I leave it as an open question whether Hadamard's conjecture that the wave equation for 3, 5, . . . space dimensions (satisfying Huygens' principle) can have any applicability to a 4-3-5 genome. In both quantum physics and in a 4-3-5 ethics, discrete approximations are the only possibility. GTR, discrete wave models and GEM can be studied to understand intrinsic properties, not just models.
36. Deleuze and Guattari, *Philosophy*, 118, 228n7: refers to G. G. Granger, *Pour la Connaissance Philosophique* (Paris: Odile Jacob, 1988, chaps 6-7. GEM nuances I. Lakatos, *The Methodology of Scientific Research Programs* (Cambridge, 1978) who vacillates between Popper and Duhem-Quine. It sublates their views by dialectically *grounding* materialisms, idealisms and voluntarisms.
37. For Kant, *Pure Reason*, 105, A 68, knowledge *is* discursive; judgment is "mediate" knowledge. In GEM, higher systems integrate not developing persons but the universe they are able to judge. "The schematism of the categories comes within striking distance of the virtually unconditioned, still Kant failed to see that the unconditioned is a constituent component in the genesis of judgment, and so he relegated it to the role of a regulative ideal" of rationality (*Insight*, 413).

38. In a "homeobox," a sequence of about 180 nucleotides encodes a 60-amino acid sequence (a homeodomain or DNA-binding protein acting as transcription factor: Klug-Cummings, *Genetics*, 250, 550). Operons, genetic units (one or more structural genes coding for polypeptides) are a negative way of controlling genes' transcriptional activity (525). If nucleotides encode amino acid triplets (amid possibly chaotic RNA transcription), GEM's potency-*form*-act triads order, liberate.
39. James Watson, *DNA: The Secret of Life*, (New York: Knopf, 2003), 36-37, 49. A protein is a molecule composed of one or more polypeptides, each composed of amino acids covalently linked together. Edwin Chargaff had encouraged them to study the ATGC bases' chemical structures..
40. Appropriating our *opera*tions means locating the immanent triplets active in our genetic and spiritual domains. In my *Logic* (97-99), I argued that the DNA double helix serves as a helpful analogy for explaining the relationship between interdisciplinary collaboration, AIRR *opera*tions and the interpenetrating cycles of psychosocial development; see also Hampden-Turner, *Radical Man: The Process of Psycho-Social Development* (Cambridge: Schenkman, 1970) 24-99.
41. Peptides contain two or more amino acids linked by the carboxyl group of one amino acid and the amino group of another. Polypeptides are an amino acid chain of 10 to 100 amino acids that are joined by covalent peptide bonds *before* assuming a functional 3-dimensional configuration. On April 1, 1948, Gamow and Ralph Alpher (adding H. Bethe's name so as mimic "Alpha-Beta-Gamma) published their big-bang theory in "The Origin of Chemical Elements" which studied the distribution of chemical elements in the universe. Positing a primeval thermonuclear explosion as origin of the universe, it argued that after the big bang, atomic nuclei were built up when initially formed pairs and triplets captured neutrons. On algorithms governing RNA's roles in producing proteins, Daniel Huson, "RNA Secondary Structure" in *Algorithmische Bioinformatik*, February 17, 2004. RNA trans*forms* DNA hereditary in*form*ation passed on from generation to generation.
42. Watson, *DNA*, 69, 67-85. William S. Klug and Michael R. Cummings, *Concepts of Genetics*, (Prentice Hall, 1997), 326-47, on how Vernon Ingram discovered the precise molecular difference causing molecular diseases. Here was conclusive "evidence that genetic mutations—differences in the sequence of As, Ts, Gs, and Cs in the DNA code of a gene—could be 'mapped' directly to differences in proteins' amino acid sequences. Ribosomes, presented with an RNA sequence of ribonucleotides, bind to it and attract the charged tRNA bonded to its amino acid. This occurs through anticodons (nucleotide triplets in tRNA molecules complementary to and able to bind to codon triplets in an mRNA molecule). Nucleosides and nucleotides are named according to the specific ATGC-U nitrogenous bases composing a building block. In laying out the issues for translating a nucleic acid sequence into an ordered polypeptide sequence, Sydney Brenner knew that it would take at least 3 nucleotides (with 64 permutations) to code for a single amino acid; he asked which of the 20 amino acids was to be incorporated into a protein chain at a particular point when there are only four DNA letters. A physical genome uses coded amino acids; a spiritual one is open to "conversions." Fig. 1 broadens my analogies between DNA-RNA coding triplets, GEM and Deleuze and Guattari's triad. Part TWO will integrate our ATGC-U AIRR-love *loci* affecting our lives with ethical discernment. An analogical chicken-and-egg problem occurs as to the universe's origin. See Stephen Hawking, '*A Brief History of Time: From the Big Bang to Black Holes* (New York: Bantam, 1988) and Paul Davies, *God and the New Physics*

(New York: Simon & Shuster).
43. Richard Liddy, *Transforming Light: Intellectual Conversion in the Early Lonergan* (Liturgical Press Collegeville, 1993) 98, 108 on Lonergan's early realization of Scotist-Suarezian influences in Scholasticism that confused knowledge with seeing—a recurrent theme in his later writings.
44. *Insight*, 434. GEM's explanatory conjugates sublate Heidegger's descriptive phenomenology.
45. Peirce, *Principles of Philosophy* Cambridge: Belknap, 1978); I, 356. He often revised his triad of agent, patient and action. GEM generalizes probable judgments (on particulars) in ways that satisfy both Peirce's view on induction and existentialists' notion of an irreducible "void" as the very pivot of thought. It "makes the transition form one particular case to another or from a particular case to the general case an almost automatic procedure of intelligence" (*Insight*, 288).
46. A. Varzy, "Boundary," *The Stanford Encyclopaedia of Philosophy*, on Peirce and on owning boundaries given their fuzziness and the epistemic ways open to us for construing such fuzziness.
47. Deleuze and Guattari, *Philosophy*, 67; they draw implications: "The merchant buys in a territory, deterritorializes products into commodities, and is reterritorialized on commercial circuits" (68). For them, Italy and Spain aborted their potential for modern philosophy; this left Germany, France and England to fashion their would-be politically viable geophilosophy (85-99), a concept that goes back to *A Thousand Plateaus* and its indebtedness to Nietzsche and Freud
47a. Lonergan, *Method*, 48, on our AIRR *operations'* plasticity and the structure of the human good. I would add that there are analogous processes of selection in genes and in our AIRR operations. Delaunay's triangulation of points that treats the points as nodes and links them using a trans*form operator* represents another analogy with quasi-infinite methods that a 4-3-5 topology interlinks. As such an o*perator* is applied to vectors as *operand*, so I map and interrelate "4-3-5 functions."
48. For Lonergan, the analogy between mathematical *operat*ors which change one function into another and biological *operat*ors, which, as "the upwardly directed dynamism of proportionate being" effect "the transition from one set of forms, laws, schemes to another set" (*Insight*, 465)
49. Emmanuel Levinas, *Totality and Infinity* (Pittsburgh: Duquesne Univ., 1969) 43, 50. Derrida's response to Levinas' notion of infinity led him to a more radical break with ontology. If war, for Derrida, is the *differance* between the Other and the finite world, GEM locates 4-3-4 *differances* between the locus of divine speech and ethics in our 4-3-5 finite living out of that speech. Deleuze mobilizes concepts of difference and repetition, not to recapture Hegel's dialectic of opposition-contradiction in which being is conceived in a univocal sense, but to transcend Hegel. GEM does so by trans*form*ing Hegel's notion of being into whatever can be intelligently grasped, reasonably affirmed and interrelated with spiritual realities—as in a co*opera*tive feedback ethics (see Part Two).
50. Edith Wyschogrod, "Derrida, Levinas and Violence" in *Derrida and Deconstructionism*, ed. Hugh Silverman (New York" Routledge), 1989, 188. She traces movements beyond egoism.
51. Bion, *Grid and the Caesura*, 51; this applies to patients afraid of being psychotic.
52. Lacan represents transcendental difference by the surface aspect of a zone (a torus-ring's three-dimensional *form*) whose peripheral exteriority and central exteriority con-

stitute a single region (Lacan, *Ecrits, A Selection*, tr. Bruce Fink). *Ecrits*, 2 initiates his "I precipitated in a primordial form." Richard Webster, "The Cult of Lacan" (Internet) exposes the obscurity of his "symbolic matrix." I avoid Freud-Lacan bio-genetic reasoning on the infantile stage in favor of Piaget-GEM stages of moral development in children's interpersonal interactions; for Lonergan (*Method*, 34), the unconscious is an *unobjectified* conscious whose objective ground is in potency.

53. P. Patton, Concept and Politics in Derrida and Deleuze," *Critical Horizons*, 44.
54. Lonergan, *Insight*, 314, on how mathematical thought tends "towards a general, complete, and ideal account of the manners in which enriching abstraction can add intelligibility and order to the material element" As with GEM's potentiality-*form*-act, Deleuze and Guattari (5), see the need to *create* concepts: "The philosopher is the concept's friend; he is potentiality of the concept."
55. Human feelings are not to be absorbed within God as infinite substance. Kant saw, better than Spinoza that philosophy cannot replace science. Our immanent AIRR exigences, however, sublate Kant's categorical imperatives by reaching transcendence through authentic, metaxic strivings.
56. The occult Chinese roots of *Feng-shui* do not diminish the impact of its aesthetic proportions; one might study the trans*form*ative loci of earlier cultures' aesthetic sense that led to *Feng-shui*, to Pythagorean harmonies and to the transpositions of such loci from, e.g., astrology to astronomy. If Neo-Darwinism, by combining population genetics with natural selection, generated a new view of evolutionary process' loci, GEM allelic conjugates iso*morph*ically interpret, integrate such loci.
57. *Insight*, 459; in both cases, having discerned a regularity of events, one advances to the abstract relation that is verified in the events. This relation implicitly defines the explanatory specifications of the events while it fixes, by their relations to one another, the conjugate *form*s. Since there are no integrators on the biological level (or on the lower levels that condition aggregates of acts), or if genetic drift and natural selection statistically change the characteristics of a species over time, GEM uses statistical and classical methods to show how these differ from ethics and spirituality.
57a. The analogy between how RNA trans*form*s DNA's four nucleotide bases and how our AIRR *opera*tions act as trans*form*ative loci may be compared with GEM's alteration of the fourfold division of classical mechanics (Newton), classical statistics (Bolzmann), quantum mechanics (Heisenberg, (Schrödinger) and quantum statistics (Bose-Einstein, Fermi-Dirac) to a twofold division. Intelligence either "anticipates the discovery of functional relations on "which relations between measurements will converge, or else it anticipates the discovery of probabilities from which relative actual frequencies may diverge though only at random." The latter procedure is statistical, the former is a mode of inquiry common to Galileo, Newton, Einstein (*Insight*, 68). GEM complements this with genetic and dialectic methods to yield four basic heuristic structures.
58. Klug and Cummings, *Genetics*, 26, 592. For J. Wells, "Inertial force as a possible factor in mitosis" in *Biosystems*, 1985; 17: 301, "an inertial force could arise in the spindle from postulated high-frequency . . . oscillations" that could be caused by changes in coherently processing electron spin alignments at the spindle poles. Matt Ridley, *Genome* (HarperCollins, 1999) on the nature-nurture aspects of our genome. ATGC bases are "letters" writing the words, paragraphs, chapters making up our genome; AIRR and 4-3-5 faith-hope-love are letters or chapters nurturing our lives.
59. Lonergan, *Insight*, 181. In his section on "the subjective field of common sense," he

concludes (206) that analysis seeks to reorient the psychic aberrations in one's stream of consciousness.
60. Lonergan, "Healing and Creating in History, *A Third Collection*, (Mahwah, NJ: 1985) 100-09, where he attacks multinational corporations for (4-2) maximizing profits to the detriment of all.
61. A 4-3-5 allelic ploidy considers evil in its factualness and attributes sin to human fallibility unlike Calvinist predestination or a Teilhard view that subsumes evil as a given of evolution.
62. Deleuze and Guattari's "4-3-4" geophilosophy *deterritorializes*. GEM contextualizes concepts within patterns of experience that do not reduce transcendence to an illusion. Its openness to transcendent realms of meaning enables it to accommodate East-Western *forms* of thought. As an in-between bridge, it functions as a parallel to Derrida's *differances* or to postmodernists views in general—but in "4-3-5 ethical ways; grammatical *forms* are "in-between alleles" whose *differances* are adjudicated in the 4-3-5 loci of our intentional *opera*tions. All the tasks and the responsibilities of life that one acquires by being born into a family, a community or tradition are located in our AIRR operations but their functions are adjusted within patterns of experience open to 4-3-5 ethics.
63. Lonergan, *Insight*, 19; 12-16. If through an inverse insight one realizes that there is nothing to be understood, one can use statistical methods to study the non-systematic. Inverse insights grasp that irrational numbers, surds, the empirical residue and other such entities lack intelligibility.
64. Watson, *DNA*, 71. Gamow and Watson's "RNA Tie Club" with a membership of 20 implied the genetic code's 20 coding amino acids. There are many diversities in how our physical and spiritual genomes' triads interface with their ATGC or AIRR "bases." RNA is both chicken and egg. In a spiritual genome, trans*form*ative co*opera*tion is enhanced through rituals, politics, social get-togethers; allelic grace (silently) enriches our lives in ways analogical to ATGC-U interactions.
65. Using *swarm* intelligence, code duality and bioscientific switch-processes, Jesper Hoffmeyer, *Signs of Meaning in the Universe* (Indiana U. 1996) argues for *some* semiotic freedom in cells. T. Strachan, *The Human Genome* (Bath: Bios, 1992). Stressing that sociobiology's "genes" are "unknown" to geneticists, Sahotra Sarkar, *Genetics and Reductionism* (Cambridge U. 2000), 191, rejects Edward O. Wilson, *On Human Nature* (Harvard, 1978) that tries to import the principles of sociobiological codes into the social sciences. If molecular biology's F-rules (structure fixes function) cannot be extended beyond biology, GEM ushers us into ethics. Scientists do not "synthesize" life; they only reassemble varying components of existing cells.
66. Richard Bernstein, *Praxis and Action* (U. of Pennsylvania, 1971), 119-22, 125, 230.
67. In persons, about 1,000 of the genome's 35,000 genes appear involved in the ubiquitin system. If gene therapy can lead to unforeseen results (Crichton's *Prey*), GEM cooperative therapy recalls our spiritual allelic foundation in overlooked metaxies of God's love or of Buddhist "nothingness."
68. Even authentic persons have inauthentic moments. GEM helps us search for non-idealist ideals.
69. *Insight*, 445. A to-be-known becomes determinate through knowing; "what is to be" becomes determinate only through its becoming. Present knowing and present reality are moments in process toward fuller knowing, fuller reality. In things of any higher genus, lower potency-*form*-act conjugates survive, but not lower things. GEM sub-

sumes such processes under the umbrella term of finality in ways analogous to Whiteheadian "creativity" and Bracken's "link" in Joseph Bracken, *The Divine Matrix: Creativity as Link between East and West* (Maryknoll: Orbis, 1995).
70. Such a procedure, which includes Husserl and GEM's appreciation of the reflective nature of judgment, allows us to establish an analogy between a geophilosophy and GEM's dialectical foundations—an analogy that this chapter reinforces by studying DNA-RNA trans*form*ations.
71. Claude Mauriac, Francois' son, adds to the tangle of sin (and mysticism) his notions of "a-literature"; his *form*less novels challenge traditional *form*s. For Frank Braio, we are in search of known-unknown *"form*less *form*alyzables" variously thematised in East-West religious traditions.
72. Lonergan, *Method*, 73, 262. In *Philosophical and Theological Papers 1958-1964*, he revised his approach to the mediation of meaning so as to include the multiplicity of analogical meanings in various cultures. My analogy between the full panoply of our emotions integrates mathematics' tensors and complex numbers; it sublates ATGC's objective properties in trans*form*ing ways Only judgments constitute a fact, arrive at objectivity or lay a plane to verify a critical philosophy. Our emerging minds work through a body-mind-spirit *triad* (*form*ed of potential trans*form*ing acts); the order or relation between trans*form*er and trans*form*ed is such that AIRR-4-3-5 *oper*ations constitute the ethically trans*form*ative process. For Thomas Kuhn, *The Structure of Scientific Revolutions* (U. of Chicago, 1970), a paradigm shift is not value-free description; it is a *praxis* whose objectivity-subjectivity mediations anticipate criteria of adequacy in choosing theories.
73. Bruce Director, "Fundamental Theorem: Gauss's Declaration of Independence," EIR, April 12, 2002, 16. Only physical action defines "magnitude." Complex numbers (ordered pairs of real numbers (a, b) together with the *oper*ations, *form* a complex number field denoted by C

$$(a, b) + (c, d) = (a + c, b + d)$$
$$(a, b) \times (c, d) = (ac\text{-}bd, bc, + ad)$$

By identifying the real number "a" with the complex (a, 0), the field of real numbers R becomes a subfield of C. The imaginary unit i is the complex number (0,1). As C is the algebraic closure of R, I work out implications of ideal loci analogously to how an Argand diagram represents points on a plane where a perpendicular axis represents real numbers, the other, pure imaginaries. One can express rational numbers as an integer or a quotient of integers, including the fractions of the *form* m/n where m and n are integers and n is not zero. Irrational numbers cannot be expressed as quotients of integers. Modern algebra uses only numbers and relations to show that a geometric problem can only be solved with a compass and ruler in a finite number of steps if its algebraic equivalent depends on a number obtained from a whole number by addition, subtraction, division, multiplication or extraction of square roots. Numbers not open to algebraic methods (*pi* etc) are *transcendental* for they cannot be the root of any algebraic or constructible equation; a complex number's modulus (numerical length of a vector representing the complex number) of $4 + 3i$ is 5.
74. If the characteristic of an R ring is the unique natural number n such that R contains a subring iso*morph*ic to the factor ring Z/nZ, GEM iso*morph*ism encompasses mathematical *morph*isms.
75. Remo Roth, "Introduction to Carl Jung's Principle of Synchronicity." The synchronicity of dreams helped Pauli tie beta radioactivity with the neutrino and antineutrino.

Brainwaves may link desynchronized synchronizations using synchronicity as well as Hausdorff topological dimensions' irregular sets and patterns. I leave such notions in their undefined nature. I explore ideal heuristics that, like Bernanos, inquire into believers' recalcitrance to implement evangelical imperatives.

76. I do not emphasize correspondence, but I believe that amplitude waves (see Feynman, *QED*) are not without their "influence" on our physical and spiritual genomes and their "interactions."

77. Freud, *The Interpretation of Dreams* (1900) ch. 7; in *Beyond the Pleasure Principle* (London: Hogarth, 1961) 49, "The dominating tendency of mental life . . . is the effort to reduce . . . internal tension due to stimuli." *An Autobiographical Study* (New York: Norton) 66. Samuel Weber, *The Legend of Freud* (Stanford Univ.) 210, on some of Freud's vicious circles. On psychic reflection, Bernard Tyrrell, *Method: Journal of Lonergan Studies*, 14, 1996, 1-35. Herbert Marcuse, *Eros and Civilization* (Boston: Beacon, 1955) rejects revisionisms of Freud by Fromm and K. Horney.

78. For Heidegger, *On Time and Being* (New York: Harper and Row, 1972) all philosophical thinking which explicitly or inexplicitly follows Husserl's call "to the thing itself" belongs to the free space of an opening of which philosophy knows nothing but which involves method. The "end of philosophy and the task of thinking" designates reflection-centered questioning. He notes that the old meaning of the word "end" means the same as place: "from one end to the other" or from one place to the other. The end of philosophy is the place in which the whole of philosophy's history "is gathered in its most extreme possibility. End as completion means this gathering." "Openness" is the possibility of encountering another present being; it grants a possible letting-appear, an opening that he likens to a forest clearing in contrast to a dense forest (57, 64-65).

79. Kant, *Pure Reason*, B 5, B 19. GEM links faith-reason alleles and the intellectual and religious conversions—a way to get us beyond Kant's transcendental idealism. It accepts the view that it was Descartes, Kant and Husserl who made it possible to treat the plane of immanence as a field of (un)consciousness. But it goes beyond Kant by linking the transcendent with the immanent field of consciousness and with synthesis. Like Kant, it ascribes immanence to the subject of synthesis as a new, subject unity but it shows that intellectual and moral conversion can be 4-3-5 allelically linked to religious conversion, to faith, grace, love, mysticism and ethics. AIRR imperatives are the link that Kant insufficiently analyzed, thus inviting a false dialectic of the ego instead of the self as 4-3-5 related with all other humans. Henry Allison, *Kant's Transcendental Idealism* (Yale, 1983) 4, opposes Strawson's standard picture of Kantian transcendental idealism, arguing that in the second edition of his first *Critique*, Kant synthesizes the sensible and intellectual conditions of apperception (an interpretation that would bring Kant closer to GEM). He ignores Lobachevskian non-Euclidian geometries in which time and space are not "*a priori*" but are *a posteriori*.

80. Edmund Husserl, *Logische Untersuchungen* (Halle: Niemeyer, 4th ed. In *Ideen zu einer reinen Phanomeologie und phanomenologischen Philosophie, I,* (The Hague: Nijhoff, 1950) 44. While factual and essential unities give objects to consciousness' straightforward regard by entering these objects of experience, each in its distinctive way, consciousness can also deflect its regard back onto these enterings and discover its own unity. Intuition helps us confirm meaning by establishing a unity which is unlike the first two. Correlating such a unity is due to our intuitions' boundary-conditions that we can accept as sources that insure that we know them correctly. Each

originary presentive intuition is a legitimizing source of cognition for one personally actualizes what intuition offers within the limits of the boundary conditions, but philosophy has never lived up to its claim (*Phenomenology and the Crisis of Philosophy*, (New York: Harper, 1965) 71.

81. Deleuze and Guattari, *Philosophy*, 142. Transcendental GEM, as open to the transcendent, is more open to Eastern notions of philosophy and religion's dependence than is postmodernism.

82. Quentin Lauer, *Phenomenology: its Genesis and Prospects* (New York: Harper, 1958, 82, 85. Such phenomenologists as Scheler and Marcel did arrive at a "self-knowledge" similar to St. Augustine's or GEM's self-constitution. For Michael McCarthy, *The Crisis of Philosophy* (SUNY, 1990) 87, Husserl's use of intuition to justify his epistemology was based on the analogy of seeing. I seek to deepen Husserl's epoche with a greater openness to reflexive transcendental feedback.

83. W. F. J. Ryan, "The Transcendental Reduction According to Edmund Husserl and Intellectual Conversion According to Bernard Lonergan" in *Creativity and Method*, 404. Husserl and GEM reject a descriptive psychologism that reduces judgments to the plane of conceptual *opera*tions.

84. In ATGC-U bases, RNA's uracil trans*form*s DNA. In AIRR feedback analogues, an isomorphic potency-*form*-act triad between our knowing and the known acts in many trans*form*ative ways.

85. *Insight*, 477. Relating total energy to the quantum, Lonergan explains metaphysics' elements by relating 1) prime potency as quantitative limitation to energy and 2) potency in knowledge and being to *finality*. There is a parallel between incomplete knowing ever heading toward fuller knowing and an incomplete universe heading toward being. As intellectually patterned experience heads toward insight and *judgments*, so potency heads toward *forms* and acts (ibid 443-46).

86. C. P. Snow, *The Two Cultures and the Scientific Revolution*, 1959, overdoes the breach.

87. Unlike words, propositions are *intersubjective* terms, *not unrepeatable*, physical occurrences. By asking whether defined terms, in fact exist, we intersubjectively seek to approximate truth.

88. "Cartesian dualism was the juxtaposition of the rational affirmation *Cogito, ergo sum* and of the 'already out there now real' stripped of its secondary qualities and of any substantiality distinct from spatial extension" (*Insight*, 413). Hobbes grants reality to mind only if it is another instance of matter in motion. John Locke, *An Essay Concerning the Human Understanding*, (New York: 1959) III, uses nominal, *not* real essences; it helps confirm British empiricism in the road that led to Hume's analysis of our knowing as a manifold of unrelated sense impressions.

89. R. Scott Hawley and Catherine A. Mori, *The Human Genome: a User's Guide* (San Diego: Academic, 1999) 5. Proteins include such structural proteins as enzymes, hormones and receptors as well as DNA-binding proteins. While proteins such as tubulin and collagen are subunits out of which cells build various kinds of scaffold and skeletons, both inside and outside of cells, enzymes direct and catalyze a host of biochemical reactions, such as digestion and energy production. As it is vital to digest food, so it is vital to digest a vast plague of phenomena tempting us everywhere.

90. The psychological present reaches into its past, anticipates its future (*Method*, 177).

91. Metaphysical equi*val*ence controls meaning (*Insight*, 502) without leaping between scientific inquiry and pseudo-metaphysical myth-making. If evolutionists distinguish

the initial conditions of physico-chemical aspects of the mass of molecules making up the cell from boundary conditions historically imprinted upon the cell at its creation through cell division, GEM meets conditions of possibility in Kant. On successive levels of integration and a principle of correspondence between coincidental manifolds on each lower level and systematizing *forms* on the next higher level (531).
92. Living tissues contains thousands of enzymes. GEM authenticates trillions of AIRR ideal actions.
93. GEM judgments reconcile such Kantian duties as justice and gratitude with our actual duties.
94. John Rawls, *A Theory of Justice* (Cambridge: Belknap, 1971) seeks to justify the substantive principles of justice on minimal, uncontroversial (partly Kantian) elements. GEM's distributive economics can validate Rawlsian "Justice as Fairness" without his veil of ignorance" premise.

CHAPTER 3

1. While Francis Galton wanted a planned human development based on his genetics, I believe that Theodor Geiger offered a more realistic, ethical alternative with his thesis that society is depersonalized by ideology (such as eugenics) but can be redeemed by ideal interpersonal bonds.
2. David Bohm, *Wholeness and the Implicate Order* (London: Routledge and Kegan) 1980. His migration from an erstwhile antipathy to mysticism to a mystic view ushers in a spiritual topology. His "hologram claims" that reality "does not exist" were anticipated by Yogacara and Berkeley. Penrose's study of consciousness based on quantum computation in microtubules and Chew's notion of "event" may also hint at scientists' search for a fifth metaxic ideal transposing AIRR loci.
3. The propositions $1 + 1 = 2$, $1-1 = 0$, $1 \times 1 = 1$ and $1 / 1 = 1$ differ as to their *opera*tions, that is to say, they differ only as conjugate terms differ from conjugate *forms* as properly understood.
4. James Fredericks, "The Metanoetics of Interreligious Encounter," *Inter-Religio*, 16, Fall, 1989; the language we speak, our beliefs shape the way we think; AIRR loci ground language and belief.
5. Steven Weinberg, *Dreams of a Final Theory* (New York: Vintage, 1993) 174.
6. GEM's genesis of methods grounds recursive rules such as those in Noam Chomsky, *Aspects of Theory of Syntax* (Cambridge: MIT, 1965). By sublating recursive patterns and restructuring Chomskian grammar insights, it sublates evolutionary views on producing sounds *and* language. If symmetry is invariance under a group of trans*forma*tions, 4-3-5 trans*forma*tors convert *forms*, respecting the in-betweens of baryon asymmetry and of a spirit *Angst* 4-3-4 haunting many of us.
7. Ronald Laymon, "Idealizations," *Concise Routledge Encyclopaedia of Philosophy* (2003), 380.
8. Diana Walker *et alii*, "Skeletor, a Novel Chromosome Protein," JCB, 18 Dec, 2001.
9. British mathematics was long handicapped by relying on Newton's synthetic me-thod. The Cambridge Analytical Society was founded (1816) to foster Leibniz' view of the calculus. Gauss' representation of complex numbers and the discovery by Abel (1824) of the imaginary period of ellliptic functions, led to the work of Cauchy (putting calculus on a firm logical foundation) of Weierstrass (stressing the analytic continuation of functions) and of Riemann. Evans M. Harrell II, "A Short History of Operator Theory"

(Internet). Clifford's reconciliation of the Grassmanian and quarternions led to other invariant *operators* and con*form*al geometry {(R. Baston, "Quarternion Complexes) *Journal of Geometric Physics*, 88, (1992) 29-52}. Hamilton used a noncommutative field or division ring involving quaternions to modify the field postulate. Einstein used Gauss and Hamilton's work and 4-D vectors that obey laws similar to those of complex numbers (based on the *physical* reality of the square roots of negative numbers). I argue that GEM functions in ways indicated in group theory (conditions of closure, associativity identity and inverses) and topology. Treating GEM as a quasi-infinite group helps one develop an analogical spiritual topology.

10. The spectral theorem evolved from spectral theory (an inclusive term for theories extending the eigenvector {non-zero vector that, if *opera*ted on by the *opera*tor, results in a scalar multiple of itself}) and eigenvalue theory of a single square matrix. As a decomposition theorem applying to normal *operators* in functional analysis and linear algebra, it notes where a multiplication *operator* can model a linear *operator*. Variational calculus implicitly uses *operators*; one calculates the first variation of a functional as a differentiation in the space of a function; here, a derivative is a linear *operator*. An infinite G group whose Cayley graph reflects large-scale geometric features reveals the group's deep properties usually hidden to other research. Division by zero approaches infinity.

11. Genetics and mathematics both have notions of determinants that respectively identify sex cells or a value associated with a square array. Lonergan (*Insight*, 465) on mathematical and genetic *opera*tors' integrating indeterminacies. I use genetics' 4-3-5 analogy and a mathematics 4-3-4 analogy to evaluate the indeterminate but creative socioethical role of AIRR-4-3-5 pivot-point loci in such a way as to bring out and link *opera*tors' upwardly directed dynamism (potency-finality).

12. Banach's book on *opera*tor theory studies functions on spaces of infinite dimensions and the trans*form*ations between the vector spaces occurring in functional analysis, in the spectrum of an individual *opera*tor or in the semigroup structure of a collection of them. If in the Dirac-von Neumann *form*ulation of quantum mechanics, self-adjoint *opera*tors (with Hermitian matrix) are 4-3-4 important, a 4-3-5 genome transposes such a notion to ethical East-West 4-3-5 feedback.

13. Being its self-adjoint *opera*tor, a Hermitian is a diagonal matrix with entries in real numbers. If the universe emerges from a Ground devoid of *form*, a *sunya*-void (prior to differentiations) is the manifest source of all; it hints at the mystic unknowing that GEM seeks beyond known unknowns.

14. A. Matamala, "Dynamical Symmetries in Quantum Chemistry." A Lie group's global structure is mostly determined by a local structure (by what happens in an identity element's arbitrarily small coordinate neighbourhood); chemists use Lie algebra to study local properties. Geometric symmetries refer to a system's external geometrical structure (rotations, inversions, translations). Dynamical symmetries refer to the particular *form* of the force law or the interaction between different parts of a system expressed in equations of motion and time; they convert, e. g., one solution of the Schrödinger equation into another, leaving the Hamiltonian as is; it allows us to *form*ulate space-translation symmetry, rotation symmetry or the time-displacement symmetry.

15. Klein gave a complete solution to the quintic by solving the related icosahedral equation. A "Klein bottle," a one-sided surface, whose inside is the same as its outside has no edges. An ant can walk across the entire surface without crossing an edge. Yet, since it has one hole and is a real Riemannian manifold, it may help us reflect on 4-3-5

valuations. Commutative sets of elements, with an equality relation and defined *operations* of addition and multiplication are a field. A non-reducible polynomial is not a field because division is not defined for some nonzero denominators. Sequencing is important in DNA-RNA and in the notion of a derived function in Grothendieck topology in which a structure is defined on an arbitrary category ("topos") with flat *morph*isms.

16. A self-isogonal Neuberg cubic is the locus of all points with pivot point at Euler's infinity point; such a cubic is a 4-3-4 analytic notion that is "transcended" in ideal 4-3-5 ethical trans*form*ations.
17. Riemann surfaces (connecting surfaces) arose from studying a polynomial equation $f(w,z) = 0$, and asking how the roots vary as w, z vary; such surfaces are determined by the function $f(w,z)$, so that the function $w(z)$ defined by the equation $f(w,z) = 0$ is single valued on the surfaces. If the open-source software movement seeks to prevent computer code from becoming hermetically sealed, distributively-*open* AIRR *loci* are not *form*ulae but trans*form*ative alleles that motivate converted ones on the analogy of how Frege, Peano and Russell coaxed mathematics into an abstract algebra *opera*ting on arbitrary symbols (Boyer, *Mathematics*, 575-98). If Gödel showed the limits of such efforts, AIRR-structured groups ground reason-faith alleles by satisfying group theory's four requirements of closure, associative law, identity elements and inverses. I use the analogy of 4-3-4 group theory to transpose it into a 4-3-5 group-theory feedback model. If Newton developed a polar coordinate system that expresses curve coordinates more succinctly than Cartesian coordinates, GEM develops a local-global symmetry that relates us to the infinite.
18. This section relies on W. W. Sawyer's Internet Home Page's "What Use are Abstract Spaces?" Vectors are entities in *n*-dimensional Euclidian space with magnitude and direction, subject to certain *opera*tions of addition and multiplication and represented by drawing an arrow. They combine with similar entities according to the parallelogram law. Because of that law, a vector has a different set of components for each coordinate system. When the coordinate system changes, the components of the vector change according to a mathematical law of trans*form*ation that stems from the parallelogram law. Two important properties of vectors are first that if we start in a particular coordinate system, we end up in the original system with components of vectors unchanged. Second, relationships among vectors will be present in the components regardless of the coordinate system. Many physical quantities take the *form* of mappings (correspondences) from one collection of vectors to another. For example, the stress at a point in a fluid is the relation between two vectors but it is also a tensor (an abstract object having a definitely specified system of components in every coordinate system under consideration). Under trans*form*ations of coordinates, the components of the object undergo a trans*form*ation of a certain nature. To account for the stress at the point in the fluid, one uses tensors that involve more than one vector. I speak of GEM-genomic *vectors* (nontechnically) so as to map AIRR-love trans*form*ative loci.
19. GEM shows that both analytic and synthetic processes consider the same reality but the order is different. "What occurs first in the systematic order is treated last in the order that traces development throughout history.... The formal difference of concepts increases the more we compare the earlier elements of the *via analytica* with later elements in the *via synthetica*." Craig Boly, S.J., *The Road to Lonergan's Method in Theology* (University Press of America, Lanham, MD, 1991, 92-93. If one seeks certitude, one begins from what is most manifest and gradually moves toward a demonstration of

what is obscure, but if one seeks understanding, one begins from those notions whose understanding does not presuppose the understanding of anything else.
20. George Gamow, *Thirty Years that Shook Physics*, (New York: Doubleday, 1966) 125. Dirac's notation made it possible to substitute quantum *opera*tors for vague function *opera*tors. Yet, he did not take into account the effects of the electron's interaction with light (Feynman, *QED*, 6); in revising Dirac's magnetic moment number, Feynman used irrational numbers to reconcile quantum mechanics and relativity. Pauli's exclusion principle helps us determine the states of electrons in atoms; "while changes of these states seem to occur statistically, still the series of states is as regular and systematic as the periodic table of chemical elements" (*Insight*, 107). I suggest that 4-3-4 quantum theorists and 4-3-5 mystics view the whole as greater than the sum of its parts.
21. Dewey, "The Modern Crisis" in *Intelligence in the Modern World: John Dewey's Philosophy*, (New York: Modern Library) 308. For GEM, Husserl's transcendent ego is based on our AIRR *opera*tions concretely *opera*ting in scientific method, in everyday living or in any pedagogy.
22. Freud's studies of causal objects and Jung's attention to subjective development complement one another Lonergan, *Method*, 67-68 (interpreting Baudoin and Ricoeur). Philosophers of mind employ the notion of the supervenience of the mental to interrelate physical and mental aspects.
23. Imaginary numbers help us analyze nature's basic forces. For W. Whewell (1794-1886), all real knowledge needs mutually irreducible empirico-intellectual components; scientific progress is due not to induction, nor from data-based theories, but to the imaginative 'superinduction' "of novel hypotheses upon known if seemingly unrelated facts" (*Concise Routledge Encyclopaedia*, 928).
24. A singularity is the singular point of mathematical analysis in a complex plane (involving z and complex number i) at which some function of the complex variable z is not analytic; but at a point arbitrarily close to the singularity the function is analytic; in a "variety," the smooth locus is dense, but there can be singularities, such as a node, a cusp on an algebraic curve, a "self-intersection" on a surface. Singularities make it difficult to analyze properties of the problem described by the variety, to carry out proofs. Hironaka solved the singularity theorem as follows: Let K be a field, and let V be an algebraic variety over K. There exists an alteration f: W→V, where W is a nonsingular variety. The theorem allows us to choose f in such a way that it is an iso*morph*ism exactly on the nonsingular part of V and to make more precise what we mean by "changing a variety into a nonsingular one." In 1996, A. J. de Jong proposed a surjective, generically finite and geometric *alteration* to replace Hironaka's algebraic approach; he adjusts Hironaka's alterations with the *morph*ism f: W→V of algebraic varieties with a "modification" if it is proper and birational. *Proper* means that f is a closed map. *Birational* means that f is an iso*morph*ism outside lower-dimensional subvarieties (it is almost everywhere). De Jong's method also works in relative situations (singularities); it allows several applications not possible in Hironaka's theory (F. Oort, "What is an Alteration?" Internet) "A morphism of projective varieties is a modification if and only if it is birational; it is an alteration if finite almost everywhere. Surjection from a set A to a set B is a function whose domain is A and whose range is B, i.e., a function from A onto B. On the one hand, every modification is an alteration; an alteration f: W→V can be factored, using Stein factorization. In De Jong's proof, one replaces a (singular) variety V by a "fibration" V→B, where all fibers are curves; one also ignores singularities or perhaps even more singularities are created. Explicit reso-

lution of singularities is then carried out in a last step. In *The Hidden Heart of the Cosmos* (NY: Orbis, 1996) 76, Brian Swimme traces the trajectories of billions of galaxies backward to find us all at the universe's "singularity-center." In GEM, prime potency, as ground of quantitative limitation in correlating the expanding universe and the emergence of additional energy, is conceived as a ground of quantitative limitation; a general heuristics relates quantitative limitation to the properties that science verifies in the quantity called "energy" (*Insight*, 444).

25. A set is a collection of elements such that two sets are equal if, and only if, every element of one is also an element of the other. Sets are not "made of" anything determinate; they only have determinate functional relations to one another. In 1874, Dedekind and Cantor both proposed that a set is infinite if its components can be arranged in a one-to-one relationship with the components of one of its subsets. Their notions in number theory and in analysis led to new ways of treating the infinitely large and small gave geometry a non-Euclidian cornerstone. Cantor sets are attractors of two homothetic figures (whose lines that join corresponding points pass through a point and are divided in a constant ratio by this point); they led to new discoveries in galaxy-modelling, fractals and to a 1981 proposal by Hutchinson of an iterated functions system linking Cantor's insights with self-adaptative complex systems and chaos theory. Fractal originally meant irregular sets or patterns whose Hausdorff dimension is not an integer and is thus greater than its topological dimension; it now means a set that is self-similar under magnification. Hausdorff dimension builds on Cantor non-dense and non-denumerable sets whose points are frontier points and each of its neighborhoods contains a set that is similar to the entire set. The Cantor C set is a fractal, a set of numbers in the closed interval [0, 1] that are not deleted if the open middle third of [0, 1] is deleted, the open middle third of each of the two remaining intervals is deleted, the open *middle third* of each of the *four* remaining intervals is deleted, etc. Continuously squaring such a set yields a fractal number. If first- and higher- order logics dispute the roles of the general and particular, GEM integrates the two. Cantor's theory of infinite-sets contradicts Kant's claim that using concepts of actual infinity leads to the antinomies of reason (McCarthy, *Crisis*, 21).

26. Mathematical analysis uses such methods as algebra and calculus as distinguished from such fields as synthetic geometry, number theory or topology. It developed initially out of *ad hoc* arguments in which curves (etc.) were analyzed by an in*f*ormal process of decomposition into infinitesimal parts. It is concerned with smooth abstract objects such as sets of numbers, sets of geometrical points or sets of functions that map numbers into numbers, or points into points. As a series converges when the sum of the first n increases without bound, so I study the convergence of what the mind conceives through 4-3-4 structures but can lead to a 4-3-5 ethics.

27. Guillen, *Infinity*, 45. Cantor, *Gesammelte Abhanlungen* (Berlin: Springer, 1932) 404, (Rudy Rucker, *Infinity and the Mind* (New York: Bantam, 1982, 3). Since the class of cardinal numbers is totally ordered, aleph-one is the second-smallest infinite cardinal number, the cardinality of the set of all countably infinite ordinal numbers. Seeking to overcome the paradox of Cantor's set of all sets, the Zermelo-Fraenkel *axiom* shows that no cardinal number is between aleph-null and aleph-one. Real analysis deals with the mathematical infinite in that its first objects and concepts are an infinite series. The group of AIRR active loci verbs, analogous to genetic loci, helps us lead our lives and contextualize analysis; it helps us posit a synthesis not subject to Aristotle's *apeiron*.

28. A hyperbola is a conic section, the locus of all points *P* in a plane and a conical

circular surface; it is the set of points whose distances from two fixed points (the foci) have a constant difference. If a hyperbola can have an irrational hypotenuse, and if Newton used Kepler's studies on the hyperbola to advantage, I focus on the AIRR loci manifest in all thinkers and in all artists in history.

29. Lonergan, *Method*, 11; transcendentals are *a priori*, going beyond the known to an unknown.

30. Lonergan, *Verbum*, 33, vii, 80; he disputes Scotus' view on a priority of concept, a view that later led Kant to sever our link to transcendence with his a priori *form*s of space and time (25). Kant's spacetime theory was eventually "junked" by physicists because human understanding develops "until it knows everything attainable within its object" (32) which is being. Opposing Kant, GEM argues that the mind itself is able to ceaselessly come up with insights which are not a fixed set of a priori syntheses. Every insight is an a priori that gets to an intelligible potentially in the sensible and to the universal potentially in the particular (*Insight*, 406). For Aristotle and Aquinas, the sensible is only *potentially* in the object and the intelligible is *potentially* in the image. Imagination is not the fault of intelligence, but that of imagination itself. One must reflect sufficiently to arrive at a true judgment. An insight feedback loop based on sound judgments and on a reflection-constituted objectivity allows us to co*oper*ate in ethical ways. Karl Rahner, *Spirit in the World* (New York: Herder, 1968) studies Aquinas, Kant, Heidegger and Marechal on the convertibility of being and intelligibility in ways that parallel Lonergan's insights. As spirits, we know by insight (conversion to phantasm); we can metaphysically reach out "beyond the world."

31. Lonergan, *Method*, 95. For Deleuze and Guattari, *Philosophy*, 120, since Cantor invoked the Platonist limit, it is odd that his *form*ulation of the limits of infinity was seen as reintroducing infinity into mathematics: it is "the extreme consequence of the definition of the limit by a number," this being the first whole number that follows all the finite whole numbers none of which is maximum. GEM mediates between *approximations* and Dedekind's focus on divisibility (not on points) by approaching irrationals in mathematics or the surd of evil through the in-betweens of trans*form*ative acbd *oper*ations and a spiritual *oper*ator. Concepts and functions are thus two different types of multiplicities: concepts are open to an infinite; functions focus on limit.

32. *Method*, 37. Kant, *Fundamental Principles of the Metaphysic of Morals* (Chicago: Regnery, 1949) 5, bases obligation on a pure will's *a priori* conceptions; morally we cannot solve problems of evil, so in *Religion within the Limits of Reason Alone*, (New York: Harper, 1960) 27-50, he accentuates evil. For John R. Silber, "Introduction" to Kant, *Religion*, xciv-cxxv, *interactions* of phenomena and noumena occur in Kant's use of *Willkur, Gesinnung, Wille* (a GEM-like notion).

33. Whitehead and Russell, *Principia Mathematica* (Cambridge U, 1950) dealt with logical paradoxes where values are presupposed by the function—not vice versa; their undetermined was already logically determined. Whitehead's *An Enquiry Concerning the Principles of Natural Knowledge* (Cambridge U.,1919), on elements that point to the divine. Arguing that "all things are vectors," his *Process and Reality*, D. Griffin and D. Sherburne, ed. (Free Press, 1978), would displace notions of static stuff with that of *fluent energy* within a bipolar physico-mental makeup.

34. Gilles Plazy, *Cezanne ou la Peinture Absolue* (Milan: Garzanti, 1988) 133. Cezanne carefully studied the golden section rectangle and the composition of Piero della Francesca's art infused with a geometry of proportion. Basing his art on perception, he reinterpreted art by *form*-space relations; this influenced Cubists who reached conclusions

analogous to those of topologists.
35. John H. Newman, *Grammar of Assent* (New York: Doubleday, 1955) anticipated GEM on judgments of fact and of value. Byrne, "Analogical Knowledge of God and the Value of Moral Endeavor" *Method: Journal of Lonergan Studies*, 11, 103-35 and Joseph Cassidy, *Extending Bernard Lonergan's Ethics: Parallels between the Structures of Cognition and Evaluation*, Ph. D Dissertation, Saint Paul U, Ottawa, 1995 have debated the role of the virtually unconditioned in judgments of value in view of Cassidy's contention that since such judgments concern future possible good of orders, which do not yet exist, they cannot give rise to a virtually unconditioned.
36. Chaim H. Tejman's Website offers a "Grand Unified Wave Theory" "Everything Equation" in which photons are comprised of equal amounts of magnetic and energetic properties and which "corresponds" to the principles of quantum mechanics as exemplified in highly energetic photons whose loops contain nearly identical levels of energy. It "holds true for all the *form*ations that exist in the universe. However, in different phases, the proportion between the energetic and magnetic loops varies." Tejman constructs 3-D models to illustrate how wave *form*ation creates everything in the universe. Energetic matter swirls and spins but allows photons to retain structural integrity so that in phase transition equations, magnetic-energetic balance is kept:

$$\text{Photon} = \frac{\text{Magnetic (loop)}}{\text{Energetic (loop)}} \cdot \frac{\text{Energetic (loop)}}{\text{Magnetic (loop)}} = 1$$

for a more sober, detailed view of photons' magnetic interaction, Feynman, *QED*, 56.
37. Decio Krause and Antonio Coelho, "Identity Theory, Indiscernibility, and Philosophical Claims" April 26, 2001 (Internet) referring to Church's *Introduction to Mathematical Logic*.
38. Rollo May's *Love and Will* and Peek's *The Less Travelled Road* have opened horizons on love.
39. An Euclidean space is a generalization of the 2- and 3-dimensional spaces.
40. Expressing vectors in a system of perpendicular axes permits simpler ways of handling n-dimensional problems such as finding the coefficients in a Fourier series; building on Fourier series in representing a vector in 3-dimensional space, Frechet extended the concept of convergence from Euclidean space by defining metric spaces as sets where a distance between points is defined. He showed that notions of open and closed subsets extend to metric spaces. Fourier theory can then project onto orthogonal planes. Since one can choose a set of perpendicular directions in various ways, to each choice of axes there corresponds a way of finding the coefficients in a series; one uses simple polynomials, not sines. Lebesgue's integral generalizes Riemann's integral by extending the concept of the area below a curve to include discontinuous functions; it expands the scope of Fourier analysis that shows that arbitrary functions are representable by infinite series of sines and cosines. If orthogonal functions are defined so that products of functions can equal one or zero (1—0), or if 19th century algebra combined properties of abstraction with an ability to apply them, GEM uses 4-3-5 group theory to bridge the worlds of science and ethics.
41. Arthur Young, *Mathematics, Physics and Reality*, would seem to support a 4-3-5 structure's ideal and realist aspects. Relying on Gauss' insight on the special ideal geometric relationship of complex numbers that create an axis at right angles to the real, and together with two kinds of numbers create a plane, he argues against viewing time as a fourth *countable* dimension. Rather, just as lines are determined by two

points, a triangle by three points, a volume by four points, so it is better to view time as determined by five points; since redundancy would be detrimental in that it produces internal stress, he opts for a five-point view that stores energy and "implies reversal of entropy." The energy is stored in the extra internal diagonal made possible by the addition of a fifth point in a volume. If we think of the minus sign in the square root of 1 (i) as representing oppositeness, "the square root of oppositeness is halfway to the opposite, and if the opposite is 180 degrees, the diameter of a circle, the square root of oppositeness is 90 degrees, or 1/4th of a circle." All the roots of unity can be shown on the same circle (plane) that displays minus one and its imaginary roots and can be expressed in terms of square roots (located by the two coordinates already established). In the case of both GEM and mathematics, ideals and reality have profound hidden interconnections, adumbrated in Pascal's triangle, Fibonacci numbers, in Gauss' work.

42. Lonergan, *Method*, 50; liberty is "not indeterminism but self-determination," seeking the good.
43. The zeta function includes a number of infinite zeroes on a line involving real numbers; the Riemann Hypothesis is that all non-trivial zeroes of this function lie on a critical line + it as t ranges over the real numbers. The function has important trans*form*ation applications in physics.
44. As do amino acid triplets, mathematics and geometry have triad notions that handle values of infinity. A trigonometric function, for example, increases or decreases without limit as an angle approaches another given angle in a counterclockwise or clockwise direction; a trisectrix is the locus of a curve symmetrical to the x-axis with line x =-a as asymptote passing through the origin.
45. *Insight*, 497; just as a trihedral is a figure *form*ed by three noncoplanar lines that intersect in a point, so GEM rethinks geophilosophical triads by putting all things on a trans*form*ative basis that moves beyond Hegel's abstract, tripartite logic and transcendently closures postmodernist doubts.
46. Guillen, *Infinity*, 84. Manifold is a continuous space whose points can be assigned coordinates, the number of which are its dimension; the surface of a sphere is 2-dimensional while spacetime is 4-dimensional. Monge and Carnot's synthetic geometries treating each step in analytic calculations as corresponding to some geometrical construction complement Descartes' analytic geometry.
47. Tensors are *form*ed by the addition and subtraction of tensors of equal rank and like character, or by the contraction with respect to two indices of different characters. Distributional tensors are *tensor fields* whose coefficients are distributions are expanded in a vector space. Tensor fields are analogues of vector fields—if such fields are algebraically closed and of positive characteristic. An intractable case is that of fields of characteristic zero, where transcendental methods such as the Riemann-Roch Theorem are used. A tensor can be decomposed into a deviator that determines the properties of a tensor field and an isotropic tensor that provides a uni*form* bias. The complex part of a Grassman ring used in a noncommutative geometry "gets around" distributive Boolean variables. Riemann surfaces arose from studying a polynomial equation f(w,z) = 0, and asking how the roots vary as w and z vary; such surfaces depend on function f(w,z), so that the function w(z) defined by the equation f(w,z) = 0 is single valued on the surfaces. Ricci-Riemann tensors admit analogues in a subanalytic category for scalar curvature. Riemann-Christoffel curvature tensors use a coordinate-free differential calculus as in Einstein's GTR. Christoffel generalized the method of quadrature, by using the symbols [ij, k] (basic tensor analysis). A metric tensor generalizes the notion of

"distance" into arbitrarily many dimensions; a tensor of order zero is a scalar that consists of a single number; a tensor of order one is a vector defined at a point or points or varying from point to point in a vector field. In 4-D spacetime, a vector has four components; in an n-dimensional space, a tensor of order one has n components. If tensors (arrays of numbers that trans*form* according to certain rules under a change of coordinates) are definable in all orders, if B. Heim's uni*form* field theory goes beyond mathematics to bridge life, psyche and spirit, or if amino acids are *opera*tional trans*form*ative triads, potency-*form*-act is a generalized triad that underlies such a trans*form*ative body-mind-spirit triad that affects our ability to devise theories. Degenerate points, basic constituents of tensor fields, play a role similar to critical points in vector topology. Studying a tensor field's behavior in a close neighborhood of its degenerate points can lead to a simple topological skeleton connecting these points. Since the integral lines of eigenvectors (or hyperstreamlines) in a tensor field never cross each other (except at degenerate points), one can reconstruct the whole tensor field based only on a small fraction of the data.

48. Einstein, *The Meaning of Relativity*, (Princeton Univ., 1955), 58; redshift, due to motion of a source away from an observer, can imply an expanding universe. The equivalence principle refers to the *intrinsic* rather, than to the extrinsic qualities of gravity and acceleration. Lorentz's trans*form*ation (used in STR) depended on W. Voigt's trans*form*ation equations that preserved the wave equation unlike those of Galilean spacetime trans*form*ations of the *form* x' = x-vt and t' = t where arguments of arbitrary f, g functions trans*form* into x'+vt'-t' and x'+vt'=t' respectively. For Voigt, any fixed v, x+t and x-t are functions of x'+t', x'-t'. The relativity difference between two frames in STR or GTR contain non-verifiable elements that involve a difference in the gravitational potentials between two observers' frames. STR-GTR complexities remain within 4-3-4 invariance that, I believe, *partly* in*form* possible AIRR-4-3-5 ethical-spiritual transpositions.

49. John Baez, "Einstein's Equation" Internet. We cannot imagine curved 4-dimensional spacetime; so physicists use a 2-dimensional sphere to help us visualize "tangent vectors" on the sphere. If we parallel transport a tangent vector from the north pole to the equator by going straight down a meridian, we get a different result than if we go down another meridian, then along the equator. Curved spacetime need not be embedded in higher-dimensional flat spacetime for us to understand its curvature, or the concept of tangent vector. Tensor calculus is important in GTR; it enables us to handle concepts of 4-dimensional spacetime. If a topological space is metrizable or if a distance between points can be defined so the space is a metric space such that open sets in the original space are open sets in the metric space, AIRR loci are open sets that enable various transpositions. If Lorentz and Poincare's notions of invariance modify STR I retrieve the irrational in Pythagoras in ways that relate the invariants of 4-3-4 mathematics to our AIRR-4-3-5 mystical in-betweens.

50. Tensors include multidimensional arrays with two types (covariant and contravariant) indices. A vector is an array of dimension one for its components can be visualized as being written in a column or along a 1dimensional line. Euclidean spaces are "flat" since their metric tensors define distance such that Pythagoras' Theorem is true. In non-Euclidian spaces, metric tensors define the square of the hypotenuse to be different from the sum of the squares of the two sides. A covariant vector field is a covariant tensor field of order one (a contravariant vector field is a contravariant tensor field of order one); if tensors trans*form* with rules, AIRR ideals trans*form* us ethically.

51. Einstein, *Relativity*, 62. It is impossible to introduce coordinates on a surface with a simple metrical significance. Gauss used curvilinear coordinates which, apart from satisfying conditions of continuity, were wholly arbitrary. Only later were these coordinates related to the metrical properties of the surface. Riemann tensors and the genetic code's 20 amino acid triads have redundant capacity; AIRR permutations are virtually infinite. Information systems use probabilities to decide permutations; a 4-3-5 spiritual topology invites mathematicians to explore possibilities of setting up series of deductive expansions that can help empirical scientists (*Insight*, 314).
52. Wolfgang Rindler, *Introduction to Relativity* (Oxford: Clarendon, 1982) 83, notes: "To equate *all* mass with energy required an act of aesthetic faith, very characteristic" of an idealist Einstein.
53. Michael White and John Gribbin, *Stephen Hawking* (Washington, DC: Henry Press: 1992) 115.
54. Lonergan, *Insight*, 23; 142-48; 171. Since reference frames are an endless multiplicity, "their intelligible order cannot be more than descriptive." The positive object of inquiry consists in the data inasmuch as they refer to initial axes of coordinates (K) and to other axes (K') moving with a constant velocity to the axes, K; the negative element of inverse insight occurs in "invariant," that is, the trans*form*ation from one set of axes to another does not lead to any modification "in the form of the mathematical expression of the appropriate physical principles and laws" (128). In Minkowski space, the functions of the coordinates of an infinitesimal interval that specify the differentials of a Riemannian manifold are unity or zero, but there are 4 dimensions within the chosen frame of reference. If the frame orders concrete spacetime, the special reference frames are some precise point in space and some precise instant in time; but if the frame is mathematical, then any point-instant whatever can serve as special reference frame. In GTR, coefficients are symmetrical; in the Generalized Theory of Gravitation, the coefficients are antisymmetrical (147).
55. Quantum field theory uses field + quantization where quantization *form*s a Hilbert space with all the eigenvectors orthogonal to each other; commutation rules must apply. A Hilbert space yields dual-space reflexivity and generalizes linear trans*form*ations. Gauge theories (that express electromagnetic fields as scalar-vector potential variables) generalize GTR's equivalence principle; requiring that Lagrangians (invariant under certain trans*form*ations) have local-global symmetries, their importance is due to their successful mathematical *form*alism in unified quantum field theory.
56. Patrick Heelan, "The Logic of Framework Transpositions" in *Language Truth and Meaning*, (Notre Dame, 1972), 101; *Quantum Mechanics and Objectivity* (The Hague: Nijhoff) 1965.
57. Iris Young, *Justice and the Politics of Difference* (Princeton U., 1990) analyzes the basics.
58. Heelan, "Logic," 103-05. In his meta-context language, the logical sum ('p or q') of the two sentences 'p' and 'q 'is mapped on the least upper bound of the two languages. His work can be related to Heisenberg's work on noncommutative matrices that led to the uncertainty relations that are closely related to Fourier (harmonic) analysis; this has made their interpretation controversial.
59. The author of "Toward a General Theory of Process" (Google) lumps "Cantor's dust" with atonal music and with pointillism as infinite sets of points, all of which indicate a breakdown of clear distinctness in identity relations. Extra-mathematical factors that led to the mathematical establishment's "attitude toward (Cantor's) *Axio*m of Choice . .

. led to tragic developments" (ibid).
60. Clark, *Einstein*, 104; Einstein knew of Lorentz's work prior to 1895. STR is the realization of the fact that the bearing of the Lorentz trans*form*ation transcends its connections with Maxwell's equations and is concerned with the nature of spacetime in general (97), i. e. the increase of mass, the shortening of length and the dilation characteristic of a moving body *form* the basis of STR.
61. "Russell and Set Theory," Palo Alto Institute for Advanced Study (Internet) adds: "If we have e.g. the set $\{1, 2, 3 \ldots n+1\}$, the nth successor set of $\{1\}$, and we then make that set a member of another set, we should either expect this new member to remain fixed at $\{1, 2, 3 \ldots n+1\}$ (and not continue to grow as more successor sets of $\{1, 2, 3 \ldots n+1\}$ are constructed) as we continue, and finally finish, the construction of a new set, or we should not be surprised when we get dynamic entities whose properties are changing with time." With time, a set often alternates from being a member of itself and not being a member of itself. "The latter makes sense in computer theory, . . . less sense in strict automata theory where the accent is on algorithms that halt by definition, and makes no sense in classical mathematics where such dynamism has never had a place in its 'timeless' logic." When defining or constructing sets, we must not forget the state of the elements of sets and their members, including their dynamic relations in time. Set theorists define sets solely by their members, but when we consider the membership properties of sets in other sets, one can doubt that x is be considered as a property of y if a set or sets are defined solely by their members.
62. Field theories study the properties of mathematical fields (where addition, subtraction, division and multiplication are well-defined). Maxwell's field theory uses equations to unify the field of electromagnetic forces. GTR's field equations describe how spacetime itself constitutes objects' dynamic contexts. If a unified field theory seeks to unify fundamental forces of nature, our AIRR feedback poly*morph*ic loci enable us to co*opera*te in 4-3-4 science and/or in living a 4-3-5 ethics.
63. Byrne, "On the Foundations of the Theories of Relativity," *Creativity, Method*, 480.
64. Schrödinger illustrates his psi function with an imaginary cat, penned up in a steel chamber, having a fifty-fifty indeterminacy chance of surviving. This indeterminacy chance, "originally restricted to the atomic domain becomes transformed into macroscopic indeterminacy, which can then be *resolved* by direct observation" (his 1935 essay on Internet). Unleashing love means that GEM complements the *resolving* of atomic or macroscopic indeterminacies with AIRR-love ideals.
65. Latent metaphysics is the first stage of metaphysics in which empirical, intellectual and rational consciousness are immanent and *opera*tive in all human knowing; see Lonergan, *Insight*, 391-410.
66. Clark, *Einstein*, 19, 598. Passive resistance is a noble option; I argue that Einstein's pacifism or secular religiosity could find a better grounding in GEM's metaxy than in a Spinozist substance.
67. Albert Einstein, *The World as I see It* (New York: Covici Friede, 1934) quoted in Damasio, *Spinoza*, 279-80. "Material reality cannot perform the role or function of spiritual reality but spiritual reality can perform the role and function of material reality (Lonergan, *Insight*, 520).
68. Christopher Dawson, *Religion and Culture* (New York: Sheed-Ward, 1948).
69. J. Listing coined "*topology*" for the study of connectivity in 3-D Euclidean space (1847). Like set theory, topology studies limits not considered in finite mathematics. Set topology describes sets in terms of topological properties such as being open,

closed, compact, etc, space being a set of points with subsets *open* in their intersecting sets of *opera*tions. In such spaces, one explains limits in terms of relationships between sets, not of distance. A single quantum of action is like a reality that can be molded, stretched or twisted but whose volume is fixed. Erik Bollt, "Stability of Order: An Example of Horseshoes 'Near' a Linear Map (*International Journal of Bifurcation and Chaos*, 9, 10 (1999), 2081 ff argues for a new kind of bifurcation route to chaos by "horseshoes, in which rather than creating/destroying a horseshoe by creating/destroying transverse homoclinic points, the horseshoe is sent/brought to/from infinity." Given an arbitrary linear map, with an arbitrary matrix, he suggests continuously de*form*ing the matrix to the nearest hyperbolic saddle. If Einstein encouraged unorthodox ideas such as Kaluza's on unifying electromagnetism with gravity that only bore fruit later, if Yang Mills quantum theory describes elementary particles using geometrical structures, if the Atiyah-Singer index theorem links topology and analysis by exploring a topological space of a manifold and differential *opera*tors (linear *opera*tors defined as a function of a differentiation *opera*tor) or if Dirac mapped an electron's probability amplitudes, I link GEM transpositions by mapping how thinkers in various disciplines can AIRR-interface.

70. Combinatorial methods represent an object as the union of simpler objects. Analysis studies points and limit processes depending on a measure of closeness between numbers, functions or points; it applies limit processes to sequences of single functions' values: calculus arose from mechanics; Fourier series, from acoustics. Three schools dispute mathematics' foundations: 1) logicism uses *form*al *axio*ms to organize the subject. 2) Hilbert's *form*alism accepts the synthetic a priori status of much of arithmetic and geometry; for it, real mathematics' judgments constitute mathematical knowledge; ideal mathematics' pseudo judgments are like Kant's ideas of reason. 3) Brouwer's intuitionism responded to the discovery of non-Euclidian geometries by denying the a priori status of that part of geometry that could not be reduced to arithmetic by e.g. coordinates.

71. A GEM "spindle" includes prayer (partial immersion in God) that avoids total immersion a la Spinoza. In GEM, all is relational (but not relative), enabling us to interweave faith and reason.

72. Guillen, *Infinity*, 100. I use GEM's directed dynamism of finality in examining religious reality.

73. Lonergan: *A Third Collection*, 17; he then compares reason-faith horizons.

74. An exterior E, as inferior *bound* of the sum of its measures, is equal to its interior "I-*measure*." Mathematics generalizes concepts of length and area to arbitrary set of points. In other sets, such as of curved regions or AIRR infinite series, a *measure* defines sets' upper and lower bounds. In GEM, the bounds are AIRR operations themselves as *applied* in literature, science or daily life. I generalize AIRR's open feedback in the broadest way possible (to include union and intersection).

75. For Lior M. Burko, "Structure of the Black Hole's Cauchy-Horizon Singularity" (PhRvL, Dec. 22, 1997) this singularity is a spherical charged black hole perturbed nonlinearly by a scalar field.

76. G. Haselhurst, "Ernst Mach," Internet. String theory applies to bosons with *integer* spin and to photons, gluons, gravitons' carrying forces; superstring theory studies bosonic string theory and the matter making up the universe (fermions: electrons, quarks). If quantum gravity synthesizes quantum mechanics and relativity, a theory based on the 4 basic forces and 3 quarks is integrated in a 4-3-5 metaxy so as to reconcile ideals with

matter's underlying quark makeup. M-theory's heterotic strings and 11 dimensions (some curled up in Calibi-Yau manifolds) are being studied.

77. Hawking, *Time*, 24, 134. An imaginary curve or surface is a term used to provide continuity in speaking of equations' loci; the imaginary part of the curve or surface correspond to imaginary values of the variable satisfying the equation. Important to understanding Einstein's argument on tensors and Hawking's work on singularities is the notion of "envelopes" (tangents to a given family of curves). When a solution of a differential equation cannot be obtained from the general solution normally used, one can set an envelope of a one-parameter family of curves that has a common tangent with every curve of the family. As one obtains the equation of the envelope by eliminating the parameter between the equation of the curve and the partial derivative of this equation with respect to this parameter, so Einstein used tensor fields to arrive at the definition of single objects whose domain is a single point or a region which involves a notion of singularity.

78. Hawking, *Time*, 121-22; he uses the in-betweens of real and imaginary numbers and of reason.

79. Fritjof Capra, *The Tao of Physics* (New York: Bantam, 1976), 7-15, 145. He praises Eastern mysticism for its notion that good and evil are different aspects of "the same phenomenon." In *Belonging to the Universe*, he and Steindl-Rast recognize Western mysticism's holistic aspects.

80. White and Gribbin, *Hawking*, 262, on the snag that defies solving complex quantum equations.

81. Lonergan, *Insight*, 4-31, 298. Theorists of science, confusing imagination's representative and heuristic functions, assumed that they can paint a picture of the really real—but this is unverifiable.

82. Capra, *Tao*, 193. Einstein, *Relativity*, 57, argues that "the law of the equality of the inert and the gravitational mass is equivalent to the assertion that the acceleration imparted to a body by a gravitational field is independent of the nature of the body." Referring to Newton's equation of motion in a gravitational field, he adds that "It is only when there is numerical equality between the inert and gravitational mass that the acceleration is independent of the nature of the body.

83. Lonergan, *Insight*, 459-467. In the organism, both the underlying manifold and the higher system are unconscious, but in intellectual development both the underlying manifold of sensible presentations and the higher system of insights and *form*ulations are conscious. As opposed to logic, GEM's study of genetic insights reveals the need to interpret all data. Different levels of expressions envisage a flow of sensible events that originates in the cognitional and volitional sources of meaning of a speaker or writer and terminates in a reproduction of sources of meaning in a hearer or reader. This occurs without imposing upon an interpreter "any Procrustean bed." The transitions from generic potentiality of an oak or an infant differ vastly, but both proceed from generic potentiality to specific determination. In the animal there is psychic development supervening upon organic development, but "in man there is intellectual development supervening upon psychic and psychic upon organic." We use the same heuristic structure in studying both.

84. Stephen Covey's seven habits of "highly efficient people" are qualified with a certain humanity.

85. Ronald Clark, *Einstein: The Life and Times* (New York: World, 1971) 95, as to whether STR was influenced by Michelson-Morley's experiment. Newton's absolute

space and absolute time "possess the twofold merit of exhibiting an 'obvious' view and of inviting criticism that goes to the root of the matter" (*Insight*, 152). GEM and this book converge with Buddha's empathy notion.
86. S. Teslik, Council of Institutional Investors, *New York Times*, 2-22-04, on company executives who, lacking a sense of boundary between personal and business expenses, hide excessive pay by dividing it up into many pieces; they are oblivious to how executive perks anger other employees.

CHAPTER 4

1. Lonergan, *Method*, 10. Lonergan's focus on Western theological method restricts his appeal.
2. G. Butterworth, "A Developmental-Ecological Perspective on Strawson's 'The Self,'" quoting Reed (1994) in *Journal of Consciousness Studies*, Vol. 5, (2), 1998, 132-40. GEM sublates unified theories of 4-2 cognition such as Newell's with its own rules that avoid infinite regress.
3. Yves Raguin, "The Outside and the Inside," on Internet. Gilbert Ryle, *The Concept of Mind* (London, 1949) sought to dispel the "Cartesian Myth" that distinguishes between the inner and outer world by advocating a *logical behaviorism*. He later moved toward a reflective thinking which promised to evade the Cartesian category mistake and his own behavioristic thinking. GEM lets our *inner ideals transform* us so we can *renew outer* realities through a reflective spirituality.
4. Robert Forman, "What does Mysticism have to Teach us about Consciousness," April, 1996. Dogen, Eckhart, al-Hallaj were all apophatic mystics; one may not be aware of a specific content or thought, but something persists in such a PCE contentless consciousness, known in Buddhism (Zen) as *sunyata* (void) or *samadhi*. In *Silent Music* (New York: Harper & Row, 1974) William Johnston explores mystical love and silence in the *Gita* and in writings of St. John of the Cross.
5. *Maitri Upanishad*, 6:19 (R. Hume, 436). St. Teresa of Avila, *Interior Castle*, in *Oeuvres*, 3, 421, quoted in W. James, *The Varieties of Religious Experience* (New York, Penguin, 1983).
6. *Anatman* does not merely replace Hinduism's *atman*, self, nor is it to be confused with a "not-self" used in Hindu philosophies; it means the "not self" (meta-SAS) idea of man's true nature.
7. Joanna Macy, *Mutual Causality in Buddhism and General Systems Theory* (Albany: SUNY, 2001) 36, stresses mutual causation in the Chain, but her "objective causal law" is to be modified by Ernest Wood, *Zen Dictionary* (New York: Penguin, 1957) 82, who notes that the Chain's no. 3 is consciousness *of*, not mere awareness; consciousness includes trans*form*ative *potentia activa*.
8. The principle of charity, demanding that we judiciously interpret the truth or rationality of what others say or think, is key to how a 4-3-5 ethics interprets various theories of causation. The principle is to be applied to texts such as the *Lotus Sutra* that make maximal claims for Buddha or to traditional notions of cause and effect such as those of Vedic speculation on *karma-moksa* or Aristotle's four causes which all have to be revised in the light of relativity and quantum physics. Galen located the *opera*tional centers of the human body in the rational, animal and vegetative souls of the Aristotelian tradition. This teleological paradigm lasted for 14 centuries and was the basis for the West's rational foundation of human biology "designed" by God. In the Dark Ages,

this view was preserved by Islam and retransmitted to the West. For me, the body has a genetic makeup; mind is the source of AIRR *operations*; spirit opens us to a Buddhist-Christian metaxy.

9. For Douglas Berger, "Nagarjuna," *Internet Encyclopedia of Philosophy*, disciplined scepticism underlies Buddhist teaching. Buddhists' doubt has affinities with Austin's per*form*atory language.

10. Early Yogacarins did not accept the ultimate reality of subjective consciousness (*vijnana*). For them, only *suchness* and our consciousness of momentary events are real. Ueda, Yoshimi "Two Main Streams of Thought in Yogacara's Philosophy," *Philosophy East and West*, 17, 1967 155, on the Dharmapalan lineage for whom the external world merely trans*form*ed an *ultimately real* subjective consciousness. Thomas Kochumuttom's *A Buddhist Doctrine of Experience* (Delhi: Motilal, 1982) interprets Vasubandhu in the light of Dignaga's distinction between the realms of things-in-themselves and our verbal expressions. We are conscious of either self or ideas, or living beings or non-living beings; ordinary categories of experience, thought or consciousness (*forms* of subjectivity and objectivity) do not represent things in themselves; the five senses or integrating consciousness have meaning only with reference to objects (49). Apart from being the subject of our categories, consciousness is "nothing." Yogacara can only be called an idealism in the sense that the *form* "in which a thing is thought to be grasped is purely imagined (*parikalpita*)"; it is no sure guide to the thing-in-itself, nor does it imply "that there is nothing apart from ideas or consciousness." Citing Vasubandhu's *Trimsatika* (42), he interprets akara, as a mode of grasping an object or as a *form* through we perceive things (53). He denies subjectivity-objectivity *duality*. A co-existing "void non-void" applies to *each* being, but not monistically. He differs from Paul Griffiths, *On Being Buddha*: *The Classical Doctrine of Buddhahood* (Albany: SUNY, 1994) who interprets akara in *Abhidharmakosa* as "mode of appearance" to support a monistic rendering of "maximal Buddha." For W. Rahula, *Zen and the Taming of the Bull, Towards the Definition of Buddhist Thought* (London: Fraser, 1978) 79, Nagarjuna and Vasubandhu do agree in principle.

11. Nishitani Keiji, The Standpoint of Zen," *Eastern Buddhist*, Spring 1984, 21. Frederick Streng, *Emptiness: A Study in Religious Meaning* (Nashville: Abingdon, 1967) offsets Griffiths, *Buddha*, 144, who questions the sixth consciousness' reorientations. Rucker, *Infinity*, argues that some set theorists make a point similar to those who assert that "the mind does not attain God, but to what is beneath Him" (218); in Buddhism's holistic *prajna*, one "grasps reality from the inside" (231).

12. Using "threads" of tradition, Gide's literary testament sees Theseus return to Ariadne. In GEM, spindle-threads relate a potential totality of genetically and dialectically ordered viewpoints by interrelating our AIRR alleles on a GEM spindle that accommodates and links *loci* of various fields

13. Magliola, *Derrida*, 89 and Internet article; for him, Zen *koan* are analogous to correspondence theory (realism vs. Nominalism). A 4-3-5 metaxy amplifies on truth's relations to ideals and to matter by investigating moral and physical truths as do Kant or Aquinas, not as Russell or Moore. On Nagarjuna's death of thought (*drstijnana*) as birth of *prajna*, T. R. Murti, *The Central Philosophy of Buddhism: A Study of the Madhyamika System* (London: Allen-Unwin, 1955), 140. For Paul Griffiths, "Pure Consciousness and Indian Buddhism" in Forman, *Consciousness*, pure consciousness overlaps with an unmediated, nondualist experience which does not include any structural opposition between subject and object. While Husserl denies that consciousness

can be nonintentional, mystics would stand against those who insist that mystical experience is always mediated by concepts, a view that owes much to Kant. Kant reacted against metaphysical idealism that posits the mind as the only ultimate reality, the physical world being either an unreal illusion or not as real as the mind that created it. Such an idealism tried to avoid solipsism by positing an overarching mind that envisages and creates the universe. For Kant, thoughts without content are empty, while intuitions without concepts are blind. GEM realism roots concepts in 4-3-5 subjects.

14. J. Jespersen and Jane Fitz-Randolph, *From Quarks to Quasars* (New York: Atheneum) 118.
15. Locke, *Understanding*, II, ch. 2, no. 4 on ideas; ch. 7, no. 25 on secondary qualities; without the latter, our "ideas" can ground neither objects nor ethics. *Insight*, 436, on Lockean substance.
16. Tao Jiang "Storehouse Consciousness and the Unconscious: A Comparative Study of Xuan Zang and Freud on the Subliminal Mind," *AAR*, March 2004, 1, 119. Nagao Gadjin *Madhyamika and Yogacara*, (Albany: SUNY, 1991) 115, on basis (non-basis) of *alayavijnana* trans*form*ation.
17. The *Discourse on the Awakening of Faith*, an ascetic text attributed to Asvaghosha, explains how one can attain a change of heart or be freed from delusions through prayer and faith. Like Ignatius' *Spiritual Exercises*, the *Discourse* is a classic reflecting on the ascetico-mystical aspects of arriving at self-transcendence. It could help sincere persons, including atheists, learn spiritual values. It is allied to *Tathagatagarbha* (Perfect One in embryo) and *Avatamsaka Sutra* traditions and to claims that all have the Buddha nature—creating a space for a matrix of the Perfect One.

CHAPTER 5

1. Claude Shannon, *A Mathematical Theory of Communication* (*Bell System Technical Journal*, 1948, 27) 379). If meaning is "irrelevant to the engineering problem," it is paramount in GEM.
2. Gregory Bateson, *Steps to an Ecology of Mind* (University of Chicago, 2000) 139. I thank Eric Casino for calling my attention to parallels between Lonergan and Bateson.
3. Lonergan, *Method in Theology*, 138; subject specialization focuses more on the mediated phase; the field approach stresses the mediating phase over the mediated one. GEM gives full attention to both phases, and links their "dynamic interdependence and unity" (145) that I "4-3-5 apply."
4. As amino acids are subunit building blocks covalently linked in DNA-RNA to *form* proteins and as anticodons are vital to that process, so presentations and representations are first steps in the cognitional and conversion processes that GEM integrates in the functional specialties.
5. Lonergan, *Method in Theology*, 133. In dealing with comprehensive viewpoints or reason-faith alleles, GEM is more open and resilient than Spinozist or Hegelian logics. Crucial to integrating philosophy and spirituality is how a 4-3-5 structure dialectically mediates faith stances. A certain from self is required. As Gauss based his plane geometry upon the concept of the distance ds between two infinitely near points, so spirituality requires a certain distantiation from self so as to invite deeper levels of integration based on feelings-reason loci that are iso*morph*ic with, yet trans*form*ative of reality; AIRR loci are thus loci for integral world cooperation. Calculus seeks the vanishing point; cybernetics garners the in*form*ation that a monitor sends to a controller to meas-

ure differences. GEM links our heart's imponderables with our culturally devised symbols.
6. Conze, *Buddhism: Its Essence*, 111; 136. For Stcherbatsky, *Conception of Buddhist Nirvana*, (Leningrad, 1927) 36, the religious revolution moved from an atheistic, soul-denying philosophy teaching the path of personal Final Deliverance and an absolute extinction of life, to establishing a High Church with a Supreme God a host of Saints and clericalism. Ethically, the revolution was from the ideal of a private salvation to that of a universal, unconditional deliverance of all beings.
7. Bion focuses on personal, therapeutic interaction; diphase GEM includes the societal.
8. Erik Erikson, *Young Man Luther* (New York: Norton, 1958) 251; *Identity and the Life Cycle* (International U) 1959. Walter Conn, *The Desiring Self: Rooting Pastoral Counselling and Spiritual Direction in Self-Transcendence* (New York: Paulist, 2000) links such themes to GEM by distinguishing the often confusing meanings, of "self ," "ego," "person," "I" and "me." He uses the Augustinian theme of interiority to arrive at a unifying drive for integration. The Chomsky-Piaget debate on language specificity in learning is balanced by the sets of rules in games in which individuals are involved in competitive 4-3-4 situations. *Method*, 279, on group theory mediation. The self can be understood in an individualist, subjective sense, as a relational self, or as the self of Indian thought (*purusa*: the essence that lies in the body; *jiva*: "life" or *atman*: "breath") which is negated in a Buddhist non-self; epic writers know that a person must lose self to find it. As opposed to individualism, most meanings of a true self imply some *form* of self-transcendence. By asking what makes one "worthwhile" to self and others, I am moving beyond a pragmatic "self."
9. *Collected Works of Lonergan*, 15, *Macroeconomic Dynamics: An Essay in Circulation Analysis* (U. of Toronto: 1999). GEM's economics' triad links production, consumption based on a redistributive function that coordinates supply and demand; it guides economists and ethicians in coordinating, in two phases, people's decisions made on the basis of ideal income-outlay factors.
10. Mumford stressed larger contexts of community action to improve the quality of life.
11. David Tracy's notions of God-language and analogical imagination within pluralist contexts are helpful for approaching public-truth claims. Lonergan, *Method*, 61, on his use of Susanne Langer, *Feeling and Form: A Theory of Art Developed from Philosophy in a New Key* (Scribner, 1953).
12. Lonergan, *Method*, 178. Common meaning is not easily reached; meaning is common inasmuch as community exists and functions and in the measure "that there is a common field of experience, common and complementary understanding, common judgments or . . . an agreement to disagree".
13. Kathleen Williams, *Lonergan and the Transforming Immanence of the Transcendent: Towards a Theology of Grace as the Dynamic State of Being-in-Love with God*, PhD dissertation (1998).
14. History, histone and histogram all have the same "web" root that I use in linking ATGC-AIRR; the web idea is used pan(en)theistically in Indra's net, in Nishida's Kegon; I sublate such "webs" so as to integrate the transcendent needs and worldly values of our errant, globalizing societies.
15. Lonergan, *Method*, 175; a critical historical method needs a philosophically in*formed* GEM.
16. Lonergan, *Method*, 180. Sandra Harding, *Is Science Multicultural? Postcolonialism, Feminism & Epistemologies* (Indiana UP, 1998) seeks to strengthen science in the

interest of justice and equality. Instead of simply embracing total relativism, she seeks to reconstruct objectivity.

17. Globalization" is a misnomer if it handicaps the weak. GEM adds hermeneutic, mystic facets overlooked in John Tomlinson, *Globalization and Culture* (Polity, 1999); "*deterritorialization*" falls short if it lacks coherently applicable *ethical* policies that can develop, apply new social rules.

18. Dunne, "Lonergan," 5. Intermediate between judgments of fact and of value are apprehensions of value connected with the ontic value of persons or a qualitative value in beauty (*Method*, 38).

19. To take a speck out of a neighbor's eye, one must first remove the plank out of one's own eye.

20. Dunne, "Bernard Lonergan," ibid, 7. Freedom integrates intelligence's higher system in psychic representations; higher-system integrators' conjugate *form*s work on lower physical and biological manifolds (*Insight*, 469). Finality serves a purpose, even if no immediate uses come to mind.

21. Alfred Schutz, *The Phenomenology of the Social World* (Evanston: Northwest U., 1967) 8. GEM's explanatory conjugates can integrate and sublate Heidegger's descriptive phenomenology.

22. Peirce opposed Descartes' abstract, individualized notion of doubt. Mead stressed heightened awareness rather than Peircean categories. On the "bifurcation" between Peirce and Mead, H. Joas, "Symbolic Interactionism, in A. Giddens and J. Turner, *Social Theory Today* (Cambridge: Polity, 1987), 87. Pointing out shortcomings in Mead's symbolic interactionism, Winter's intentional ethics and his view of the social origin of meaning are more nuanced than C. K. Ogden and I. A. Richards, *The Meaning of Meaning* (London: Routledge-Paul, 1923) 11, and their triadic notion of the sign, thought and imputed reference (Raymaker, *Buddhist-Christian*, 10-17).

23. Gibson Winter, *Elements for a Social Ethics* (New York: Macmillan, 1968) 109. Thomas Csordas, *Body/Meaning/Healing* (Palgrave, 2002) has a Merleau-Ponty perspective that can be complemented by Winter and GEM to show the limitations of an embodiment not sufficiently linked to a heuristics. With Winter, I seek a social ethics that does more than what R. M. Hare *The Language of Morals*, (Oxford Univ., 1952) is able to do. Hare's utilitarian ethics is on the right path in moving ethics beyond emotivism into the realm of rational judgments; yet, in the face of conflicting ideologies, one must ask what is a "most felicitous outcome" Hare's notion of thick evaluative concepts that go beyond the thin concepts of "good, bad, right or "wrong," are "world-guided" in that particular facts must obtain for them to be applied. If the genetic code needs 3 stop codons to terminate protein synthesis, only thick evaluative alleles end deliberation.

24. Ehrlich relied on a sense of justice, ideals (*Encyclopedia Britannica*, 1986, Vol. 4).

25. Because our life and our intellects are "gifts," I seek to empower Nietzschean voluntarism with a receptivity to what is beyond us—a receptivity which is necessary to trans*form*ative feedback. Ideal, in-between politics seek to go beyond winner-take-all by empowering, enfranchising losers.

26. Lonergan's study of *oper*ative-co*oper*ative grace in Augustine and Aquinas initiated GEM.

27. Lonergan, "Healing," 106. Andrzej Werbert, "The Case of the Wolf Man" in *On Freud's Couch*, ed. I. Matthis and I. Szecsody (London: Jason Aronson, 1998) 202, notes how Freud reconstructs fragments of a case, "filling in the gaps (*Lucken*)," a

"filling" that lacks emptying.
28. Henri Maspero, *Le Taoisme et les religions chinoises* (Paris: Gallimard, 1971) 46, 279-91. Edwin O. Reischauer and John K. Fairbank, *East Asia: The Great Tradition* (Boston: Houghton Mifflin, 1960) 28, 68. A Chinese Emperor's tenure depended on *jen*; to keep the absolute nature of their Imperial system, the Japanese banned *jen*. Previously, Japan's encounter with Buddhism in 539 CE, had opened Japanese religiosity to syncretism. Nakamura Hajime, *Toyojin no Shii Hoho*, 3 (Tokyo: Shunjusha, 1962) and Allan Grapard, *The Protocol of the Gods: A Study of the Kasuga Cult in Japanese History* (U. of CA, 1992), on Kasuga's syncretist influence.
29. Ruth Benedict, *The Chrysanthemum and the Sword* (Tokyo: Tuttle, 1946) 219. "Higher Law" in the Japanese code meant that obligations to persons high in the hierarchy determine relations with persons lower down. The code did not enjoin loyalty to loyalty; it made the ties of one's social status override other obligations. Good intentions, in the American sense, were irrelevant. In the Meiji era, faced with "superior" Chinese and Western civilizations, Japan *adapted* both of these to its needs. Its absolutist Constitution restored the Emperor as symbolic focal point of political integration; it set up the Emperor system as a spiritual focus for the state, one that would transcend class or social strata but exploited attitudes based on feelings-obligations.
30. For Doi Takeo, *The Anatomy of Dependence*, tr. by John Bester (Tokyo: Kodansha, 1971), the Japanese are raised with a sense of dependence (*amae*) on intimates leading them to divide the world into inside and outside relations. *Amae*, the "key" to Japanese psychology, is like Freudian assimilation, a basic *form* of emotional ties with an object (23, 38, 78) which invites feelings of *dependence* in personal relationships but *excludes* unrelated others. Admitting that his worlds are "not clearly defined in reality," Doi *uncritically* accepts Motoori's "value of no value" and "principle of no principle." If Western freedom threatens Japan's older value system, those spoiled by *amae* may become *borderline*, troubled persons. While Westerners favor independence, Japanese prefer a passive trans-self/*amae* promoting group cohesiveness but demoting outsiders. Psychic conversion may help us reach religious or moral conversion in the light of *amae* etc. For Peter N. Dale, *The Myth of Japanese Uniqueness* (London: Croom Helm, 1986) 62, Doi distorts both Freud and Balint's passive object love for, like many "Japanese-identity" writers, he *opera*tes "in a mythical universe." Freudianism is not popular in Japan that favors introspective gratitude.
31. Heinrich Zimmer, *Philosophies of India* (Princeton: Bollingen) 1951, 524. The West has mixed up in "soul," "elements that belong to the mutable sphere of the psyche (thoughts, emotions, and similar elements of ego-consciousness, and on the other, what is beyond, behind or above these: the indestructible ground of our existence, which is the anonymous Self' (79) beyond the ego. In D,'*The Universe is a Green Dragon: a Cosmic Creation Story* (Santa Fe: Bear, 1984), 129, Brian Swimme argues that the powers of nature such as fire and tornadoes reveal the cosmic dynamic of "self-organizing" activity that he likens to the way humans create art or organise other activities.
32. Sin is a non-intelligible non-being—as is a mindless theft that a thief "excuses" with lies (G. Sala, "From Thomas Aquinas to Bernard Lonergan": Internet). Joseph Grassi, *Informing the Future: Social Justice in the New Testament* (New York: Paulist, 2003), on evil's corporate nature that, as in biblical times, requires a corporate response—the aim of my AIRR 4-3-5 matrix.
33. Mystic prayer (oratory) characterizes St. Philip Neri's Oratorian movement and the

oratorios of Schutz and Bach whose choruses so powerfully express the Gospel's dynamic themes. GEM artists live a *noblesse-oblige* ethic respecting privacy but recognizing its limits. A spiritual spindle integrates 4-3-5 trans*form*ative loci in the psychic, social, mystic-prayer and ethical dimensions of human subjectivity by "co*oper*atively appropriating" AIRR ideals. Focusing on the transgressions of these ideals enables us to "link" our patterns of experience with Nishida's loci-based experience which I translate into GEM diphase loci, lest his Zenist views be closed off from "allelic grace."

34. Wayne Proudfoot, *Religious Experience* (Berkeley: Univ, of California, 1985) 233.
35. Steven Katz in Forman, ed. *The Problem of Pure Consciousness*, in *Philosophy East and West*, 50, 2, April 2000, 10. "Language, Epistemology, and Mysticism," in *Mysticism and Philosophical Analysis*, 22-74, ed by Steven Katz (London: Sheldon, 1978). I find parallels in how rationalists such as Parmenides, Confucianists, Advaitists or Wolff provoke idealist counter arguments tinged with empiricism as in Plato, Taoism, Ramajuna's *Visisatadvaita* (modified nonduality) or Kant.
36. Anne Taves, "Religious Experience and the Divisible Self," AAR, 71, 2, 2003, 321; Leigh Eric Schmidt, "The Making of Modern Mysticism," ibid, 275. If James was influenced by Renouvier's Neo-Kantianist desire to philosophically ground moral action, GEM adds 4-3-5 loving experience.
37. Sakashita Shotaro, *Satori*, tr. by J. Raymaker, *Japan Mission Journal*, Winter 1999, 219-226. Jacqueline Stone, *Original Enlightenment and the Transformation of Medieval Japanese Buddhism* (U. of Hawaii, 1999) on how *hongaku* (a putative "original enlightenment") "migrated" from the realm of principle (*ri*) to an ideological "realm of actuality (*ji*)." Dogen rejected such "*hongaku*" as caught in *atma-vada* substantialism and devoid of *experiential* enlightenment.
38. Gale E. Christianson, *In the Presence of the Creator: Isaac Newton & His Times* (New York: Free Press, 1984. *Encyclopedia Britannica*, 1986, Vol. 23, "The History of Mathematics," 615.
39. Friedrich Schleiermacher, *The Christian Faith* (New York: Harper, 1963) Vol. I, xi.
40. Louis Roy, "Consciousness according to Schleiermacher," *The Journal of Religion*, 1997, 220.
41. Lonergan, *Method in Theology*, 286. The data "on the dynamic state of other-worldly love are the data on a process of conversion and development. The inner determinants are God's gift of his love and man's consent, but there are also outer determinants in the store of experience, . . . in the accumulated wisdom" of a religious tradition. An ability to love depends on psychic maturity. The basic terms and relations derived from AIRR bases include the patterns of experience and various realms of meaning, our diverse heuristic structures—all of which involve emergent probability.
42. Buddhist transcendence is exemplified in David Loy, *Lack and Transcendence* (Atlantic Highland: Humanities Press, 1996) and in Nishida's use of Indra's net (*Avatasamka Sutra*). This net, part of Indra's heaven, includes infinite proportions with a jewel located in each of its eyes. Nishida's locus locates, symbolizes the cosmos and its infinitely 4-3-5 dependent relationships.
43. GEM is aware of God's challenging immanent and transcendent presence. Metaphors are best understood through hermeneutics. GEM's theology takes seriously the biblical imperatives of love which it locates not in the metaphors of language but as perfecting AIRR *oper*ations *oper*ating in all persons; it invites us all to co*oper*ate in meta-SAS ways that reflect cultural-interfaith diversity.
44. David McMahan, "Modernity and the Early Discourse of Scientific Buddhism," *AAR*,

December, 2004, 4, 897-933, addresses well notions of cause in Buddhism and modern science.

45. Karol Wojtyla, "Subjectivity and the Irreducilbe in Man, in *The Human Being in Action, Analecta Husserliana*, Vol. VII (Dordrecht: Reidel, 1978) 113-49; *The Acting Person, Analecta*, Vol. X, (Boston: Reidel, 1979). His "dynamized" persons and their acts (*Action*, 63-85) is close to GEM. For him, phenomenologists overlook the essential unity of experience and attribute the unitary nature of experience to "its allegedly being composed" of a set of sensations or emotions. He corrects phenomenological claims on our dynamic ability to integrate self within reality.

46. Nishida *Intuition and Reflection in Self-Consciousness* (Tokyo, 1917) explores consciousness using Fichte's *Tathandlung* as transcendental *a priori*; his *From the Acting to the Seeing Self* (Tokyo, 1927) initiates his *sunya* phase beyond Fichte's Idealism. He seeks a realm of reality suffused with his own mystical experience which he called the Realm of non-self or "nothingness."

47. James Heisig, *Philosophers of Nothingness* (Honolulu: Univ. of Hawaii, 2001), 50, 72-73.

48. Heisig, *Nothingness*, 74; 65, on relating Nishida's "self-identity" views to other ambiguities.

49. Van Bragt, Introduction, *Religion and Nothingness* (Berkeley: U. of CA, 1982), xxx.

50. Keiji Nishitani, *Nothingness*, 113; 119-67. Van Bragt stresses *soku* as "locus" (*Pratitya*).

51. Joan Stambaugh, *Impermanence is Buddha-nature: Understanding of Temporality* (Hawaii U., 1990) examines (128) how Dogen, Blake and Holderlin "kiss" momentary joy. I let love *loci*, as analogue of uracil mRNA, "kiss" a mystic undifferentiated unity bypassing Kant's *noumena*. For Dogen, since being and time are inseparable, we must appropriate the moment in our actions; to learn one's own self is to forget one's self. His notion of constant Zen practice, like love, can serve as an AIRR-basis for East-West, being-nothingness encounters. GEM's view of logical and mystical *form*s of predication helps us explain how in Zen, we become conscious of a *cosmic* unconscious or how we sublate the power of words by discovering their sources. Lonergan, *Method in Theology*, 110, argues that "mystery is the unknown. Without a transcendental notion of being as the to-be-known, transcendent mystery" comes to be named a foundational "void." A subject not being universal, Nishida seeks to free the predicate from a subject's entitative nature. Watsuji Tetsuro, *Climate—A Philosophical Study*, (Tokyo:1951) favors *de-aru* verb predications rather than Nishida's *ga-aru* that stresses subjects' concrete existence. While Heidegger remains within a Kantian framework focusing on "What makes X possible?" Watsuji and GEM transpose that question. What for Heidegger constitutes the fundamental, mysterious, open transparency "that characterizes human awareness in contrast to the equally mysterious opacity of other beings" is, for Watsuji, the unity of the three ecstases of time—past, present and future (Stambaugh, viii). Since all consciousness is *of* something, there is no such thing as a Cartesian worldless subject.

52. Nishitani, *Religion*, 108-09. Tanabe Hajime opposes Nishida's *self-power* view with an *Other-Power* one which links the absolute with the existential trans*form*ation of subjectivity by grace; it is an Eastern analogue of Voegelin's metaxy parallel to my *Logic*'s Tatalytic mediations. For Voegelin, being drawn by the Father is not just human nor strictly divine but an "in-between."

53. Lonergan: *A Third Collection*, 196, adds: "As movement is from the mover but in

what is moved, so the drawing from the Father" in a suppliant is from the 'Beyond.' It is an "in-between" occurring in more that a mere "SAS-me."

54. John Keenan, *The Meaning of Christ* (Maryknoll, NY: Orbis, 1983), 113, 152; he criticizes the phenomenology of religion *not* because phenomenologists practice phenomenology. Rather than practicing it, they adopt "philosophical frameworks that, however adequate" to some parts of religious phenomena reduce other parts to data congruent with their own chosen agenda. *Mahayana* theology *may* reduce Christian awareness to a philosophical framework but it as a *set of* interconnecting themes that interpret the meaning of faith within a 4-3-5 GEM framework.

55. Dom Helder Camara's work of fostering justice in the slums of Brazil was undermined by his successor; but the undermining only gave rise to a wider movement to help conscientize the poor.

56. Plato's later dialogues moved his ethics beyond *The Republic*'s theory of ideas.

57. In Hinduism, "*Om*," based on a coalesced *au* plus *m*, represents such key triads as the three worlds of earth, atmosphere and heaven, the major Hindu gods, Brahma, Vishnu and Siva and the sacred Vedic scriptures, *Rg*, *Yajur* and *Sama*. As paramount Hindu mantra, *Om* embodies the essence of the universe; it is uttered at the beginning and end of Hindu prayers. Christians of the Middle Ages, guided by such Popes as Leo the Great, Gregory the Great and Innocent III, and Islamic teachers such as Al-Hallaj and al-Ghazzali all advocated 4-3-5 ideals of interrelatedness, realizing that many strive to be united with the Ultimate Spirit despite our body-mind limitations. Michael O'Callaghan, "Rahner and Lonergan on Foundational Theology," *Creativity and Method*, 123-40, on a dialectic that respects a person's uniqueness in appropriating one's heritage. The Pope and bishops cannot personally evaluate all philosophical systems, but the Church accepts what is true. In doing so, it puts its authoritative seal in official pronouncements that theologian are then called to interpret. A poetic, critical instinct may also be quite helpful in such endeavors.

58. A. J. Marr, "The Spandrel of Virtue: Radical Behaviorism and the Science of Optimism"; I see *virtue* as an ideal ability and willingness to confront the "4-2 *viral* slime" that confuses so many.

59. Tad Dunne, in "Bernard Lonergan" *The Internet Encyclopedia of Philosophy*", 6-10. I speak of GEM's 4-3-5 virtue-ideals so as to avoid the contentious issue of a fifth level in GEM.

60. Daniel Yankelovich, *New Rules* (Random House, 1981) advocates an ethic of self-commitment that gets us beyond Maslow's fallacious "self-psychology." Insights into intellect-in-process or the scale of values apply on individual and world-in-process levels (*Method*, 29, 39). *Insight*, 240, is not optimistic as to a "cosmopolis" that rises above politics due to human bias and the surd of sin. GEM (AIRR bridge to confront evil) 4-3-5 sublates commonsense practicality so as to save it.

61. Lonergan, *Method*, 365-66. *Insight*, 231. David Roy, "Bioethics as Anamnesis," *Creativity and Method*, 336. Reagan's deregulation bloated the national debt at the expense of future generations.

62. Bion, *Grid and the Caesura*, 46; he searches for a "method by which . . . particular interpretations can be put into an order before establishing which one is to be given precedence." This is not a matter of talking, but of an ordering of the splits made by a practiced mind at the right moment.

63. If Jean-F. Lyotard, *The Postmodern Condition: A Report on Knowledge*, tr. by G. Bennington and B. Massumi (U. of Minnesota, 1984) notes inabilities to integrate de-

notative scientific and evaluative languages and reduces *phronesis* to cleverness, John Caputo, *Radical Hermeneutics* (Indiana U., 1987) offers a meta-*phronesis* way for helping us (4-3-5) cope in postmodern times. With Lyotard's paralogy, GEM feedback breaks up and recombines theories—but in 4-3-5 ways.

64. In his 1996 seminar on Deleuze, Victor Vitanza argues that Deleuze and Guattari prioritize the 3rd person over the 1st person. According to Vitanza, the making of sense in their epistemology has no connection to the individual person but is merely the product of the 1st and 2nd person. In reviewing Gillian Howie, *Deleuze and Spinoza: An Aura of Expressionism*, (Palgrave, 2002), in *Notre Dame Philosophical Reviews*, (Nov. 11, 2002), Todd May argues that Deleuze retains Spinoza's view of substance and modes and of the univocity and immanence of being but *not* his claims on attributes or his determinism. At stake in how Hegel and Deleuze appropriate Spinoza are the notions of how the unfolding of the virtual into the actual (immanent causality) allows for causal relations among elements of the actual (transitive causality). By focusing on the "1st person" appropriating self and that person's relationship with other persons and the rest of reality, GEM allelically obviates causality problems by locating these in AIRR self-correcting judgments.

65. Deleuze and Guattari, *Philosophy*, 118. "The different status of intensive ordinates in each case derives from this since they are internal components of the concept, but only coordinates of extensive abscissas in function, when variation is no more than a state of variable." (47, 60, 218). Like Narcissus, who spurned the love of Echo and pined away in love for his own image in a pool of water, so they spurn religion to pine away with conceptual images. I locate feeling and affects within an ethic that affect the psyche and one's personal relations. An uncertainty principle places limits on experimentation; GEM, too, must reckon with the limits of actualizing ethical ideals.

66. Lonergan, *Method*, 257; see note above on Cantor, the cognitive realm and infinity.

67. David Kalupahana, *A History of Buddhist Philosophy* (Honolulu: Univ. of Hawaii, 1992) on Dignaga as being in the Nagarjuna-Vasubandhu empiricist tradition that steered clear both of the extremes of absolutely real, pure experiences and of absolutely unreal mental constructions. On Berkeley's attack of Locke's theory of abstract ideas and on Dignaga's denial of the existence of universal ideas, Ewing Chinn, "The Anti-Abstractionism of Dignaga and Berkeley," œ,*Philosophy East and West*, 44, 1994, 55-77; the question is how far do names refer to spatiotemporal objects.

68. Roy, "Bioethics as Anamnesis," *Creativity and Method*, 332. Hans Jonas, "Introduction," *Philosophical Essays* (New Jersey: Prentice Hall, 1974, xvi). GEM's secular-yet-theocentric approach reinforces the Church's teachings on social justice. Lest we marginalize such teachings, we must grasp reason-faith's allelic AIRR complementarities and how they might interface in a global ethics. The 02-12-2004 issue of *The New York Times* reported two revolutionary facts of science; first, the cloning of human embryos, and second, the potential of producing ultra-high-speed fiber optic equipment at the equivalent low-cost personal computer industry prices, thus blurring the line between computing and communications. While cloning humans presents us with a new ethical dilemma, the superb digital machines (not limited by physical distance) signal both the speed of "progress" and the need to devise rules to deal with dizzying change. A spiritual genome invokes and examines all facets of such debates in the light of reason and a 4-3-5 faith.

GLOSSARY

GEM generalized empirical method. Lonergan's succinct term for the dynamism by which the universe and the human making of history are discernible through our data of sense and of consciousness and which becomes conscious in and is consciously and intentionally deployed by each human being. I interpret this dynamism as our spiritually genomic AIRR operations plus a 4-3-5 love ethics. The mark of such a 4-3-5 ethics is that it is not reduced to mere analytical structures.

AIRR the four ("4") basic operations that characterize a person's everyday performance. These have their ground in GEM, in the four levels of conscious intentional operations common to all human persons. The abbreviation stands for the four "AIRR" imperatives that urge each person to "*be* A) attentive, I) intelligent, R) rational and R) responsible." The first three "AIR operations" were Lonergan's initial field of interest in his book *Insight*. He brought the fourth "R) responsible operation" into sharper focus in his *Method in Theology*. I allude to "AIRR operations" as GEM's *basic triad* ("3") in analogy to amino acid triplets. Lonergan, on occasion, alluded to, and many of his interpreters speak of a fifth imperative ("5") as that of "*being* in love" with God and neighbor: (= my AIRR-4-3-5 acts).

AIRR-4-3-5 feedback structures as trans*form*ative feedback structures– the "AIRR" and "4" refer to GEM's basic operations, the "3", to its potency-form-act triad knowns or what is to-be-known by the first three operations. "AIRR" and "5" are GEM's key trans*form*ational, foundational reality. These AIRR-4-3-5 feedback structures, as trans*form*ative, characterize both physical and spiritual genomes— but in analogical ways. Our AIRR operations operate on the analogy of DNA-RNA interchanges. Our AIRR operations must be supplemented, as is DNA, with a fifth feedback operational function that moves AIRR from being a mere immanental reality to a self-transcendent, (AIRR-4-3-5) one, to "*being-in-love*," and that enables humans to cooperate in self-giving, ethical ways.

4-3-4 modes: the manner, in which we use AIRR operations in mathematics and other analytical procedures. It restricts us to the immanental.

4-2 reductionist methods that neglect the set of our 4-3-5 trans*form*ative operational, AIRR-love abilities, reducing these to body-mind automatisms.

dharma Buddha's universal truth common to all; the void of self-nature as affirmed for Buddhists.

dharmas (plural) are the interrelated elements of the empirical world, or the cosmic factors and events that combine momentarily; how they combine or influence us is debated.

dhyana a type of meditative prayer rejected by Zen because of its residual dualism.

Hongaku-shiso original state of enlightenment, a belief rejected by critical Buddhists.

karma belief that one's past actions influence one's future lives in reincarnation.

mu Japanese for Taoist *wu*, nothingness; in compounds it denotes no-thought, non-action, etc. For Nishida, *mu* as absolute, is the reality, akin to *nada* or *Nichts*, that underlies and interrelates all.

nama-rupa mind-matter; collective name for Buddhist categories of psychophysical analysis.

nirvana the state of freedom from desire and from *samsara*; in Mahayana, it is related to *sunyata* (*ku*) and to *dharmakaya*, the unchanging, true reality of a Buddha as apophatic.

Nirvikalpa an apophatic that epistemologically frees us of thought *form*s to touch the absolute.

paramita in Mahayana, one of the advanced virtues (e.g. *prajna*) practiced by boddhisatvas.

prajna Zen meditation without object; wisdom enabling one to be grasped by Ultimate Mind.

pratitya-samutpada
Buddhist principle of causation dependent origination constituting all things; as *sunyata*, it is deemed be a flux of phenomenal events interrelated in a chain of twelve links.

samsara central Hindu-Buddhist belief that one continues being reborn until freed from karma.

skanda five changing aggregates sensation, perception, *form*, consciousness and active mind.

sunyata voidness of ultimate reality, understood not as a negation but as undifferentiation or as dynamic self-determination out of which all apparent entities, distinctions and dualities arise. Because all things are related or dependent (*pratitya-samutpada*), they are "Empty."

tathata the is-ness, suchness of things; *ku*-voidness or *sunyat*a is suchness, and vice versa.

tathagata "Who has come in truth," *interpreted* as Buddha's hidden principle, his Dharma body.

vikalpa imaginary, conceptual thought forms that keep phenomena foundationally unexplained.

INDEX

Subjects

(Most terms are identified schematically rather than exhaustively.)

Abhidharmakosa, 179
AIRR, 4, 7, 17, 18, 24, 30, passim
Alleles, 3,5-8, 15, 16, 18, 116 passim
Amae, 183
Anatman, 178
Apperception, (transcendental), 163
ATGC-U nucleotides, 5, 6, 17, 30, 41, 55, 164, passim
Axiology, 9, 19, 88, 140
Batin, 128
Buddhist Chain, (see *pratitya-samutpada*)
Categories, 6, 16, 20, 34 passim
Centromere, 39
Chaos theory, 10, 11, 117, 141, 143
Complex numbers, 64
Conjugates, 54, 55, 77, 152, passim
Citta-caitta, 107
Dialectic, 126-128
Differance, 11, 41
DNA-RNA, 27, 30, 31, 41, 116, passim
Emptying, 105
Feedback in GEM, 5, 23, 114-149
Geophilosophy, 35, 37
Inbuilt Bridge, (AIRR and GEM), 5, 25
Insight, 6-7, 27, passim
Isomorphism, 13, 36, 55, 130, 140
Judgments, 11, 18, 30, 40, 72, 131, 143
Karma, karmic, 106
Kasuga Cult, 183

Kegon, 139
Known unknowns, 55
Koan, 179
Locus, 4, 19, 107, 116, 137, 154
Madhyamika, 107
Mahayana, 12, 139
Matrix, 23, 26, 31, passim
Metaphysical Equivalence, 55, 164
Metaphysics, 8, 55
Metaxy, 6, 7, 26, 33, 85, 109, 126
Nama-rupa, 106
Nirvana, 131
Noble Truths of Buddhism, 75, 107, 135
Objectivity and objectification, 10, 114
Operators and Mapping, 10, 40, 62, 76, 89
Paramartha, (absolute truth), 108
PCE, (pure consciousness event), 105
Postmodernism, 7, 8, passim
Potency-Form-Act, 8, 10, 15, passim
Prajna, 141, 142
Pratitya-samutpada (Buddhist Chain), 106, 107
Rhizome, 10, 61
Skandha, (five aggregates), 107
Soku, (as used by Nishitani), 139-141
Spindle, (in meiosis, mitosis and GEM), 41, 61, 85, 176
Spiritual genome, 3, 4, passim
Spiritual topology, 10, 41, 65, 91, 94,
Sunyata, 12, 44
Tao, 12, 111, 140, 141
Topos, 137, 166
Vectors, (Vector-*loci*), 64, 79
Vikalpa, 107

Void in Buddhism, (see *sunyata*)
Virtue, 5, 8, 9, 20, passim
Yogacara, (practice of *yoga*), 107-109, 135, 136
Zen, 21, 128, 132

Names
(This index is selective rather than exhaustive.)

Abe, M., 132
Allison, H., 163
Aquinas, St. Thomas, 70, 71, 118, 183
Aristotle, 18, 37, 50, 70, 71, 89, 134, 137, 151, 154
Augustine, St., 52, 70, 130
Austin, J., 178
Bartusiak, M., 151
Bateson, G., 19, 112, 181
Benedict, R., 183
Berkeley, G., 147
Bernstein, R., 161
Bion, W., 20, 21, 25, 37, 45, 50, 120, 155, 159, 186
Bloom, A., 152
Bohm, D., 165
Bohr, N., 76
Boole, G., 82, 83
Braio, F., 162
Brentano, F., 13
Broglie de, L., 76
Buddha (Gautama), 6, 8, 21, 42, 55
Byrne, P., 85, 170
Cantor, G., 68-71, 85, 169, 170
Capra, F., 93, 177
Caputo, J., 186
Cauchy, A., 67
Cayley, A., 62
Cezanne, P., 11, 27, 33, 35, 72, 140, 170
Chomsky, N., 181
Comte, A., 118
Conze, E., 180
Crick, F., 32, 43
Cusa, N., 9, 26, 156
Damasio, A., 28, 29, 156, 157
Dedekind, R., 67, 68, 79, 169

Deleuze, G., 8-13, 36, 37, 45, 59 153, 161, 164, passim
Derrida, J., 21, 34, 154, 159
Descartes, R., 36, 54, 71, 78, 172
Dewey, J., 66, 168
Dilthey, W., 27, 157
Dirac, P., 65, 66, 108, 160
Dogen, 154, 185
Doi, T., 183
Dunne, T., 156, 177, 182
Eccles, J., 24-26, 155
Eckhart, Meister, 132
Einstein, A., 84-85, 87-88, passim
Erikson, E., 117, 181
Feynman, R., 23, 90, 92, 155
Fichte, J. G., 11, 33
Foucault, M., 11
Fourier, J. B., 10, 64, 74, 171
Frechet, M., 72-75, 128, 119
Frege, G., 72, 73, 90, 167
Freud, S., 50, 66, 113
Galileo, G., 53, 54, 60, 64
Galois, E., 49, 63, 82
Gamow, G., 31, 81, 167
Gauss, C. F., 45, 48, 66, 67, 80, 131, 171
Geertz, C., 22
Gödel, K., 34
Guillen, M., 155, 169, 172
Guattari, F., see Deleuze
Hawking, S., 81, 92, 176
Hawley, R. S., 164
Heelan, P., 82-83, 174
Hegel, G. F., 6, 33, 36, 52
Heidegger, M., 7, 124, 152, 163, 172, 180
Heisenberg, W., 65, 160
Heisig, J., 185
Hilbert, D., 24, 67, 75, 85, 88
Hume, D., 9, 24, 76
Husserl, E., 15, 42, 50-52, 95, 112
Jesus, xii, 6, 8, 42, 55, 95, 112
John Paul II, Pope, 184
Jung, C. G., 49, 50
Kalupahana, D., 188
Kant, I., 10, 11, 19, 51, 133 passim
Keenan, J., 141, 185
Kepler, J., 38, 69, 91, 133, 140

Kierkegaard, S., 8, 13
Klein, F., 15, 63, 65, 166
Klug, W., 158, 160
Kochumuttom, T., 179
Kronecker, L., 71
Kuhn, T., 162
Lacan, J., 37, 159
Lamb, M., 156
Lauer, Q., 165
Leibniz, G., 50, 73, 152, 156
Levinas, E., 21, 36, 50, 159
Lobachevsky, N., 66
Locke, J., 54, 107
Lonergan, B., (expounder of GEM), x, 4, 6, 10, 13, 16, 151, 153, 159, passim
Loy, D., 184
Lyotard, J. F., 186
Mach, E., 79, 84
Macy, J., 178
Magliola, R., 6, 179
Massumi, B., 10
Maspero, H., 182
McCarthy, M., 164, 169
Mead, G. H., 123, 124
Mendel, G., 4, 38
Minkowkski, H., 82
Monge, G., 67
Mori, C., 164
Nagarjuna, 107, 108, 133
Newton, I., 95, 133, 165
Nietzsche, F., 8, 11, 77, 146
Nishida, K., 10, 18, 49, 130, 137-139, 146
Nishitani, K., 18, 139-141, 179
Parmenides, 6, 135
Pascal, B., 6, 7, 55
Pauli, W., 49
Peirce, C. S., 33, 34, 182
Piaget, J., 117, 181
Plato, 6, 7, 9, 10, passim
Poincare, H., 18, 50, 63, 137
Popper, K., 24, 27, 155
Proudfoot, W., 131, 184
Pythagoras, 6, 23, 48, 67, 76, 80

Raguin, Y., 104
Rahner, K., 152
Rawls, J., 165
Raymaker, J., 151, 182, 185
Riemann, B., 78, 81, 167, 172
Roy, L., 186
Rousseau, J. J., 152
Rucker, R., 169, 179
Russell, B., 75, 167, 170
Sartre, J. P., 12
Schleiermacher, F., 133, 184
Scheler, M., 164
Schopenhauer, A., 50, 116
Schrödinger, E., 30, 65, 160
Schutz, A., 123, 124,
Scotus, Dun, 71, 170
Shannon, C., 112, 180
Snow, C. P., 53, 164
Socrates, 9, 42
Spinoza, B., 8-10, 28, 29, 88, 152, passim
Stambaugh, J., 152, 185
Strachan, T., 161
Suzuki, D. T., 132
Tanabe, H., 185
Teilhard de Chardin, P., 104
Teresa of Avila (St.), 24, 133
Tracy, D., 180
Van Bragt, J., 181
Vasubandhu, 179, 188
Voegelin, E., 6, 9
Watson, J., 32, 43, 154, 156, 158
Watsuji, T., 184
Weber, M., 124
Weierstrass, K., 165
Weyl, H., 63
Whitehead, A., 152, 170
Wiggers, J., 4, 155
Winter, G., 124, 182
Wojtyla, K., see Pope John Paul II
Zermelo, E., 75
Zimmer, H., 183

AUTHOR'S BIOGRAPHICAL NOTE

John Raymaker, of French-Belgian parentage, was raised in Richmond, Virginia. He attended St. Charles College (Baltimore, MD) and Catholic University. Ordained a priest for the Missionhurst Fathers of Arlington, Virginia, he served as a missionary in Japan from 1965 to 1970, and again from 1979 to 2003. He has also been exposed to many Hispanic and Vietnamese communities while doing parish work in San Antonio, Texas, Tottori, Japan, in Richmond, Virginia and Boston, MA.

After obtaining a Ph D in interdisciplinary studies with a dissertation on Bernard Lonergan and Gibson Winter's social ethics (1977, Marquette University), he went back to Japan and served on the staff of Oriens, Tokyo, a Catholic ecumenical and publishing center. He taught at several Universities including Hosei and Junshin Universities.

From 1996 to the present, he has been engaged in writing books on Lonergan's method which he interprets as a "spiritual genome." He married Christa Hussong of Homburg, Germany in 2003 and has been a long-time member of the Federation of Christian Ministries which advocates new forms of ministry to supplement and cooperate with present forms of established ministries.

www.ingramcontent.com/pod-product-compliance
Lightning Source LLC
Chambersburg PA
CBHW021405290426
44108CB00010B/395